DEPARTMENT OF HEALTH

The Children Act
Guidance and
Regulations

Volume 3
Family Placements

A NEW FRAMEWORK FOR THE CARE
AND UPBRINGING OF CHILDREN

LONDON HMSO

© Crown copyright 1991
First published 1991
ISBN 0 11 321375 1

KN
176
G725
Vol.3.

Preface

The guidance in this volume is issued under section 7 of the Local Authority Social Services Act 1970. It is one in a series of such books designed to bring to managers and practitioners an understanding of the principles of the Children Act and associated regulations, to identify areas of change and to discuss the implications for policies, procedures and practice. It is not intended that any one handbook should be read as a discrete entity. The Children Act was conceived as a cohesive legal framework for the care and protection of children. Each volume of guidance should therefore be read in conjunction with the others in the series and cross-references are made where appropriate. The need to build on sound practice and the multi-agency, multi-disciplinary co-operation identified in **Working Together** and the **Principles and Practice Guide** is also reinforced throughout the Act.

The guidance is written as if the Children Act is currently in force and refers in the past tense to legislation which is repealed by the Act and guidance which is withdrawn in consequence. A glossary of terms and index will be provided for the guidance as a whole.

Contents

4   FOSTER PLACEMENTS

5   PLACEMENT OF CHILDREN IN CARE WITH PARENTS

9   AFTER CARE

10   REPRESENTATIONS PROCEDURE

CHAPTER 1 INTRODUCTION

1.1. This volume is about family placements. The Children Act 1989 brings together most private and public law relating to children, replacing complex and fragmented legislation with a single statute. Part III of the Act places new emphasis on local authorities' duty to provide services to support parents in bringing up children in need in their own home and to work in partnership with parents in looking after children away from home. Reference to "parents" includes any person with parental responsibility unless otherwise indicated.

1.2. The first provision in Part III is the general duty to safeguard and promote the welfare of children in need (section 17). In addition Part III addresses the general duty of a local authority toward children being looked after by them. "Looked after" is the new term used in the Act which covers all children accommodated by a local authority, whether this is by voluntary arrangement or because of a care order (references to *in care* are to children subject to a care order). Emphasis is placed upon the need to make plans for children looked after in partnership with those who are important in the child's life and to involve those people and the child, subject to his understanding in reviewing such plans. This is reinforced by the requirement to provide a representations procedure. The Part III provisions supported by those in Schedule 2 are intended to put beyond doubt the powers and duties of local authorities in assisting families to provide appropriately for the good health, proper care and development of their children.

1.3. Within this document the provision of residential accommodation is discussed as a service provision only so far as over-arching principles of the legislation and the general duties of the local authority apply to the process of decision-making, planning, review and representations. Guidance on residential placements is in volumes 4 and 5 in this series. Equally, child protection issues are referred to within this document but readers will need to refer to Volume 1 which covers Part V of the Act for detailed guidance on the new court orders available under the Act. That guidance, this volume and the volume on residential placements should be read in conjunction with the Department's publications, **Working Together, Principles and Practice in Regulations and Guidance and Patterns and Outcomes in Child Placement**.

1.4. When reading this guidance, reference should be made to the full text of the relevant regulations in Annexes A – G.

CHAPTER 2 ARRANGEMENTS FOR PLACEMENT OF CHILDREN

2.1. This Chapter gives guidance on arrangements for placement and planning to safeguard and promote the welfare of children looked after by the local authority or accommodated by a voluntary organisation or registered children's home without the involvement of the local authority. The agency looking after or accommodating the child is henceforward referred to as *the responsible authority* unless otherwise indicated. The Arrangements for Placement of Children (General) Regulations and guidance reflect the emphasis in the Children Act on partnership between parents, children and the responsible authority and between the responsible authority and other agencies, as being the most effective means of meeting the needs of the individual child. These regulations and guidance together with the regulations and guidance relating to specific types of placements provide a statutory framework within which responsible authorities should work with children and families and act as good parents.

CHILDREN WHO ARE LOOKED AFTER BY THE LOCAL AUTHORITY

2.2. A child is looked after by a local authority if he is in their care by reason of a court order or is being provided with accommodation for more than 24 hours by agreement with the parents or with the child if he is aged 16 or over (section 22(1) and (2)).

2.3. Under voluntary arrangements the local authority does not obtain parental responsibility for a child looked after, but is obliged to comply with the appropriate regulations. Although a care order gives the local authority parental responsibility for the child, any person who is a parent or guardian retains their parental responsibility and may continue to exercise it to the extent that their actions are not incompatible with the care order (see section 2(8) and section 33(3)(b) of the Act). This reflects the intention underpinning the Children Act that parents should be encouraged to exercise their responsibility for their child's welfare in a constructive way and that where compulsory intervention in the family is used it should where possible enhance rather than undermine the parental role.

2.4. Children who are kept away from home under an emergency protection order (EPO) where they are accommodated by or on behalf of the local authority are "looked after" children (under an EPO the applicant has parental responsibility for the child). So too are those children on remand or under supervision with a residence requirement requiring them to live in local authority accommodation and those children in police protection or arrested and at the police's request accommodated by the local authority. These children are not in care.

Welfare

2.5. The primary duty of the local authority is to safeguard and promote the welfare of a child who is looked after and to make such use of services available for children cared for by their own parents as appears to the authority reasonable in the case of a particular child (section 22(3)(b)). Although the Child Care Act 1980 requirement in respect of promotion of a child's welfare, "throughout his childhood" is not reproduced the intention is still that both the immediate and long-term needs of the child should be considered and provided for in the local authority's planning for the child. In undertaking that planning for a child in care the local authority is required to give the same attention to the wishes and feelings of the child, parents and others as they must when providing accommodation under voluntary arrangements. The local authority should also take into account and consider fully the child's religious persuasion, racial origin and cultural and linguistic background. Children with physical and/or sensory disability or mental handicap will require particular consideration and the accommodation provided for them should not be unsuitable to the needs of the child (section 23(8)).

Family Links

2.6. When a child is being looked after by the local authority, the local authority is required to make arrangements for that child to live with a member of his family unless to do so would be impractical or inconsistent with the child's welfare (section 23(6)). "Family" in the context is any person falling within the scope of section 23(4) of the Act or a relative, friend or other significant person in the child's life (such as, where a child is in care, a person in whose favour a residence order was in force immediately before the care order was made). This requirement is intended to ensure that the Act's emphasis on the promotion of the upbringing of children within or by their families is applied equally to looked after children. The accommodation provided should be near the child's home so far as is reasonably practicable and consistent with the child's welfare (section 23(7)(a)). The provisions of paragraph 8 of Schedule 2 (provision for children living with their families) and paragraph 10 (maintenance of the family home) can be used together to achieve reunification of a family when the child is living apart from some or all of his family but is not looked after by the local authority. This would be a matter for consideration also when a local authority is notified of a child accommodated by a health or local education authority or others (sections 85 and 86).

2.7. The same emphasis on the importance of family links is found in the requirements that a child be accommodated near his family home (section 23(7)(a)) and that siblings be accommodated together as long as this is practicable and consistent with each child's welfare (section 23(7)(b)).

Protection of the Public

2.8. If it appears necessary in the public interest to protect members of the public from serious injury from the actions or behaviour of a child, the local authority may exercise its powers in a manner which is not necessarily consistent with its duties under section 22. This reservation is set out in section 22(6). A further limitation on the welfare duty is contained in sections 22(7) and (8) which states that the Secretary of State may, if it is considered necessary to protect members of the public from serious injury, give directions to a local authority and, that where such directions are given the local authority shall comply with them even though to do so is inconsistent with their duties under section 22.

Arrangements for Placement of Children (General) and Review of Children's Cases Regulations

2.9. The Arrangements for Placement of Children Regulations place a new duty on local authorities, voluntary organisations and registered children's homes in making arrangements to place a child to draw up and record an individual plan for the child. (The Review of Children's Cases Regulations require that the plan is reviewed and amended as necessary on a regular basis—see Chapter 8). In these Regulations, the expression "*arrangements*" is used (see Regulation 3). This is referred to in the guidance by the social work term "*plan*". The primary purpose of planning and review is to safeguard and promote the welfare of a child living away from his family. Planning is required from the earliest possible time after recognition of need or referral where the provision of accommodation (whether under voluntary arrangements or on a compulsory basis) is likely to be necessary. Thereafter, the plan should be reviewed on an ongoing basis. All the necessary considerations for the child's welfare, including the child's wishes and feelings and the wishes and feelings of the parents and others the responsible authority are required to seek and take into account, must be given due attention. There is no statutory requirement to plan, review and monitor the case of a child who is provided with a service other than accommodation. However good practice requires that in cases when the local authority is providing a significant level of services to a child (including where that service is provided to a member of his family) to extend the same philosophy and principles which are outlined below to the management of those cases (see section 17 and Part I of Schedule 2 to the Children Act).

PARTNERSHIP AND PARTICIPATION

2.10. One of the key principles of the Children Act is that responsible authorities should work in partnership with the parents of a child who is being looked after and also with the child himself, where he is of sufficient understanding, provided that this approach will not jeopardise his welfare. A second, closely related principle is that parents and children should participate actively in the decision-making process. Partnership will only be achieved if parents are advised about and given explanations of the local authority's power and duties and the actions the local authority may need to take, for example exchanges of information between relevant agencies. The general duties of responsible authorities in sections 22, 61 and 64 of the Children Act are primarily based on these principles. These duties require responsible authorities to consult parents and others and the child (where he is of sufficient understanding) before any decision is made affecting a child who is about to be or is already being looked after by a local authority, or who is accommodated in a voluntary home or registered children's home. This new approach reflects the fact that parents always retain their parental responsibility. A local authority may limit parents' exercise of that responsibility when a child is looked after by a local authority as a result of a court order, but only if it is necessary to do so to safeguard and promote the child's welfare (section 33(3)(b) and (4)).

2.11. Planning and review of a child's case with the involvement of parents will provide the basis of partnership between the responsible authorities and parents and child. The development of a successful working partnership between the responsible authorities and the parents and the child, where he is of sufficient understanding, should enable the placement to proceed positively so that the child's welfare is safeguarded and promoted.

2.12. The successful development of partnership with parents should in most cases avoid the need for care proceedings or emergency action. Although genuine partnership will be easier to achieve in the absence of compulsory measures, the same kind of approach should be taken in cases where a child is in the care of the local authority as a result of a court order. This will be achieved by:

(a) consulting and notifying the parents about decisions affecting the child;

(b) promoting contact between the child and his parents and family where it is reasonably practicable and consistent with the child's welfare; and

(c) by seeking to work with the parents to achieve a safe and stable environment for the child to return to (where this is judged feasible) or by finding a satisfactory alternative placement for the child.

PROVISION OF ACCOMMODATION BY VOLUNTARY AGREEMENT

2.13. The provision of accommodation for a child by the local authority under voluntary agreement with the parents will occur when the parents suggest that kind of arrangement to the local authority, specifically request such provision or accept proposals made by the local authority. The parents contribute their experience and knowledge of the child to the decision. The local authority brings a capacity to provide services, to co-ordinate the contribution of other agencies and to plan for and review the child's needs. Such placements fall within the scope of the Arrangements for Placement of Children Regulations which require the local authority to agree a plan with the parents for the placement of the child. The plan should take into account the wishes and feelings of the child where he is of sufficient understanding. The Review of Children's Cases Regulations require a review of that plan on a regular basis. Accommodation may also be provided to a child aged 16 or over, despite parental objection if the child agrees (section 20(5) and (11) of the Act). In these cases, the local authority will be working closely with the child to agree the plan for providing accommodation.

2.14. Agreements between parents and the responsible authority should reflect the fact that parents retain their parental responsibility. The responsible authority's responsibilities under these Regulations should not detract in any way from the parents' continuing parental responsibility. Their continuing involvement with the child and exercise of their responsiblity should be the basis of the agreed arrangements; all concerned in the arrangements should be aware of this. One agreement may cover several short-term placements such as a respite care arrangement if the conditions of Regulation 13 are satisfied (see paragraph 2.16 below and guidance on agreements in paragraphs 2.63–2.67).

CHILDREN LOOKED AFTER WHO ARE SUBJECT TO A COURT ORDER

2.15. The Arrangements for Placement of Children Regulations apply to all cases where a child subject to a court order is looked after by a local authority on a compulsory basis.

SHORT-TERM PLACEMENTS

2.16. Regulation 13 allows for a defined series of short pre-planned placements (eg for respite care, phased care and family link schemes) to be treated as a *single placement* for the application of these regulations. A plan for the child is required and all the requirements of the Regulations apply, but need not be repeated for each episode of accommodation so as long as the conditions in Regulation 13 are met. The conditions in Regulation 13 are:

"(a) all the placements occur within a period which does not exceed one year;

(b) no single placement is for a duration of more than four weeks; and

(c) the total duration of the placements does not exceed 90 days."

All the placements should take place with the same carer for a family placement and at the same establishment for a residential placement ("at the same place").

MAKING THE PLAN

2.17. The Arrangements for Placement of Children Regulations place a statutory duty on responsible authorities to draw up a plan in writing for a child whom they are proposing to look after or accommodate in consultation with the child, his parents and other important individuals and agencies in the child's life (Regulation 3). Planning for the child should begin prior to placement. After placement, the plan should be scrutinised and adjusted (if necessary) at the first review four weeks after the date the child was first looked after and at subsequent reviews.

2.18. In some cases, such as an emergency or immediate placement, it may not be possible to draw up a long term plan prior to placement. However, a provisional outline plan should always exist. The firm plan should then be drawn up as soon as possible after the child has been looked after or accommodated. Once a plan has been drawn up it should be notified to the child and his parents. Persons who have been consulted and other relevant individuals should be notified on a need to know basis. This notification should normally take place prior to placement. Where this is not possible, notification should be given as soon as possible after placement. Any amendments made to the plan at the first or subsequent reviews should be recorded in writing and notified to those consulted or involved in the reviews as required by the Review Regulations.

2.19. Where a child is provided with accommodation under agreed voluntary arrangements the plan for the child will have been agreed with the parents. It will form the basis of a written agreement between the responsible authority and the parents. However, where the accommodation is being provided as the result of a self-referral for assistance to a local authority by a child aged 16 years or over the agreement should be between that child and the local authority (see paragraphs 2.63–2.67 re agreements). Where a child is looked after subject to a court order, the local authority should still seek to work in partnership and reach agreement with the parents, wherever possible. The arrangements made must be recorded in writing and a copy given to the parents (see paragraph 2.68 on provision of information to others).

THE PURPOSE OF PLANNING

2.20. The purpose of planning is to safeguard and promote the child's welfare as required by the general welfare duties in sections 17(1) and 22(3) and 61 and 64 of the Act. The drawing up of an individual plan for each child looked after will prevent drift and help to focus work with the family and child. This will be achieved in broad terms by:

(a) assessing the child's needs;

(b) determining what objectives have to be met to safeguard and promote the child's welfare;

(c) consulting with parents, the child and others whom the local authority consider are relevant;

(d) appraising fully the available options to meet those objectives;

(e) making decisions only after full consultation with the child, his parents and other agencies and individuals with a legitimate interest;

(f) identifying which individuals are to undertake which tasks; and

(g) setting a timescale in which tasks must be achieved or reassessed.

WELFARE OF THE CHILD

2.21. Regulation 4 and Schedules 1–3 of the Arrangements for Placement of Children Regulations list matters to be considered by the responsible authority, so far as is reasonably practicable, when drawing up a plan for a child who is to be looked after or accommodated. This list covers different aspects of the child's welfare, but is not intended to be exclusive and does not repeat matters already covered in the Act. There may well also be other matters for consideration in individual cases. The Act and the Regulations indicate the need to cover the following aspects in relation to the child's welfare:

● the child's needs;

● the ability of the parent to adhere to an agreed plan (relevant except in cases where a child is looked after subject to a court order);

● parental responsibilities and the parents' capacity to provide for the child's needs;

● the wishes and views of the child having regard to his understanding;

- the provision of services under Part III of the Act in respect of children looked after by a local authority;
- what is necessary to fulfil the responsible authority's duty under the Act to safeguard and promote the child's welfare;
- the type of placement best suited to the child's needs (taking into account the duty in relation to children looked after by a local authority to place the child near his home and with siblings if applicable);
- what is necessary to make the appropriate provision for the child's religious persuasion, racial origin and cultural and linguistic background;
- any needs the child may have because of disability. This may include a consideration of the type of accommodation to be provided, the suitability of the carer, the need to arrange any specific assessments (for example, under the Education Act 1981) and for any physical and/or sensory disability or learning difficulty;
- the local authority's duty under section 23(6) to enable the child to live with a parent, other person with parental responsibility for the child, relative or friend. Where the child is in care, a person in whose favour a residence order was in force immediately before the care order was made, or other person with a legitimate interest in the child;
- Reunification issues not covered above;
- the arrangements proposed for contact with regard to the duty on the local authority in paragraph 15 of Schedule 2, to promote and maintain contact between the child and his family or contact under directions from the court;
- the requirement in Regulation 6 that a voluntary organisation or the person carrying on a registered children's home should endeavour to promote contact between the child and his parents, other persons with parental responsibility or a relative, friend or person connected with him; and
- the arrangements to be made for the child's health and education. (Health and education are dealt with more fully below).

2.22. All factors relevant to the welfare of the individual child must be taken into account in assessing the child's needs and making decisions about the child's welfare. None of the separate factors involved should be abstracted and converted into a general pre-condition which overrides the others or causes any of them to be less than fully considered. The only general policy that is acceptable in making decisions about placing children is that all relevant factors should be considered. Different factors will obviously vary in importance in relation to different children or in relation to the same child at different times. It will be right in those circumstances to weigh different factors differently. But it is not right to define any factor as of such general significance or primacy that it overrides or qualifies the duty to consider together all factors bearing on the welfare of the child as an individual.

Health Care

2.23. Responsible authorities should act as good parents in relation to the health of children looked after or accommodated by them. Health care implies a positive approach to the child's health and should be taken to include general surveillance and care for health and developmental progress as well as treatment for illness and accidents. The health care of all children looked after by local authorities or accommodated by voluntary organisations or in registered children's homes should be provided in the context of the child health surveillance programmes in the area which are designed to provide child health surveillance and promote the physical, social and emotional health and development of all children. (**Health circular HC(F)(89)20/ HC(89)(32) Health Services Development – Promoting Better Health**: Management of General Medical Services (7.11.89) (paragraphs 34/35) advises on joint development and implementation by DHAs and FHSAs of agreed child health surveillance programmes).

2.24. Regulation 7 requires responsible authorities, when drawing up a plan for a child, to ensure that the child is provided with health care, including any specifically recommended and necessary immunisation and any necessary medical and dental attention. This will include registering the child with a registered general medical practitioner and entering into a contract with a general dental practitioner to enable the child to be offered the full range of NHS dental treatment. (This contract will need to be renewed annually). In the case of children with disabilities and those with special needs, consideration must be given to continuity of specialist care. Use of NHS provision and school health services should be the same for the child being looked after or accommodated as it is for any other child. An informed and sensitive approach is especially necessary for these children since they will often have suffered early disadvantage and may be at risk because they have not received continuity of care.

2.25. The responsible authority's plan for the child should include health care arrangements which should be kept under review (see Regulation 6 and Schedule 2 of the Review of Children's Cases Regulations). Responsible authorities and district health authorities should make arrangements for professional advice to be available to responsible authorities to interpret health reports and information, assist in preparing and reviewing the arrangements for health care and assist in decisions relating to the child's care. One way of providing for this would be to agree that a designed doctor should undertake this work.

2.26. Responsible authorities should be alert to the health care needs of children from ethnic minority groups and make sure that they receive appropriate health care. Social workers should put carers in touch with a named health professional who can provide carers with an understanding of particular health conditions such as sickle cell disease and thalassaemia and help them to respond appropriately to such conditions.

2.27. Responsible authorities are required by Regulation 7 to arrange for a medical examination and written health assessment of a child before placement if reasonably practicable unless an assessment has been carried out within the last three months (but see also paragraphs 2.30–2.32). In the case of an immediate placement, the authority should arrange for a health assessment as soon a possible thereafter. The health assessment may be an initial assessment when a child is first placed or may be a reassessment in the case of a child who has been placed for some time or who has been placed again after an interval. The aim of this requirement is to provide a comprehensive health profile of the child and provide a basis for monitoring the child's development whilst he is being looked after or accommodated.

2.28. There is a requirement in Regulation 6 of the Review of Children's Cases Regulations for medical examination and written health assessment of children during placement to take place at least once in every period of six months before the child's second birthday, and at least once in every period of twelve months thereafter. Up to school age, it is recommended that medical examination and written health assessment should take place and should follow, and use wherever possible, information gained from the schedule of development surveillance prescribed by the district health authority in which the child is placed. It is also recommended that medical examination and written health assessment should take place prior to each change of school or at intervals specified in the plan for the child.

2.29. These requirements provide only a basic framework for practice. Arrangements for ensuring that children receive proper health care during placement will involve the responsible authority, parents, the child, other carer, GP, community child health doctor, health visitor, the school health service and, depending on the child's needs, specialist and domiciliary services. Regulation 5 of the Arrangements for the Placement of Children Regulations requires health authorities to be notified of each placement. Responsible authorities and health authorities should together aim to develop effective arrangements for the communication of information relating to a child's health to all the health professionals who are involved with the child.

Consent to Examination or Treatment

2.30. Responsible authorities should have clear policies and procedures in relation to consent to the medical examination and treatment of children who are placed by them and should make these known to the health authority and the child's carers. The arrangements for this should be clearly set out in each plan or agreement. These will vary according to whether a responsible authority does or does not have parental responsibility for the child. The arrangements should enable carers to seek and obtain any specifically recommended immunisations and medical and dental treatment for a child, without delay or confusion. There may be occasions when parents refuse consent to a medical examination or treatment and the child is not of sufficient understanding to make the decision. In such cases where a child is in care and the local authority has not acted to restrict the parents' exercise of parental responsibility under section 33(3)(b) in this respect then they must do so to comply with these Regulations and to ensure that necessary medical examinations and treatment are made available to the child. When a child is not in care and the parents refuse consent, the local authority may have to resort to obtaining an appropriate court order (including for example, a section 8 specific issue order or an emergency protection order or child assessment order).

2.31. The relevant individual health professionals should be aware of and co-operate with the arrangements which are made. The most convenient arrangement is likely to be where a carer has delegated authority from the parent or the local authority for routine treatment and minor procedures. If the parent holds the child's health record, it may be appropriate for it to be given to the carer for the duration of the placement. The need for operations and major treatment should be discussed with parents, and their consent obtained subject to the exercise by a local authority of its powers in section 33(3)(b) in respect of a child in care. Parents should be kept informed of their child's state of health and it should be agreed in each case whether this should be done by the carer or the authority.

2.32. Children of sixteen and over give their own consent to medical treatment (**see also HC(90)22 Health Service Management: Patient Consent to Treatment or Examination**). Children under sixteen may also be able to give or refuse consent depending on their capacity to understand the nature of the treatment; it is for the doctor to decide this. Children who are judged able to give consent cannot be medically examined or treated without their consent. The responsible authority should draw the child's attention to his rights to give or refuse consent to examination or treatment if he is 16 or over or if he is under 16 and the doctor considers him of sufficient understanding to understand the consequences of consent or refusal. There is no prohibition on placement if it is impossible to persuade a child to be medically examined. But it is a responsibility of the authority, and part of the carer's task, to help and encourage young people to understand the importance of health care and to take responsibility for their own health.

Education

2.33. Schedule 3 to the Regulations sets out the considerations about a child's educational needs which form part of the planning process. Children who are looked after or accommodated have the same rights as all children to education, including further and higher education and to other opportunities for development. Some children's perception of their ability may have been undermined and their true potential may not be immediately evident. As children who may be damaged and vulnerable, they often need extra help and encouragement and opportunities to compensate for early deprivation and for educational disadvantage arising from changes of placement while in care. In planning for a child, responsible authorities should have regard to the importance of continuity of education and of taking a long term view of a child's education; providing educational opportunities and support; and promoting educational achievement. It is also important to recognise the value of peer group relationships made in educational settings. The aim should be to help all children to achieve their full potential and equip themselves as well as possible for adult life. However expectations must be realistic. Responsible authorities have the responsiblity of acting as a good parent in relation to the child's education.

2.34. Regulation 5 requires responsible authorities to notify the local education authority of placement. Arrangements for liaison and coordination should aim to ensure that information reaches those who need it in good time, especially the school. Special care and support is needed where a change of school cannot be avoided. Responsible authorities should ensure that the carer's role and responsibility towards the child are understood by the school. In many cases carers will exercise the parental role in relation to the school in day to day matters but there will be cases where parents continue to play that part. It will be up to the social worker to clarify such arrangements with the school if any confusion seems likely to arise, in order to avoid loss of confidence and cooperation.

2.35. Carers have an important contribution to make to a child's educational progress and development. They are in a good position to observe and to help identify and assess both the child's real capabilities and any difficulties, fears and development deficits. Carers will need to be supported in this role. With the help of the carer and through school reports and direct contacts with the school, the child's educational progress must be kept under review along with other aspects of the child's welfare. Difficulties should be explored and help provided, including where appropriate, arrangements for access to specailist services within the local authority's educational provision.

2.36. Social services departments and education authorities should collaborate to safeguard the interests of children with statements of special education educational needs under the Education Act 1981 and in accordance with sections 5 and 6 of the Disabled Persons (Services, Consultation and Representation Act 1986). Local authorities should see that the parent's rights are exercised in respect of requests for assessment, monitoring and reviews. Whether or not the local authority has parental responsibility they should act in consultation with parent and foster parent.

2.37. Children should be encouraged and given opportunities to develop and pursue leisure interests and any special gifts they may have, and to share in the activities of their peers. Even where a child is looked after or accommodated for a relatively short period, the aim should be to provide opportunities for development so that the child can benefit as far as possible from the placement; and to identify the help the child may need to sustain new interests on return home.

2.38. Where a local authority propose to place a child in an establishment at which education is provided for children accommodated there, there is a duty in section 28 of the Children Act 1989 for the local authority to consult the appropriate education authority before doing so and inform them of the arrangments that have been made for the child's accommodation. When the child ceases to be accommodated the local authority is required to inform the appropriate local education authority. The aim of this provision is to ensure that appropriate educational facilities are available for the child.

2.39. The appropriate local education authority means:

(a) the local education authority within whose area the local authority's area falls; or,

(b) where the child has special educational needs and a statement of his needs is maintained under the Education Act 1981, the local education authority who maintain the statement.

2.40. A child's ethnic origin, cultural background and religion are important factors for consideration. It may be taken as a guiding principle of good practice that, other things being equal and in the great majority of cases, placement with a family of similar ethnic origin and religion is most likely to meet a child's needs as fully as possible and to safeguard his or her welfare most effectively. Such a family is most likely to be able to provide a child with continuity in life and care and an environment which the child will find familiar and sympathetic and in which opportunities will naturally arise to share fully in the culture and way of life of the ethnic group to which he belongs. Where the aim of a placement is to reunite the child with his or her own family, contact and work with the family will in most cases be more comfortable for all and carry a greater chance of success if the foster parents are of similar ethnic origin. Families of similar ethnic origin are also usually best placed to prepare children for life as members of an ethnic minority group in a multi-racial society, where they may meet with racial prejudice and discrimination, and to help them with their development towards independent living and adult life.

2.41. These principles should be applied with proper consideration for the circumstances of the individual case. There may be circumstances in which placement with a family of different ethnic origin is the best choice for a particular child. In other cases such a placement may be the best available choice. For example, a child may have formed strong links with prospective foster parents or be related to them. Siblings or step siblings who are not all of the same ethnic origin may need placement together. A child may prefer and need to remain close to school, friends and family even though foster parents of the same ethnic origin cannot be found in the locality. A child with special needs may require carers with particular qualities or abilities, so that choice is limited. The importance of religion as an element of culture should never be overlooked: to some children and families it may be the dominant factor, so that the religion of foster parents, for example, may in some cases be more important that their ethnic origin.

2.42. For a child whose parents are of different ethnic groups, placement in a family which reflects as nearly as possible the child's ethnic origins is likely to be the best choice in most cases. But choice will be influenced by the child's previous family experience and, as with all placement decisions, by the child's wishes and feelings. In discussing and exploring these with a child, responsible authorities should be ready to help the child with any confusion or misunderstandings about people of different ethnic groups which may have arisen through previous family or placement experience. Children of mixed ethnic origin should be helped to understand and take a pride in both or all elements in their cultural heritage and to feel comfortable about their origins. Carers must be able to provide this, with the help and support of others where necessary. This applies equally whether a child is placed with a minority ethnic family or with a white family or a family including members of differing ethnic origins. Where it has not proved possible to make a placement which entirely reflects the child's race and culture, an independent visitor could provide a link with child's racial and cultural background (if the criteria for appointing an independent visitor apply).

THE PLANNING PROCESS

2.43. A plan to meet the child's needs may exist before a specific placement is considered; either because of the degree of service provision to the child living in his family home, or because the child is moving from one plannned placement to another. Where no plan exists the planning process must begin once a child in need has been identified as being likely to require accommodation. Contingency planning for the possible accommodation of a child while efforts continue to support the family and keep the child at home may achieve a more successful and less disturbing transition for the child. Chronologically, the planning process should comprise the following typical stages: *inquiry*, *consultation*, *assessment* and *decision-making*. These are described in the following paragraphs.

Inquiry

2.44. Inquiry consists of:

(a) Working with the child and his parents, other members of the family (and other involved adults) to obtain their wishes and views. It is at this stage that work to develop partnership with parents, to encourage continuance of the parental role and to help the child and parents share in decision-making must start. Patterns of working and attitudes established now will in most cases influence all future work.

(b) Collecting information about the child and his family. The level of consultation will depend on the circumstances of the individual case. This will involve approaching other involved professionals (eg GP, community child health doctor, school teacher, health visitor, police, child psychologist etc) and other individuals (eg relatives, family friends etc) as necessary.

Consultation

2.45. It is essential when planning a placement to consult all those concerned with the child from the outset. The need for consultation should be explained to the parents and the child. The responsible authority should co-ordinate the involvement of all relevant agencies, and all the individuals who are significant in the child's life and the child so that a plan is drawn up which meets the child's individual needs.

2.46. Sections 22(4), 61 and 64 of the Children Act 1989 state that before making any decision with respect to a child whom they are looking after or propose to look after or accommodate, the responsible authority should obtain and take account of the wishes and feelings of—

(a) the child;

(b) his parents;

(c) any person who is not a parent of his but who has parental responsibility for him; and

(d) any other person whose wishes and feelings the authority consider to be relevant (see paragraphs 2.51–2.52 for guidance).

The Child

2.47. The child's views should be sought in discussion with the child, subject to the child's understanding (see sections 22(4)(a) and (5), 61 and 64 of the Children Act). It will always be necessary for the child's views as expressed to be discussed, recorded and given due consideration before a placement decision is made and at every review meeting and at case conferences. The implications and options in the plan should be explained, discussed and if necessary, reassessed in the light of the child's views. The social worker should be aware and acknowledge that there may be good reasons why the child's views are different from those of his parents or the responsible authority. The more mature the child, the more fully he will be able to enter into discussion about plans and proposals and participate in the decision-making process. When older children are involved, and particularly in a case of self-referral, there may well be a different perception of the child's needs and interests as seen by the child and his parents. With young children, the social worker should make efforts to communicate with the child and discover his real feelings. All children need to be given information and appropriate explanations so that they are in a position to develop views and make choices.

2.48. Providing children with reassurance and helping them with their anxieties about a placement is essential to the success of a placement. Children should feel that they have been properly consulted, that their views have been properly considered and that they have participated as partners in the decision-making process. However, they should not be made to feel that the burden of decision-making has fallen totally upon them, nor should they be forced to attend meetings if they choose not to do so. The reasons for this choice should be explored so that they are given real opportunities to understand the good reasons for taking part in meetings. The possibility of the child being accompanied to a meeting by a person who is able to provide friendly support should be considered. Where the child has communication difficulties appropriate specialist provision will need to be made so that it is possible for the child to express his views and for those views to be considered. Such provision could include someone with the appropiate communication skills such as a sign language interpreter. In the case of a child whose first language is not English, an interpreter should be provided if necessary.

The Family

2.49. The child's family, parents, grandparents and other relatives involved with the child should be invited to participate actively in planning and to make their views known. The Children Act 1989 requires that parents (including the unmarried father who may not have parental responsibility) should generally be involved in all planning for the child, and should be kept informed of significant changes and developments in the plan for the child. Similarly, members of the child's family or others who play a significant part in the child's life should be involved in the making of arrangements for the child. Such sharing of information and participation in decision-making should be the norm subject only to the overriding best interests of the child.

2.50. In drawing up a plan, therefore, responsible authorities should ensure that the parents of the child, the child himself and other significant persons are given the opportunity and appropriately helped to express their views on the objectives of the plan and on how the responsible authority proposes that the objectives should be achieved. How far their views influence outcomes will depend on the circumstances of the individual case. Where the child is to be provided with accommodation by voluntary agreement, the responsible authority will be working with the parents in the child's best interests on the proposed plan and arrangements to implement it. In child protection cases, parents' views about the proposed plan should not be allowed to prevent the local authority from carrying out its duty to protect the child. If agreement cannot be reached with the parents on a voluntary basis, and lack of agreement makes it impossible to implement a suitable plan, it may be appropriate to apply for an order under Parts IV or V of the Act.

Others

2.51. To meet the requirements of the Act (section 22(4)(d)), responsible authorities will need to use their discretion to consult all the relevant statutory agencies which are and have been previously involved with the child and his family and other relevant agencies and persons before a child is looked after or accommodated. The responsible authority should explain and make sure that parents and children understand why there is a need to consult and what the consultation process involves and obtain the relevant consent. It is essential that other agencies involved with the child are consulted about the needs of the child and his family so that the proposed plan is based on as complete an assessment as possible. People to be consulted in addition to the child, his parents and any person with parental responsibility may include:

(a) the district health authority;

(b) the child's general medical practitioner;

(c) the appropriate local authority, where it is proposed that the child (who is not looked after by that authority) will be placed in their area;

(d) the local education authority (and school);

(e) any other person whose views the responsible authority consider should be sought. For example; child's extended family, a guardian ad litem, a worker in a voluntary agency involved with the child and his family, a former foster parent, the officer in charge of a home where the child had previously been placed, a teacher who has been significantly involved with the child or a community leader.

2.52. Responsible authorities should seek to identify and make contact with specific officers in other agencies who will be contacted when pre-placement enquiries are made and who will consult colleagues in the field involved with the child and report back. The parents and the child, if he is of sufficient understanding should be informed of who is to be consulted and that the information gathered will be properly safeguarded. Existing carers, including foster parents, a head of community home, etc should already be involved in day to day planning for the child but a specific opportunity to contribute to formal planning or review considerations should be arranged.

Recording Consultation

2.53. It is important that the information obtained during consultation is clearly recorded in writing on the child's case record so that it will be easy for someone unfamiliar with the case to see:

(a) what the considerations in arriving at decisions were;

(b) how the objectives of the plan have been decided upon; and

(c) how proposals for achieving these objectives have been reached.

In this way the decision-making process will be clear for the record. This discipline will assist the responsible social worker to ensure that all the necessary factors in relation to the child's welfare are considered fully. (It will also inform the line management supervision process).

Assessment

2.54. Using the information gathered together in the inquiry process it will be possible to make a full assessment of the child's needs in relation to safeguarding or promoting his welfare, taking into account any services the responsible authority or other agencies may already be providing. The assessment should link in to other assessment processes. The Act provides that a local authority may assess a child's needs for the purposes of the Children Act at the same time as any assessment under:

(a) the Chronically Sick and Disabled Persons Act 1970;

(b) the Education Act 1981;

(c) the Disabled Persons (Services, Consultation and Representation) Act 1986; or

(d) any other enactment.

2.55. Joint assessment in appropriate cases will help to ensure that the child's needs are not addressed in isolation and that the child is looked at 'in the round'. Working in collaboration with other agencies will help to identify how the responsible authority and other agencies can best meet the child's needs.

2.56. In assessing the need for local authority provision of services due account needs to be taken of the particular needs of the child ie health, disability, education, religious persuasion, racial origin, cultural and linguistic background, the degree, (if any) to which these needs are being met by existing services to the family or child and which agencies' services are best suited to the child's needs.

2.57. Assessment must identify a child's ethnic origins, religion, special needs and family experience to provide as comprehensive a guide as possible to the child's needs. Necessary experience and expertise should be provided for in staffing of services and through relationships with other professions and services and with the community. In some areas the local community may include too great a variey of ethnic groups to be reflected fully in composition of staff. In others, local authorities may be called on only rarely to provide a service for a child or family from a minority ethnic group. In both these circumstances, local authorities will need to identify sources of advice and help so that the necessary experience, expertise and resources are available when needed. Care is needed so that the terms 'black' and 'black family' are not used in isolation in such a way as to obscure characteristics and needs. In assessing the needs of a child with communication difficulties or a child with a parent with communication difficulties, it is important that local authorities are aware that a sign language interpreter, large print, tape and braille may need to be provided if communication is to be effective.

2.58. The Department's publication **Protecting Children: A Guide for Social Workers undertaking a Comprehensive Assessment (HMSO 1988)** contains much useful guidance which is applicable to all assessments of children by social workers.

Decision-making

2.59. During the process the social worker will be deciding on the best approach to the case by identifying the child's needs, obtaining and taking into account the wishes and feelings of the child, his parents and others involved with the child, seeking the advice of other professionals in the consultation process and will be considering:

- is the best approach the provision of services (including if appropriate) accommodation by voluntary agreement;
- whether of not child protection action is needed (which may often include provision of accommodation for the child by voluntary agreement); or
- is it compulsory care subject to a court order that is required.

3 60. Decision-making will entail:

- translating the assessed needs into aims and general objectives;
- listing and appraising the specific options available (or which may need to be created) for achieving these objectives;
- deciding on the preferred option, setting out the reasons for the decision.

2.61. The proposed plan will explain in detail how the objectives can be achieved ie if and what sort of accommodation is needed; what other services for the child and services for parents or other members of family or the child's carer need to be provided; services which might be provided by other agencies such as the health authority or a voluntary organisation; likely duration of the placement; and arrangements for sustaining family links, promoting contact and reunification of the family.

Contents Of The Plan For The Child

2.62. There is no prescribed format for a child care plan (but see the considerations in Regulation 4 and Schedules 1–4). The plan should be recorded in writing and contain the child's and his family's social history and the following key elements:

- the child's identified needs (including needs arising from race, culture, religion or language, special educational or health needs);
- how those needs might be met;
- aim of plan and timescale;
- proposed placement (type and details);
- other services to be provided to child and or family either by the local authority or other agencies;
- arrangements for contact and reunification;
- support in the placement;
- likely duration of placement in the accommodation;
- contingency plan, if placement breaks down;

- arrangements for ending the placement (if made under voluntary arrangements);
- who is to be responsible for implementing the plan (specific tasks and overall plan);
- specific detail of the parents' role in day to day arrangements;
- the extent to which the wishes and views of the child, his parents and anyone else with a sufficient interest in the child (including representatives of other agencies) have been obtained and acted upon and the reasons supporting this or explanations of why wishes/views have been discounted;
- arrangements for input by parents, the child and others into the ongoing decision-making process;
- arrangements for notifying the responsible authority of disagreements or making representations;
- arrangements for health care (including consent to examination and treatment);
- arrangement for education; and
- dates of reviews.

Agreements

2.63. Regulation 3 which governs the making of arrangements (the plan) requires that a responsible authority should draw up a plan in writing. Where a child is not in care the responsible authority should reach agreement on the plan with the parents, other person with parental responsibility, or if there is no such person, the person caring for the child. Regulation 4, governs the considerations on making and contents of arrangements and requires at 4(2) that where practicable the plan should include details of the matters specified in Schedule 4 to the Regulations. Where a child is provided with accommodation by voluntary agreement the plan should form the basis of a written agreement between the responsible authority and the parents or if there is no such person, the person caring for the child prior to the provision of accommodation. The agreement must set out the role for the parent in the day to day life of the child. This will have been discussed and agreed in negotiations between the responsible authority and the parents with the involvement of the carer.

2.64. Regulation 5(3) requires the responsible authority to produce a written copy of the agreement which incorporates the detail of the plan for the child and the arrangements made. There is no requirement for the agreement to be signed, but in cases where the parent, although consenting to the plan does not wish to sign the agreement, the responsible authority will wish to sign the document to indicate their commitment to the plan for the child. A copy of the agreement should be sent to the person with whom it is made. The child should also receive a copy in a form appropriate to his understanding. The older child of 16 or over should be encouraged to sign the agreement when he has referred himself to the local authority and is to be provided with accommodation by the local authority by virtue of their powers under section 20 (3), (4) and (11). Again, there is no requirement that the agreement should be signed.

2.65. Where agreement is reached with one person with parental responsibility, the responsible authority is entitled to act on that if that parent has a residence order in his favour (section 20(9)). In other cases, the local authority can act unless another person with parental responsibility is willing and able to provide accommodation for the child or arrange for accommodation to be provided for him and objects to the proposed arrangement (section 20(7)). If accommodation is being provided in accordance with an agreement and the other person subsequently objects and can provide accommodation or arrange for accommodation to be provided, again the local authority would have to comply with their request.

This advice would not apply in respect of arrangements concerning a child aged 16 or over (section 20(11)).

2.66. An agreement should include arrangements for the child leaving accommodation, such as a period of notice to allow time for preparation of the child for this event and to ensure that the child's wishes and feelings are taken into account. Where a child is provided with accommodation by voluntary agreement for a substantial period and has become attached to the carer, this will be important if the child and the carer are to have a sense of stability and security. An agreement should also include a statement of the steps each party should take if another party decided to change the agreement. For example, if the local authority was unable to provide a service it had agreed to provide or proposed to move the child to another carer, the agreement might state that the parent would withdraw the child from accommodation. Or if the parent decided to take action which was harmful to the child the agreement might state that the local authority would consider applying for an emergency protection order.

2.67. Although the Regulations do not require a local authority to reach agreement on the planned arrangements for a child in their care, it is the intention, so far as is practicable, and in the child's best interests that arrangements should be made in partnership with parents. Where the interests of the child or the non co-operation of the parents require that initial arrangements are made without agreement, part of the planned work should be to try to establish a working relationship for the future. A child's interests are likely to be served best if the parents are encouraged to keep in touch and take an active role in planning for the child. This will be the case even where the long-term plan for the child is that he remains in care.

Notification

2.68. It is essential that those involved in the decision-making process are notified of the decision (Regulation 5) so that they may have an opportunity to make any necessary arrangements for their involvement in the placement or to make their views on the placement decision known. Careful note should be taken of the provision in regulation 5(3) about the notification of information to third parties. Such notification should only contain the amount of information it is necessary to divulge. The responsible authority will need to identify others who were not involved in the decision-making process but who will be involved with the child and have a need to know of the placement arrangements. Consideration should be given, in the light of circumstances of an individual case, of the need to notify people who have been involved in the child's life but who are not specified in Regulation 5.

2.69. All responsible authorities should notify the local authority in whose area the child is placed, providing sufficient information for the local authority to fulfil their duties in respect of registration of placements. Responsible authorities should notify the specific officer in other agencies already identified and consulted about these placements (see paragraph 2.52). These officers should be asked to disseminate the information as appropriate to their colleagues in the field who are or will be involved with the child including, in those cases where a child protection case conference has been consulted, the members of the case conference.

2.70. Once the plan has been decided upon, it should be notified in writing to the parents, the child, other carers, representatives of other agencies involved with the child and others with a sufficient interest in the child. Good practice requires that the responsible authority's social worker explains personally to the parents and the child what the plan entails and the reason for reaching the decisions therein. This should be done in addition to any explanations given during the assessment and planning process.

2.71. Where a child's or parent's first language is not English, an interpreter may be required. Sensorily impaired children and adults may need a specific format of any formal written notification. For blind or visually impaired people it could be braille, on tape or in large print. Deaf or hard of hearing impaired people have a range of communication needs depending on the type of deafness and the age of onset. Appropriate provision should be made for a child or parent with such communication difficulties. This may range from making available someone who is a clear speaker with understanding and knowledge of the speech and language difficulties of hearing impaired people, to an accredited sign language interpreter. Interpretation resources will also be required for a child who uses Makaton.

Format of Notification

2.72. The written notification of the agreement (or of the plan if no agreement has been reached) should include:

- a summary of the proposed arrangements and the objectives covering details of the placement and its likely duration;
- arrangements for contact;
- who is responsible for implementing the plan;
- the role of the child's parent on a day to day basis;
- arrangements for or issues of reunification; and
- contingency plans if the placement is unsuccessful.

Where a child is provided with accommodation by voluntary agreement, the notification should also set out the arrangements for the ending of the placement. The oral explanation given by the responsible social worker to the parents and the child will supplement this. In exceptional circumstances where a child is in care or subject to an emergency protection order, the carer's name and address may be omitted from the notice; this would be when the local authority has reasonable cause to believe that informing a person would prejudice the child's welfare (paragraph 15(4) of Schedule 2). Where it is necessary to take this exceptional decision to safeguard a child's interests, the circumstances and reasons should be recorded on the child's case record and notified to the parent in writing. The letter of notification should also refer to the representations procedure which each local authority is required to set up under the Children Act (see Chapter 10). It will be helpful to enclose an information leaflet so that the parents, the child and others notified of the arrangements are aware of the channel open to them for making representations or complaints.

IMPLEMENTATION OF DECISIONS ARISING FROM THE PLAN

2.73. One of the most important aspects of planning is to ensure that the decisions arising from the plan are implemented. This is best done by ensuring that all those involved in the planning and subsequent review process know clearly who is responsible for implementing which decisions and when. The value of the plan will rapidly diminish if objectives are not met in part or in whole because there has been poor communication, lack of clarity about who is responsible for what and the relevant timescales. Therefore the letter notifying the proposed plan should make it clear who is responsible for the implementation of different components of the plan.

MONITORING THE SUPPORT AND SUPERVISION OF THE PLACEMENT

2.74. The regulations relating to specific placements provide for support and supervision of the placements. Arrangements must also provide for line management supervision and monitoring of the social worker's performance in supporting and supervising the placement. Good records will play a key part in this appraisal of the worker's performance in relation to the placement's aims and objectives. The examination by the line manager of records should precede as well as accompany periodic discussions about the placement.

INTER-AGENCY ARRANGEMENTS IN ENGLAND AND WALES

2.75. Where a child is placed by a local authority (the local authority) under these Regulations in the area of another local authority (the area authority) the local authority should inform the area authority of the placement and provide sufficient information for the area authority to be able to complete their register in accordance with Regulation 10 (see paragraphs 2.79 and 2.80). The local authority should notify also the other relevant authorities, the district health authority, the local education authority etc of the placement and arrangements for supervision.

2.76. A local authority with responsibility for the care of a child may arrange for any or all of their functions in relation to the child to be performed by another local (area) authority (section 101 of the Local Government Act 1972). In such cases the local authority should provide the area authority with all the information which is needed to discharge the local authority's duties in accordance with these Regulations and the other Regulations relating to specific placements. Regulation 12 requires the area authority to keep the local authority informed of the progress of the child and, in particular, make reports to the local authority following each visit to the placement and each occasion on which the child is seen (in accordance with sections 17(5) and 27 of the Children Act 1989) and following each review. The authorities are required to consider together as necessary and at least after each review what action, if any, is needed.

PLACEMENT OUTSIDE ENGLAND AND WALES

2.77. A local authority may arrange (or assist in arranging) for a child for whom they are providing accommodation by voluntary agreement to live outside England and Wales with the approval of every person who has parental responsibility for the child (paragraph 19(2) of Schedule 2). In the case of a child who is in care, the court's approval must be sought (paragraph 19(1) of Schedule 2). This may only be given in certain circumstances, namely where: every person with parental responsibility for the child consents or his consent is dispensed with under paragraph 19(5), the child himself consents (if he has sufficient understanding), suitable arrangements have been made for the reception and welfare of the child in the new country and living there would be in the child's best interests (paragraph 19(3) and (4) of Schedule 2). Where the child is moving to another jurisdiction within the British Islands (ie the United Kingdom, the Channel Islands and the Isle of Man) the effect of the care order may be transferred to the relevant public authority in the receiving jurisdiction under regulations to be made by virtue of section 101 of the Act (see also the specific requirements in the Foster Placement (Children) and the Placement of Children with Parents etc Regulations).

RECORDS

2.78. Accurate, comprehensive and well organised records are essential to good practice. They are the basis, as social workers and carers change, for a clear and common understanding of the plan for the child, the arrangements made, agreements which have been reached and decisions which have been made and the reasons for them. Careful recording of agreements and decisions relating to the plan for the child, the aim of the placement and of the child's progress in the placement enables the implementation of planning decisions to be monitored effectively and kept under review. The responsible authority's records will be one important source of information for the child who is permanently placed away from his birth family.

2.79. Regulations 8 and 10 require responsible authorities to keep two sets of records:

(a) a case record for every child placed by the responsible authority; and

(b) a register of all children in the local authority's area who are placed under these Regulations whether by the local authority or another responsible authority, and of all children placed by the local authority outside their area.

Different requirements in respect of registers apply to voluntary organisations and registered children's homes. The detail of Regulations 10(2), 10(4) and 10(5)–(7) should be studied.

Registers

2.80. The register provides a record of the identity and whereabouts of every child placed by a responsible authority. The local authority's register will provide a means of immediate reference to basic information about any child placed in an area as local authorities have to register children placed by them and other responsible authorities in their area. They also have to register children placed by them (the local authority) outside their area.

Case Records

2.81. A child's case record should include all the information about family history, involvement with the authority and progress which is relevant to the child being looked after or accommodated. The case record will be an integrated case record for all purposes. Regulation 8(2) in respect of the material to be kept in the record requires that the case record contains:

(a) a copy of the arrangements made for the child (the plan);

(b) copies of any written reports in the responsible authority's possession concerning the welfare of the child; this will include family history and home study reports, reports made at the request of a court, reports made of visits to the child, his family or his carer, health reports etc;

(c) copies of all the documents used to seek information, provide information or record views given to the authority in the course of planning and reviewing the child's case and review reports (see also Regulation 10 of the Review of Children's Cases Regulations);

(d) details of arrangements for contact and contact orders and any other court orders relating to the child; and

(e) details of any arrangements made for another authority, agency or person to act on behalf of a local authority or organisation which placed a child.

It is also recommended that any contribution the child may wish to make such as written material, photographs, school certificates etc. should also be included.

2.82. The record should be kept in such a fashion that it is easy to trace the process of decision-making and in particular so that the views of the child and his parents can be easily found and related to the sequence of decisions taken and arrangements made. In addition, any papers temporarily placed in the record which are the property of the child should be identified as such and marked for return at the appropriate time.

2.83. The child's record should be separate from management records, records relating to a foster parent or residential care matters which are not solely concerned with the individual child. Where some information on one of these other records is relevant to the child a duplicate entry should appear in the child's record. Records should not be amalgamated even in the case of siblings although a degree of cross-reference and duplicate entry will be necessary.

Safekeeping of records

2.84. Regulation 9 and good practice require that authorities should take steps to ensure the safekeeping of records. This requires not only arrangements for the physical security of the records but effective procedures to restrict access to the records to those who are properly authorised and need access because of their duties in relation to a case.

Access to Records

2.85. The Children Act requires authorities to give access to records to persons duly authorised by the Secretary of State (such as the Social Services Inspectorate) and to guardians ad litem appointed by the court. Access by the Local Commissioner is provided for in the Local Government Act 1974. Other legislation affecting social work records is the Data Protection Act 1984 and the Access to Personal Files Act 1987, which give individuals rights of access to certain information about themselves. The Data Protection Act applies only to computerised records, and the Data Protection (Subject Access Modification) (Social Work) Order 1987 (SI 1987/1904) under the Act provides for certain information to be exempted in prescribed circumstances from the right of access as does the Data Protection (Miscellaneous Subject Access Exemptions) Order 1981 (SI 1987/1906) which maintains existing restrictions, including in relation to adoption records.

2.86. The Access to Personal Files Act 1987 and the Access to Personal Files (Social Services) Regulations 1989 similarly provide for subject access to information which is kept manually by local authorities (not voluntary organisations or persons who carry on a registered children's home) and the circumstances in which information is exempt from the right of access. The Department of Health issued a circular (LAC(88)17) in September 1988 containing guidance on the safeguarding of personal information held in local authorities records for the purposes of their Social Services functions and on the disclosure of that information to others within the authority and to other organisations. The Department has issued two circulars on the Data Protection Act and Social Work Order (LAC(87)10 and LAC(88)16) and a circular on the Access to Personal Files Act and the Access to Personal Files (Social Services) Regulations 1989 (SI 1989/206) (LAC(89)2) which relate to the client's own access to his records. The latter also includes an amendment to LAC(88)16 and its own detailed guidance on the handling of requests for information made by or on behalf of children.

2.87. Responsible authorities should act in accordance with the above guidance and with their own legal advice in matters relating to the disclosure of information held in the records. It is good practice that information held about an individual should be shared with him unless there are special reasons for withholding it covered by the legislation and guidance mentioned.

Retention of Records

2.88. Regulations 9 and 10 specify the length of time for which records are to be kept. These should in some cases be regarded as minimum periods rather than an inflexible rule. Responsible authorities should consider their policies on retention in relation to their records as a whole and to individual records, bearing in mind the purpose and value of retention of the different records.

2.89. Entries in the register must be kept until the child to whom the entry applies reaches the age of 23 or for five years after the death of the child before reaching that age.

2.90. The child's case record must be kept until the seventy-fifth anniversary of his date of birth or fifteen years from the date of death in the case of a child who dies before reaching the age of eighteen.

CHAPTER 3   A FOSTERING SERVICE

INTRODUCTION

3.1. Foster care is frequently the preferred way of providing care and nurture for children who need to be looked after by a local authority. In recent years there have been notable changes and developments in foster care and in the demands made on social workers and on foster parents. Foster parents may more appropriately be called foster carers or care givers in some circumstances and schemes. This guidance, to be consistent with the primary legislation and the Regulations, uses the legal, familiar and widely-used term. Fostering is more and more recognised as a skilled task needing training and support and foster parents have an important role in the professional team concerned with a child's care. Authorities have moved towards the development of a fostering service with specialist workers and recruitment and training programmes. The regulations do not require the establishment of such a distinct service although experience has shown its value; they do, however, separate the functions of approving the foster parent and approving the individual placement for the child.

3.2. The Foster Placement (Children) Regulations 1991 replace the Boarding-out of Children (Foster Placement) Regulations 1988. Authorities should note that the new regulations provide for approval of a foster parent rather than a household. The regulations provide that any local authority or any voluntary organisation which is also the responsible placing agency, (an approving authority) can approve a foster parent but a foster parent cannot then be approved by any other agency. Any local authority or voluntary organisation (a responsible authority[1]) may place a child with an approved foster parent subject to the consent of first, the approving authority and second, any other responsible authority which at present have a child placed in the foster home. This scheme is intended to provide better regulated and more convenient use of foster homes. It offers scope for co-operation and harmonious working together by the authorities and the foster parent, while introducing safeguards against indiscriminate and ill-considered shared use of foster homes. The scheme effectively gives the approving authority 'first call' on the foster home by giving them a veto on further use which in their view would jeopardise the welfare of the child or children already placed. There must, of course, be no interference with the freedom of the foster parent to choose to work for one agency rather than another. If agreement cannot be reached between the parties, the foster parent may ask for approval to be terminated and seek approval from another agency. The new scheme should also afford foster parents some protection from feeling under pressure to accept responsibilities which may be too much for them and their families, and may not best secure the interests of the children placed. However, any scheme can only provide a framework for co-operation which must depend on good practice. The new scheme requires a measure of trust between authorities; and means that if a second authority and a foster parent wished to propose a development of the foster parent's terms of approval, the decision would lie with the approving authority.

---

[1] A responsible authority, in relation to a child means the local authority or voluntary organisation responsible for the placement of the child under sections 23(2)(a) or 59(1)(a), of the Act (Regulation 1(2)). In this guidance, 'authority' means a responsible authority. 'Local authority' and 'voluntary organisation' are used where applicable. An approving authority means the local authority or voluntary organisation responsible under Regulation 3 for approving (or not approving) the foster parent. A private or 'independent' fostering agency may *not* approve foster parents.

3.3. Regulation 3 provides that children may be placed only with a foster parent who has been approved in accordance with the regulations. The only exception is where an immediate placement is made by a local authority under Regulation 11 (see chapter 4). A foster parent may not be approved unless the approving authority are satisfied that he is suitable to act as a foster parent and his household is suitable for a child to be placed in.

3.4. Each authority will have its organisational and procedural arrangements, including management and staffing structures, for the recruitment, assessment, approval, preparation, training and support for foster parents; these arrangements make up what may be described informally as a fostering service. Authorities should ensure that policies, structures and schemes of delegation provide for proper consideration of the critical decisions which fall to be made in respect of approval of foster parents; review of foster parents; placement; and sometimes, termination of placement.

3.5. Procedures for taking overall stock at regular intervals of the available pool of foster parents who form the major resource of the service will make plans for recruitment and training more responsive to likely future needs; in respect of the numbers and range of foster placements and ensure that resources are more effectively used. Information from reviews of approval of individual foster parents will have a role to play in evaluating overall strengths and deficiencies in the fostering service; providing information about forthcoming changes in the availability of existing foster homes; and giving foster parents an opportunity to contribute to planning and developing the service.

THE FOSTERING TASK

3.6. The aims of foster placement and the skills required can be varied and wide ranging. The nature and purpose of different types of placement need to be identified and understood, so that the need for foster homes as resources can be assessed and foster parents recruited and prepared; and so that clear agreements with foster parents on the aim of placement can be reached to avoid the frustrations arising from mistaken, confused or disappointed expectations. In particular the continuing role of the parent in the child's life and the precise arrangements to ensure that parental responsibility is not diminished must be explained and agreed. Short term, respite and long term placement are convenient descriptive terms and are used as such in this guidance. They are insufficiently precise, however, for the purposes of planning for individual children. Planning needs to address the *aim* of the placement, any specific *tasks* associated with the aim and the *expected duration* of the placement. Under the Arrangements for Placement of Children (General) Regulations, the plan for the child, which is the basis of agreements with parents and foster parents, must include the expected duration of placement.

RECRUITMENT

3.7. Methods of recruitment will vary according to the outcome of objective reviews of local choice and need but are likely to include the following elements:

(a) general publicity and information giving to raise awareness and understanding in the community of fostering and the needs of children;

(b) recruitment campaigns for foster parents generally or for specialised schemes or needs or to seek a placement for a specific child;

(c) open meetings at which enquirers can learn more about fostering and meet experienced foster parents;

(d) established foster parents and local foster parent groups can be valuable assets in publicising fostering and recruitment of other foster parents.

PUBLICITY AND RECRUITMENT

3.8. Publicity and recruitment campaigns should aim to reach all groups in the community, especially where there is or may be a need for foster parents from a particular racial, cultural or religious group. Local authorities are particularly required by paragraph 11 of Schedule 2 to the Act to have regard, in publicising and recruiting for the fostering service, to the different racial groups to which children in need in the area belong. Where placements are needed or likely to be needed for children from minority ethnic groups or for children of particular religious affiliation, sustained efforts may be needed to recruit a sufficient number and range of foster parents from those groups and of that religion. Such efforts are essential if all children who need foster care are to have the opportunity of placement with families which share their ethnic origin and religion. The development and planning of fostering services should aim to ensure that the resources of the service, including the arrangements for the recruitment, assessment, approval, preparation and support of a pool of foster parents, are responsive to the demands on the service. This calls for forward planning to identify the range and estimated numbers of foster homes which are likely to be required. Publicity and recruitment campaigns, resource networks and exchange arrangements must aim to reach all groups in the community and to increase awareness and understanding generally of the needs of children. Appropriate assessment and training must be available for all foster parents.

3.9. General recruitment campaigns may result in the identification of foster families particularly suited to care for the child with special needs. However, it may be necessary to target recruiting by advertising in magazines and other specialist media. Other things being equal it may be that a foster parent with experience of a disability similar to the child's will have a particular understanding and knowledge which will benefit the child. Consultation with relevant disability organisations will assist authorities to devise appropriate recruiting campaigns.

3.10. Authorities should develop policies and guidelines in respect of publicity to recruit foster parents for individual children so that the wishes and feelings of children and their families are properly considered and to guard against disclosure of confidential information.

3.11. There is scope for inter-agency co-operation and co-ordination in joint publicity and family finding campaigns and for agreements between local authorities and voluntary organisations who have developed or propose to develop specialist fostering schemes. Such arrangements can help avoid costly duplication of effort.

ASSESSMENT

3.12. All enquirers should be given a positive and welcoming response. Even where the applicants' preferences do not meet the service's immediate identified need, mutual exploration of what is involved may lead some applicants towards undertaking a different kind of fostering. Equally, it may be appropriate to consider whether, as an alternative to fostering, applicants might be asked to work with befriending schemes, youth clubs or out of school schemes. Similarly, departments should keep in mind for future needs enquirers who initially respond to an advertisement for a specific child. Discussion should, of course, be honest to avoid unreal and unfounded expectations, for example, on the part of an applicant who accepts a child needing short placement hoping it will "turn into" a long term placement. Assessment processes should enable applicants to opt out after learning more of what is involved. It should always be clear to applicants, however, when they are being assessed as foster parents, rather than participating in exchanges of information. Similarly the enquiries and investigations to be made and the records to be kept if an application succeeds should be clearly explained. Prospective foster parents should be given a clear understanding of the selection process so that they understand the need for visits from social workers and the timescale of assessment.

3.13. Regulation 3 requires authorities to obtain information on and consider the range of factors set out in Schedule 1 in order to determine whether an applicant can be considered suitable to be a foster parent and whether his household is suitable for a child to be placed in. Regulations are framed in terms of a single foster parent but are subject to the provision in section 6 of the Interpretation Act 1978 that the singular includes the plural and the masculine gender includes the feminine gender and vice versa "unless the contrary intention appears". Where an applicant is married, both partners should be assessed and approved. The same principle should be followed whenever responsibility for the care of the child is shared by two people in a household, for example, mother and daughter. This is not intended as a check list to which there are right and wrong answers, nor is it exhaustive. The aim should be to identify all the factors which contribute to a general picture of the applicants, their family and way of life.

3.14. Authorities and those interested in becoming foster parents must understand that an authority's duty is, unequivocally and unambiguously, to find and approve the most suitable foster parents for children who need family placement. It would be wrong arbitrarily to exclude any particular groups of people from consideration. But the chosen way of life of some adults may mean that they would not be able to provide a suitable environment for the care and nurture of a child. No one has a 'right' to be a foster parent. Fostering decisions must centre exclusively on the interests of the child.

3.15. *Medical reports* will be the most satisfactory source of information about the health of applicants. In addition, members of primary health care teams who are familiar with the family may be well placed to help. Local arrangements should ensure that professional advice is available to enable health information to be interpreted and to advise on the extent to which the health of the applicant – or deteriorating health in the case of an established foster parent – may affect capacity to act as a foster parent.

3.16. Birth certificates, marriage certificates and other papers which relate to the applicant's history, such as naturalisation documents should be seen routinely. Marital status will be particularly significant should adoption ever become a consideration.

3.17. Applicants are required to provide written consent for police records to be consulted to check for previous convictions. A record of convictions will not necessarily preclude appointment but will require careful consideration and consultation with senior staff. Authorities should check their own records in respect of the applicants and other members of the household. The police should also be asked to check the records of all other members of the household with their permission. Authorities should note that the Rehabilitation of Offenders Act 1974 exceptions orders apply to these checks.

3.18. Social workers should visit on at least one occasion at a time when they can meet the entire household and explore the relationships of all the members; the extent to which other members of the household may participate in the care and daily life of a foster child; and the demands which are made on the applicants by other members of the household, such as elderly relatives requiring care.

3.19. As well as the suitability of the accommodation, the social worker should investigate access to schools, public transport and other amenities. If the fostering of a child with special needs is under consideration; is the accommodation suitable? Is the appropriate medical support readily available and will the local education system be able to provide for the child's special needs?

3.20. The social worker should make a point of communicating with the children of the family and learning about their feelings on the introduction of a foster child into the family. The impact of fostering on family and social life should be discussed and considered with the applicant.

3.21. Where the foster parent has children who are not living in the household, the extent of contact with them should be explored. When the child is over 16 and the degree of contact and involvement in the household is significant the advice at paragraph 3.17 above may be relevant.

3.22. The health visitor may be able to help the social worker form a view of parenting capacity. For example, what is the applicant's experience of caring for children of different age groups, including other people's children? The applicant should know that such views will be sought.

3.23. Where the prospective foster parent lives in the area of another authority their views must be sought. Where there has been a previous application to foster or adopt, the relevant agency should be consulted.

3.24. *Religion* and degree of religious observance and capacity to care for a child of a particular religion or from a more or less religious background than that of the foster parents: the social worker should seek to understand the extent to which religion influences the foster parent's family life. What is the element of familiarity and sympathy with and understanding of other denominations and faiths with which the foster family may have links through relatives or friends? What would be expected of a foster child by way of participation in the religious life of the family? Would this be compatible with the expectations and needs of a child and his parents? How would the applicant expect to participate in and nurture a child's religious life?

3.25. *Racial origin and cultural and linguistic background* and any special experience and knowledge relevant to the care of a child of a particular racial origin or for a child of mixed race or from a particular cultural background: does the applicant have links through his or her own background, marriage or friendship with a particular group, or a special understanding of a particular culture and knowledge of language? To what extent is the applicant prepared to develop such links and understanding?

3.26. The applicant's attitudes and expectations in relation to contact between parents and children, visits by parents and relatives to the foster parents' home and *working with parents* in pursuance of the aims of the placement and the plan for the child will be particularly important. The social worker should seek to clarify whether attitudes and opinions are dogmatic or amenable to training and change. It is essential that the applicant is aware of the day to day implications of working with parents and is prepared to accept training and support to achieve the required partnership with parents.

3.27. The *standard of living* and "*life style*" of the family will need to be assessed. What are the *leisure activities and interests* of the family? How does *employment/occupation* affect family life? Are shifts worked? What time is available for family activities? Where the principal care giver is employed outside the home, what arrangements are available or proposed to ensure proper care for a foster child after school and during sickness and holidays? What opportunities will be available to the child to associate with other families, with children in the applicant's circle and in the community; and to take part with his peers in activities appropriate to his age and interests?

3.28. Views should be formed of the *applicant's attitudes and expectations* in relation to child rearing, looking after someone else's child, understanding and perception of fostering and capacity to work in partnership with a child's family; of the applicant's capacity to provide a foster child with protection, nurture and opportunities for development; and of the applicant's preference and suitability as a foster parent for any particular group of children or for any particular fostering tasks.

3.29. A view should be formed also on the applicant's views and expectations in relation to *education*. Does the applicant recognise the need and have the capacity to provide educational support to a foster child and to encourage the development of special talents and interests, including those which call for additional or out of school arrangements? Do the children of the family attend fee paying schools? Does the applicant have the capacity to develop an understanding of particular educational methods, settings and services which they may not have encountered before? Could the applicant cope with the challenge of providing any necessary support to a child with special educational needs?

3.30. The applicant's views on *discipline* should be explored including a readiness to accept that corporal punishment is inappropriate for children in foster placements and to undertake not to use such a form of punishment. The term "corporal punishment" should be taken to cover any intentional application of force as punishment including slapping, pinching, squeezing, shaking, throwing missiles and rough handling. It would also include punching or pushing in the heat of the moment in response to violence from young people. It does not prevent a person taking necessary physical action, where any other course of action would be likely to fail to avert an immediate danger of personal injury to the child or another person, or to avoid immediate danger to property. It is well established that the enjoyment of eating and drinking is fundamental to a child's healthy physical and emotional development. Meal times are an important social occasion in the life of a child and it would be quite inappropriate for a child to be refused meals. Deprivation of food and drink should be taken to include the denial of access to the amounts and range of foods and drink normally available to children in the home but would not include instances where specific food or drinks have to be withheld from a child on medical advice. Similarly, restriction of contact ie visits to and from the family and friends should not be used as a punishment.

3.31. Applicants are required to name two referees both of whom must be interviewed. A referee should be someone who is in a position to comment on the applicant's sense of responsibility including his or her knowledge, understanding and love of children, evidence of sound relationships, his or her motivation to foster children and his or her personality. If this range of information is not available from the referees additional information on this point will be necessary. An additional interview with a member of the wider family may be helpful in establishing the importance of the wider family and their attitudes towards a foster child in the family.

3.32. The use of BAAF form F is recommended for reports on which the decision to approve or not is to be taken. The recommended terms of approval should be clear, ie, in relation to the particular type of fostering placement, number of children, children of a particular age group. Specification could arise from the assessment or from the choice of the prospective foster parent. Approval may be restricted to a specific named child or children. Subject to the requirements of legislation and guidance on disclosure of records, the content of the report should normally be shared with the prospective foster parent while avoiding disclosure of information supplied in confidence by referees or other agencies or professionals.

ASSESSMENT OF RELATIVES AND FAMILY FRIENDS AS FOSTER PARENTS

3.33. Possibilities for a child to be cared for within the extended family should have been investigated and considered as an alternative to the provision of accommodation by the responsible authority. However, even when it has become necessary for the responsible authority to arrange provision of accommodation, placement with a relative will often provide the best opportunities for promoting and maintaining family links in a familiar setting.

3.34. The Foster Placement (Children) Regulations apply to a placement of a child by a responsible authority with a relative or friend including allowing a child to remain with a relative or friend with whom the child is living when the need for accommodation arises.

PLACEMENTS PREVIOUSLY GOVERNED BY THE ACCOMMODATION OF CHILDREN (CHARGE AND CONTROL) REGULATIONS 1988

3.35. Existing placements of a child who is subject to a care order with a relative or friend will continue to be governed by the requirements of the Charge and Control Regulations 1988 (as if those Regulations were still in force) for twelve months from the day on which Part III of the Act comes into force (paragraph 21 of Schedule 14 to the Act). Thereafter, such placements will come within the scope of the Foster Placement (Children) Regulations 1991. During the twelve month transitional period, the child will be treated as having been placed with a local authority foster parent. But during that time, the local authority must make arrangements to consider approving that person as a local authority foster parent under the 1991 Regulations, if it is planned that the child is to remain with that person after the end of the twelve month transitional period.

PLACEMENTS PREVIOUSLY GOVERNED BY THE BOARDING-OUT OF CHILDREN (FOSTER PLACEMENT) REGULATIONS 1988

3.36 Existing placements of a child in an approved household under the Boarding-out Regulations 1988 will continue to be governed by the requirements of those Regulations (as if those Regulations were still in force) for twelve months from the day on which Part III of the Act comes into force (paragraph 21 of Schedule 14 to the Act). Thereafter, such placements will come within the scope of the Foster Placement (Children) Regulations 1991. During the twelve month transitional period, the child will be treated as having been placed with a local authority foster parent. But during that time, the local authority must make arrangements to consider approving that person as a local authority foster parent under the 1991 Regulations, if it is planned that the child is to remain with that person after the end of the twelve month transitional period.

APPROVAL

3.37. A foster parent may be approved to provide foster care for a particular named child or children or number and age range of children or of placements of any particular kind or in any particular circumstances (Regulation 3(5)). It is therefore possible for the assessment process to focus on the suitability of a relative or friend in respect only of the child or children concerned, where the advantages to the child of remaining within the wider family and in the care of a familiar figure may be a significant factor. Assessment of relatives as foster parents must include consideration of the extent to which the placement will affect the child's other family relationships, including contact with either or both parents. Where such contact has been terminated or restricted, the local authority will need to consider with the prospective foster parents any particular difficulties they may encounter in maintaining any conditions or restrictions on contact. Similarly, relatives may feel their loyalty strained where they are given confidential information not available to other family members, just as they may be reluctant to disclose to the authority information they already possess. The authority should be ready to provide appropriate support where difficulties arise. All these considerations are especially critical where a child has experienced abuse, including sexual abuse. In such cases, the case conference could make important contributions to reaching a decision.

3.38. Authorities should make known to prospective foster parents the arrangements for reaching decisions about approval. The arrangements must reflect the importance of the decision and the need for accountability within the authority. Local choice will vary. A local authority may wish to link decision-making in this context with their arrangements to comply with the

Placement with Parents etc Regulations. This would provide a consistency in level of decision-making and provide oversight of placement decisions. Otherwise an authority may choose to use a small panel, including a senior officer designated to make the decision or perhaps extend the role of an adoption panel.

3.39. Depending on the skills and resources available within the fostering service there may be scope for the participation of outside members with relevant expertise and experience to contribute to decision-making. An experienced foster parent from another agency, for example, could be invited to join a panel (as an individual and not as a representative of a group).

3.40. The role of a panel could be extended to include consideration, advice and recommendations in relation to decisions other than approval of foster parents, such as matching and placement; consideration of possible applications by foster parents for residence orders; and, decisions in connection with reviews of foster parents. Foster care frequently calls for decision-making in circumstances which require careful consideration and weighing of complex issues to ensure that the child's interests are best served. But while decisions must always be made with care they must often in the interests of a child be made speedily. A range of decision-making procedures for different circumstances may be necessary with guidelines to ensure professional accountability and managerial responsibility as well as the maintenance of standards.

3.41. Where a joint adoption and fostering panel is used business should be conducted so as to avoid confusion between matters falling within the scope of the Foster Placement (Children) Regulations and those falling within the scope of the Adoption Agencies Regulations. Fostering with a view to adoption, for example, is a confusing and inaccurate concept which can blur the need for distinct decisions. Similarly, it should be understood that approval as adopters does not imply approval as foster parents.

3.42. Authorities are required by Regulation 3 to give notice in writing of the decision on approval. The decision should also be communicated personally by a social worker. It is important that the notice of approval should clearly state the terms of approval in accordance with Regulation 3(5)(a). As far as possible, the reasons for refusal should be explained. It is important that a full record of the decision-making process is kept rather than a record of the decision only. A representations procedure should be available for reconsideration of the decision and to deal with an applicant's dissatisfaction with the approval process.

3.43. The outcome should also be notified to any professionals who have contributed to the assessment, such as health visitors or GPs.

REVIEW AND TERMINATION OF APPROVAL

3.44. Authorities are required by Regulation 4 to review the approval of foster parents at least once a year. Annual review will no doubt be right in most cases, although changes of circumstance such as change of address, death of spouse or remarriage or change in health will normally call for an out-of-course review. The authority's review procedure must be set out in the foster care agreement.

3.45. Reviews should focus on the foster parent rather than the current placement and should, if possible, be carried out by a social worker with responsibility to the fostering service who may not be the social worker of a child in placement. Consultation would then of course be necessary to establish how the placement is working and what the child and his parents views on this are. A review should include a visit to the foster home, discussion with the foster parent and the child, and generally meeting other members of the household. It should be an opportunity for airing and discussion of a foster parent's view of the service offered by the authority and of the foster parent's own experience and any difficulties arising. The terms of approval should be included in the review. Non use or under use of a foster home are also factors to investigate on review as the process should contribute to an understanding of the strengths and weaknesses of the fostering service as a whole.

3.46. The extent to which reviews should include a comprehensive re-assessment of a foster parent will depend on individual circumstances. An authority may decide that a full re-assessment will be needed where it is agreed that a foster parent should seek approval for a different kind of placement, perhaps to care for sexually abused children or to participate in a special scheme.

3.47. Review of approval may be needed on investigation of allegations against the foster parent made by a child or parent or other person. Procedures must first and foremost protect the child's welfare, but should also take account of the sensitivities and rights of the other parties including the foster parents . Where it is decided to leave the child in the placement during the investigation arrangements should take account of the need for additional support and supervision.

3.48. In any review under Regulation 4 the authority must seek and take into account the views of the foster parent. Foster parents should be offered the opportunity of giving their views in writing in advance of the review, although some may prefer their views to be recorded during the discussion. Any other authority which has a child in placement in the foster home or which has used the foster home within the last year must be invited to give their views which must be taken into account. It is important that both or all authorities using the services of a single foster home should contribute to the review as reviews can be an important means of maintaining a good understanding between all parties and identifying and resolving any difficulties that may arise.

3.49. The review and the decision taken should be recorded. Regulation 4 provides for the foster parent to be notified in writing of the outcome including any change in the terms of approval. Where a decision has been taken to terminate approval, the decision and the reasons should be generally discussed with the foster parent before the statutory notice is issued.

3.50. Approval must be formally terminated by the approving authority when it is decided that the foster parent is no longer suitable. It is not sufficient to avoid placing further children. Notice of termination should also be given where a foster parent decides to give up fostering unless the foster parent intends to resume after a short break. Authorities should also issue a notice of termination where although no formal notice of resignation has been received, it is clear that a foster parent does not intend to continue or resume fostering. This is important because as long as foster parents remain formally approved, their services are available to other responsible authorities.

3.51. Copies of notices of re-approval and termination are to be sent to any other authority using the foster home and taking part in the review. As a matter of good practice, the outcome of the review should normally be discussed with the other authorities before a final decision is reached. If the outcome of a review means that a child is to be moved from the foster home, plans for the termination of the placement will have to be agreed between the authorities and the foster parent. This will not apply if the child has to be removed at once to safeguard and protect his welfare. Plans will need to be made in consultation with the child, parents and other individuals significantly involved.

THE FOSTER CARE AGREEMENT

3.52. Regulation 3(6) requires the approving authority to enter into a written agreement with a foster parent at the time of approval. The purpose of the agreement is to provide written information about the terms and conditions of the partnership between the authority and the foster parent. It also provides foster parents with written confirmation of matters which should be discussed and agreed during assessment.

3.53. The matters and obligations to be covered in the foster care agreement are set out in Schedule 2 to the Regulations. These are minimum requirements. Authorities should not restrict themselves to these matters but should ensure that foster parents have a full understanding of what is expected on behalf of both foster parent and authority when a child is placed, in relation to the requirements of Regulations and the authority's policies. The authority and the foster parent will also enter into a specific agreement when an individual child is placed (see Chapter 4).

TRAINING AND SUPPORT OF FOSTER PARENTS

3.54. Preparation should begin as part of the assessment process, as the foster parent learns about foster care and what is required of a foster parent. After approval, the social worker and foster parent should agree on what further preparation and training is needed, before a child is placed and continuing beyond placement. The early months as a foster parent or the early months of a first "specialist scheme" placement can have particular importance as a period of development. Opportunities for training and support should be provided at three levels:

● support, discussion and evaluation in the home;

● participation in foster parent groups;

● participation in formal training events with other foster parents and social workers.

3.55. Social workers need access to appropriate training resources to meet the needs of foster parents. National Foster Care Association training packages have proved valuable in training programmes, including the foundation courses **The Challenge of Foster Care** and **A problem shared**. Further modules are available for development and specialism in the fostering task. The help of health professionals should be sought in local training schemes. Reading matter should also be available to foster parents. Some themes should be common to all preparation and training programmes, such as working with parents. All training should aim to enable foster parents to help and work with parents and children in the context of a multi-racial society and to develop positive attitudes towards less advantaged groups. Initial training and preparation should alert foster parents to the possibility (without undue stress on the likelihood) that hitherto undisclosed abuse of a child, including sexual abuse, may come to light during placement. Foster parents need to know how they should respond and the steps they should take. Similarly, all foster parents need to be aware that some children may have undetected health conditions to understand the circumstances and factors which suggest a child may be at risk, and the implications for family life and the child's care. There should be a clear understanding of the support which the authority has a responsibility to provide if circumstances of this kind arise.

3.56. Specialised preparation and training are needed for foster parents undertaking some tasks or participating in some schemes, for example, the care of sexually abused children, or juvenile offenders. Opportunities for continuing training should be available for all foster parents. Professionals from other services and agencies can be asked to contribute to training. Health service professionals may be willing to speak on such matters as helping adolescents with developing sexuality or the health care needs of children from minority groups.

3.57. Foster parents need support and help with difficulties that arise from the special demands of the fostering role, in addition to help that may be needed in connection with the care of a particular child. Fostering makes demands on the whole family and can be the cause of stress in family relationships. Authorities should ensure that appropriate support, advice and assistance are provided to the foster parent and foster family. A foster parent may need help in learning to deal with ambivalent attitudes from neighbours and a lack of understanding and co-operation on the part of other agencies and services. Authorities can help by demonstrating their own confidence in foster parents and by making sure that professionals in other services know of a placement and of the foster parent's responsibilties. Letters of introduction from the authority may assist the foster parent in this respect.

3.58. The role of the child's social worker includes support, advice and assistance to the foster parent, in relation to that child. It is desirable, however, for foster parents to be allocated their "own" social worker to whom they may turn for general advice and support. The support available from a specialist worker may be supplemented by links with an experienced foster parent.

3.59. The social worker should see that foster parents have access to support which is available from other sources. Within the fostering service, experienced foster parents and foster parent or foster family groups can be an important training resource and a source of support, especially to less experienced foster parents. Foster parents should also have access to the support of professionals in other services which is available to all parents in the community.

COMPLAINTS AND REPRESENTATIONS

3.60. Under the Children Act 1989 there is no statutory provision for foster parents to have access to a procedure to make representations or a complaint on their own behalf except in connection with decisions about the usual fostering limit. It is essential, however, that foster parents should be able to make representations about disputes and discuss facts connected with other aspects of their service as foster parents, including disputes about the care of a child, dissatisfaction with the services or support provided by the authority and requests for review of decisions such as refusal of approval, termination of approval or termination of a placement. Responsible authorities may therefore wish to extend their statutory Children Act complaints procedures to include complaints made by foster parents on their own behalf.

CHAPTER 4 FOSTER PLACEMENTS

CHOICE OF PLACEMENT

4.1. The general duty set out in section 22(1) of the Act apply to all decisions by local authorities (section 64(1) in the case of voluntary organisations) in relation to foster care of a child. This is reinforced by Regulation 5 which requires authorities to be satisfied that placement with foster parents is the best way of meeting their welfare duty towards a child in their care and that the specific placement is the most suitable having regard to all the circumstances. In choosing the most suitable placement, authorities can face a difficult task in meeting the assessed needs of the child. There are often practical limitations on choice which mean that the ideal placement is not available. Regular reviews of recruitment and training needs and forward planning to meet identified needs should mean that the type of foster home needed will be more likely to be available.

4.2. The making of arrangements in advance as required by Regulation 3 of the Arrangements for Placement of Children (General) Regulations will allow more opportunity for the child's needs to be carefully assessed and a plan developed before placement. Hasty or immediate placements should be avoided as far as possible. Contingency planning for a possible placement while efforts continue to keep a child at home may mean a more successful and less disturbing transition to a foster placement if the child must be accommodated. Even where time is short, a partial plan, which can be reviewed and developed, is required by the Arrangements for Placement of Children (General) Regulations and is essential to a successful placement.

4.3. Some of the considerations which influence assessment of a child's needs and choice of placement are reflected in particular statutory requirements which have been discussed in Chapters 1 and 2. Section 23(7) of the Act requires that accommodation provided for a child who is being looked after shall, so far as is reasonably practicable and consistent with his welfare, be near the child's home; and, subject to the same premise, that siblings are accommodated together. Accommodation provided for a child with disabilities should so far as reasonably practicable, not be unsuitable to the child's particular needs. Regulation 5 also requires authorities to satisfy themselves that the child's needs arising from his racial origin and cultural and linguistic background will, so far as practicable, be met; and to place a child, where possible, with a foster parent of the same religious persuasion as the child or with a foster parent who will undertake to bring the child up in that religious persuasion.

4.4. A child's need for continuity in life and care should be a constant factor in choice of placement. In most cases, this suggests a need for placement with a family of the same race, religion and culture in a neighbourhood within reach of family, school or day nursery, church, friends and leisure activities. Continuity also requires placement in a foster home which a child can find familiar and sympathetic and not remote from his own experience in social background, attitudes and expectations; a foster home in which he is most likely to be able to settle down and as far as possible feel "at home" and free from anxieties. This is equally if not more necessary where it is not possible to place a child near home or where there are special reasons for choosing a placement at a distance.

4.5. Authorities are required in making any decision to have regard to the wishes and feelings of the child subject to the child's understanding, and this applies to all decisions in relation to foster care. The more mature the child, the more fully the child will be able to enter into discussion about plans and proposals. Children need information and explanation so that they are in a position to develop views and make choices. Some authorities provide preparation and information groups for children as part of preparation for foster care. With young children the social worker should make efforts to communicate with the child and discover the child's real feelings. Providing children with reassurance and helping them with their anxieties about foster care or a particular placement is essential to the choice and success of a placement. But responsibility for making decisions lies with the authority. Children should not be allowed to feel that the burden has fallen totally upon them.

NUMBERS OF CHILDREN IN FOSTER HOMES

4.6 An important factor to be taken into account in placement decisions, and in discussions about the best use of foster homes, is the number of children who may be placed in a foster home. Paragraphs 2 and 3 of Schedule 7 to the Act prescribe a 'usual fostering limit' of three children. The limit does not apply if the chidren are siblings. This does not mean that placement of three in a foster home should be taken as a norm. In many cases the welfare of a child needing placement will be best served by being the only foster child in the family. Where more than one child is to be placed, the interests of both must be carefully considered and weighed. The needs of the foster parents' own children must also be considered. These points should be borne in mind in decisions to approve a foster parent for the placement of two or more children who are unrelated.

4.7. Local authorities have powers under paragraph 4 of Schedule 7 to grant exemption from the usual fostering limit. The factors to be taken into account in considering whether to grant exemption are set out in paragraph 4 of Schedule 7. These are:

(a) the number, ages and circumstances of children whom the person proposes to foster;

(b) the arrangements which the person proposes for the care and accommodation of the fostered children;

(c) the intended and likely relationship between the person and the fostered children;

(d) the period of time for which he proposes to foster the children;

(e) whether the welfare of the fostered children (and of any other children who are or will be living in the accommodation will be safeguarded and promoted; and

(f) the incidence within the foster home of any other child care activities (eg child minding which might influence a foster parent's capacity to provide sufficient care for children fostered).

4.8. Where exemption is granted, written notice must include the names of the children who may be fostered and any conditions which the local authority decide to attach to the exemption. An exemption might, for example, be given to allow another child to join a family for the holidays. Local authorities have powers to vary or cancel conditions attaching to the exemption.

4.9. Where a foster parent is exceeding, or wishes to exceed, the usual fostering limit and the local authority conclude that exemption should not be given, the foster parent will be treated as running a children's home, and the Children's Homes Regulations will apply. There may be cases in which local authorities are called on to decide whether an establishment is a foster home or a children's home. This can only be judged on all the facts and circumstances of the case. Small scale, domestic setting, a family atmosphere and an excellent standard of care do not necessarily mean that an establishment is not a children's home; these characteristics are, in fact, desirable in all children's homes. A few useful pointers which suggest that the reception of children is on a different basis from the extension of the family circle which is the hallmark of foster care, and that an establishment would be more appropriately treated as a children's home are:

- a fixed number of 'places' are offered;
- all places must ideally be filled, to achieve viability;
- investments have been made in the fabric of the premises to accommodate a larger number of children;
- a voluntary organisation has arranged for a couple to run an establishment with a view to providing care for a fixed number of children.

4.10. Clearly, however, there can be no fixed rules. The important aim is that the most appropriate safeguards and support should be applied in each case.

THE FOSTER PLACEMENT AGREEMENT

4.11. Regulation 5 requires a responsible authority to enter into a written placement agreement with the foster parent. The matters to be covered in the foster placement agreement are set out in Schedule 3. While the *foster care agreement* (Regulation 3(6)(a)) covers general matters relating to the foster parent and to all placements, the *foster placement agreement* (Regulation 5(6)) will set out the agreed arrangements for the care of the individual child placed. It also serves as a confirmation of what is expected from the foster parent and the authority and what has been agreed with the parent. Different requirements apply when a child is placed in an emergency or in an immediate placement (see paragraphs 4.24 to 4.26).

INFORMATION TO FOSTER PARENTS

4.12. The foster placement agreement must include a statement of the information which the authority considers necessary to enable the foster parent to care for the child. This includes the authority's plans for the child and the objectives of the placement; the role of the child's parents and the arrangements to enable them to continue their role in the child's life; the child's personal history, religious persuasion, cultural and linguistic background and racial origin; the child's state of health and need for health care and surveillance; and the child's educational needs. The statement must be provided at the time of the signing of the agreement or, where this is not possible (because the information is not available, for instance) within the following 14 days.

4.13. This requirement acknowledges the need for communication of essential information if there is to be an effective partnership between parents, authorities and foster parents. Foster parents need to have a full understanding of the background and history of children on whose behalf they are undertaking an exacting and responsible role and who will need their help in coping with living away from home. The foster parent will generally need to know the circumstances leading to the child being looked after or the child's admission to care and the child's previous experiences. The social worker should discuss with the parents and any other previous carers, and with children according to their understanding, the information which is to be given to a foster parent and why. Where there is a special reason for withholding significant information, the reason should be recorded on the child's case record.

4.14. The purpose of providing information is to enable the foster parent to care for the child. In some circumstances less information, about the child's history for example, may be needed in connection with a very short-term placement. Authorities should see however that foster parents are properly equipped with all the information they need to help a child during a placement. There is no requirement under Regulation 11 for written information to be issued when a child is placed under the emergency or immediate placement provisions but authorities should make sure that the emergency or immediate foster parent has sufficient information to care for and help the child.

4.15. Foster parents are required to undertake to treat as confidential any information about a child or his family given in confidence in connection with a foster placement. Foster parents' training should include advice on the maintenance of confidentiality and dealing with questions from family and friends. Advice should also be given on the safekeeping of documentation connected with the child and the placement, which should be returned to the authority when the placement ends.

PREPARATION AND INTRODUCTION

4.16. There are examples of intensive approaches to preparation, more usually associated with specialist schemes or with long-term placements, where foster parents are closely involved in preparation, pre-planning meetings and sharing of information. While they may not be practicable in the majority of placements, the principles of such approaches can be applied with benefit to all placements. The foster parent will need information about the child and the child's needs and history, the plan for the child, the parents' knowledge of the arrangements and degree of involvement in the plan and the child's understanding of the plan. The aim of the placement and what is expected in relation to the placement on the part of parent, authority and foster parent must be understood by all parties.

4.17. The introduction of the child to the foster placement is an important part of the preparation. Wherever possible the social worker should bring a parent or previous carer to share in the introduction. Parents have an important part in preparation and introduction. They can provide information about the child's day-to-day routines, capabilities, habits, fears, likes and dislikes. This information is essential if the foster parent is to provide continuity of care for the child and help the child to settle in. The expected role of the parent in the day to day care for the child (such as who will be in contact with the school) should be clarified in the preparation for placement.

4.18. The financial arrangements for the placement should be settled. In addition to maintenance payments, the authority should consider with the foster parent whether there are any particular needs arising from the placement: bedding, bedroom furniture, equipment, clothes. A good deal of equipment may be needed where a group of siblings is placed in a household not equipped to cater for large numbers. Children with special needs frequently involve extra expense. Authorities should be realistic and sensitive in responding fully and promptly to a need for extra expenditure, always bearing in mind that the responsibility for providing for the child lies with the authority and his parents, not the foster parent.

SUPERVISION OF PLACEMENT

4.19. Regulaton 6 provides a framework of requirements, including visits, for the social worker's task of supervising the placement and working with the child and foster parent towards the objective of the placement and the achievement of the plan for the child. These visits are separate to any visit for the purpose of reviewing approval of the foster parent. The requirements for supervision are:

- visits: the child must be seen at each visit. (Where a visit is made to discuss the foster parent's need for support or at the foster parent's request it may not be appropriate to see the child at that time. Such visits when the child is not seen fall outside the pattern of visits required in Regulation 6);

- advice and assistance to the foster parent; and

- reviews of the plan for the child (under the Review of Children's Cases Regulations – see Chapter 8).

4.20. Minimum visiting requirements are one visit within the first week of placement and then at intervals of not more than six weeks during the first year of placement, and thereafter visits at intervals of not more than three months. The frequency of visits should be determined by the circumstances of the case and the authority must arrange a visit whenever reasonably requested by a child or foster parent. Visits during the first weeks of placement can be especially important to check that arrangements made at the time of placement for schooling and contact are working smoothly, or to give any help needed during the settling-in period. The Regulations provide for the child to be seen alone if considered appropriate. The plan for the child and the placement agreement should identify where this is a consideration from the outset. The need to see the child alone will be decided upon by the responsible authority during the course of the placement. After each visit, the local authority is required to ensure that the social worker who made the visit produces a written report (Regulation 6(4)). The report should indicate that the child was seen and if not why not, and if the child was seen alone. It should also comment on the child's welfare and the success of the placement including any comments made by the child or the carer. Any matter for concern or difficulties should be highlighted so that the need for any necessary action can be discussed with the social worker's supervisor.

4.21. Visiting the child in the foster home has a number of purposes. These include:

(a) a measure of child protection; to talk to the child, to safeguard and reassure a child who may feel isolated and vulnerable and who is away from family and friends. The standard of care should be observed and the child's bedroom sometimes seen. Some visits should be unannounced, in order to provide a balanced perspective of the quality of life in the foster home. A foster parent presenting a "brave-face" would not alert a social worker to their need for help and support in a particularly stressful time in the placement. Visits should occasionally take place when all the members of the household are at home. The child should sometimes be seen alone, perhaps outside the foster home. This reinforces the child protection element. It also helps child and social worker to get to know each other and build up a relationship of trust. Both child and foster parent should feel free to get in touch with the social worker at any time;

(b) an opportunity to evaluate and monitor the achievement of goals, with the child and foster parent, and to contribute to the review of the plan, to monitor, with the help of the foster parent, the child's educational progress; and generally to identify where help is needed;

(c) monitoring the contact arrangements; and

(d) to give support to the foster parent.

4.22. Visits should not be neglected because a placement is going well. Ongoing review of the plan for the child requires that visits take place at least at the frequency the Regulations require. The social worker will not be equipped to identify and help with pending difficulties if no care has been taken to establish a relationship with a child and foster parent. Nor will it be possible otherwise to assess fully long term situations. If, for example, in a long term placement, visits and support seem genuinely superfluous and parents are no longer involved with the child, the case for a residence order application could be considered.

4.23. There are some circumstances where visits in excess of the minimum frequency will be especially necessary. For example, where the role of the child's parents is changing, the child's needs have changed, or perhaps because a lone foster parent has not been allocated a social worker of his "own". There will inevitably be periods in any placement when a foster parent or the placement may be under particular stress.

IMMEDIATE PLACEMENTS

4.24. The powers in Regulation 11 are not available to voluntary organisations. In an emergency Regulation 11 allows a child to be placed with a person who is an approved foster parent. Such a placement with an approved foster parent (Regulation 11(1) and (2)) may be arranged for a period not exceeding 24 hours, even though the requirements of Regulation 5(6) (placement agreement) have not been satisfied. Before such a placement is made, the local authority should satisfy the provisions of Regulation 5(1)(a) (welfare of the child) and obtain a written agreement covering the details in Regulation 11(4)(a)–(e). These duties are:

"(a) to care for the child as if he were a member of the foster parent's family;

  (b) to permit any person authorised by the local authority or (if different) the area authority, to visit the child in the foster home at any time;

  (c) where regulation 7(1) or (2) applies, to allow the child to be removed from the home of the foster parent at any time by the local authority or (as the case may be) the area authority;

  (d) to ensure that any information which the foster parent may acquire relating to the child, or to his family or any other person, which has been given to him in confidence in connection with the placement is kept confidential and is not disclosed except to, or with the agreement of, the local authority; and

  (e) to allow contact with the child in accordance with section 34 of the Act (parental contact etc), with any contact order (as defined in section 8(1) of the Act) and with any arrangements made or agreed by the local authority."

4.25. Regulation 11(3) allows immediate placement with a relative or friend and requires that the relative or friend should be interviewed, the home inspected and information obtained about the other members of the household. As for emergency placements with approved foster parents the authority should be satisfied that the placement is in the child's best interests and should make a written agreement covering the details in Regulation 11(4)(a)–(e) (see above). The authority should, in practice, make the fullest enquiries possible in the circumstances, including where possible checks with the police locally to satisfy themelves that nothing is known which suggests that the relative or friend is not a suitable person to be entrusted with the child. Where possible, the parent's views or those of other relatives should be sought.

4.26. These powers are intended to be used exceptionally in unforseen circumstances and not for an admission to care for which contingency plans could have been made. Where such planning has not been possible the powers may be used with benefit where it would clearly be advantageous to a child to be placed with or to remain in the care of a familiar figure in reassuring surroundings. Authorities should guard against inappropriate use of the powers and it is recommended that local procedures should provide for authorisation at a senior level. An immediate placement may last no longer than six weeks and the child must be visited at least weekly. The placement may only continue beyond six weeks if during that period the relative or friend is approved as a foster parent.

SHORT-TERM PLACEMENTS

4.27. Regulation 9 allows for a series of *pre-planned* short-term foster placements, of a particular child with the same foster parents to be treated as a single placement for the purpose of applying these Regulations. The length and timing of the individual placements within the arrangement need not be specified in advance but no single placement may exceed four weeks and all the placements must occur within a period which does not exceed one year. The total duration of time in the placement during the arrangement is not to exceed 90 days.

4.28. The authority is required to visit a child in such a placement from time to time as circumstances require and when reasonably requested by the child or foster parent. The minimum visiting requirements are one visit during the first placement in the series followed by a second visit if more than six months pass from the beginning of the first placement in the series while the child is in the placement.

4.29. The sort of short-term placements which may come under Regulation 9 are schemes variously known as 'respite care', 'phased care' and 'family link' schemes. Under such schemes an authority makes arrangements for a child who normally lives with his family to spend short periods of time with an approved foster parent. Schemes are usually for the benefit of children with disabilities and their families, to provide the parents with a break and the child with the stimulus of a change of scene. Schemes may also be used for other children in need to take the 'heat off' at intervals and prevent family breakdown. Some children placed in short-term respite schemes may normally live in long-term foster placements.

4.30. Once the arrangements are in place, the carers and the parents may be able to operate them with minimal involvement from a social worker, ie the child may be taken to and from the foster home by the parents for the number of weekends or weeks specified in the arrangment. Sometimes an arrangement may provide specifically for say, one weekend per month or two months; or an arrangement may provide for a certain number of weekends or weeks, the timing to be agreed between foster parent and parents according to circumstance. In some cases a 'package' of services is agreed, including a specified amount of child minding and baby sitting. The Arrangements for Placement and Review Regulations also make similar provision for a series of short-term placements to count as single placements.

PLACEMENT OUTSIDE ENGLAND AND WALES

4.31. A local authority may arrange (or assist in arranging) for a child for whom they are providing accommodation by voluntary agreement to live outside England and Wales with the approval of every person who has parental responsibility for the child (paragraph 19(2) of Schedule 2)). In the case of a child who is in care, the court's approval must be sought (paragraph 19(1) of Schedule 2). This may only be given in certain circumstances, namely where: every person with parental responsibility for the child consents or his consent is dispensed with under paragraph 19(5), the child himself consents (if he has sufficient understanding), suitable arrangements have been made for the reception and welfare of the child in the new country and living there would be in the child's best interests (paragraph 19(3) and (4) of Schedule 2). Where the child is moving to another jurisdiction with the British Islands (ie the United Kingdom, the Channel Islands and the Isle of Man) the effect of the care order may be transferred to the relevant public authority in the receiving jurisdiction under regulations to be made by virtue of section 101 of the Act. Voluntary organisations are prohibited by Regulation 10 from placing a child outside the British Islands. Both voluntary organisations and local authorities may place a child within the British Islands, but outside England and Wales. The Regulations do not apply outside England and Wales and Regulation 10 therefore requires agencies to take steps to ensure that equivalent requirements are met where placements are made outside England and Wales.

4.32. Circumstances in which the question of a placement outside England and Wales may arise include those in which:

(a) it would be in the interests of a child to be placed with a relative or other person elsewhere in the British Islands: Scotland, Northern Ireland, the Isle of Man or the Channel Islands;

(b) a foster parent moves to a new address elsewhere in the British Islands and there are reasons in favour of continuing the placement; and

(c) a foster parent is required to go overseas for a tour of duty or service posting and there are reasons in favour of continuing the placement.

4.33. Where it is clearly in a child's interests and consistent with the plan for the child to be placed elsewhere in the British Islands, and the foster parent is approved under the Regulations, appropriate arrangements for supervision should be made with the relevant authorities. Local authorities should follow the principles which apply to similar arrangements which may be made with area authorities in England and Wales to supervise a placement on their behalf.

4.34. Where a foster parent plans to move permanently or temporarily elsewhere in the British Islands, similar considerations apply as to any proposed move by a foster parent beyond the locality. The authority will need to weigh the advantages and disadvantages of continuing the placement, bearing in mind the views of the parents, the plans for the child, the objectives of the placement and implications for contact. The child's wishes will be a critical factor; the consent of the parents (or those with parental responsibility) is essential where the child is not in care. Whether or not the child is in care, parents should be involved in the decision-making process.

4.35. Other factors arise when the proposed move is overseas, including the increased difficulty of continuing any contact arrangements and the difficulty of supervising and reviewing the placement. If the foster parent is in the armed services, it should be possible to make arrangements with the Soldiers, Sailors and Airmens Families Association (SSAFA). Where the authority believe that supervision is not required, consideration can be given to the possibility of an application by the foster parents for a residence order. This will have the advantage of bringing before the court any conflict between the child's interests and wishes and the parent's wishes.

4.36. A decision to allow a foster parent to take a child overseas (except for a holiday) should not be made except where there are exceptional circumstances and adequate and realistic arrangements can be made to safeguard the child's welfare and meet the requirements of the Regulations. It should be agreed only where the stay overseas is for a definite and limited period.

THE END OF THE PLACEMENT

4.37. A placement may come to an end in a variety of ways. Planned endings occur where the objective of the placement has been achieved or partly achieved, or it has been decided that the objective cannot be achieved and the plan has been reviewed. Placement may end in:

● a move to another placement;

● return to the child's family;

● return to the family, but continuing support and services are needed and the child is expected to return for further periods of respite care; and

● leaving the placement for independent life.

4.38. The aim should be to achieve a planned ending to a placement with careful preparation and transition, whether to their family, another placement or adoptive placement. Foster parents have an important role to play in preparing and reassuring the child, assisting gradual introductions by taking the child on visits to the new carers and receiving visits from them, and by helping the new carers to understand the child's habits, routines and needs.

4.39. A child's return to his family may need equally careful preparation, and child and family may need support over the settling-in period until the child is re-integrated into the family. Other services under the Act may be appropriate (see Volume 2 in this series). A period of gradual re-introduction may be needed, depending on the length of time the child has been away from home and the extent of changes in the family. The need for continuity is equally critical at the end of a placement as at the beginning. Children often return to different addresses, new babies in the family, new step parents and step brothers and sisters. Sometimes a child must change schools and leave behind friends and interests acquired during foster placement. Parents, too, need to be prepared for changes in the child's habits, interests and routines; and for the possibility of disturbed behaviour while the child is settling in.

4.40. It is sometimes appropriate for contact between former foster parents and child to continue for a time through visits, telephone calls or letters. In most cases it is helpful to foster parents to be given news of how the child has settled into his new life. Feedback of this kind can contribute to their development in the fostering role.

4.41. Unplanned endings may happen where a crisis leads the authority to remove the child immediately or the foster parent asks for the child to be removed or the child insists on leaving. Where a child is accommodated by agreement with a parent under voluntary arrangements, a parent may remove the child without notice. Foster parents will need advice on handling those cases in which it may be necessary to seek an emergency order to prevent totally inappropriate and unplanned removals where this would be likely to cause significant harm to a child (for example, a drunk parent coming to "collect" his child in the middle of the night).

4.42. Local authorities have a duty under Regulation 7 not to allow a child to remain in a foster home if the authority considers that it would not be in his interests to stay there. Where necessary (where a child is at risk of harm, for example) the child should be removed immediately. Authorities have power under Regulation 7 to remove in these circumstances any child who is placed with foster parents in their area by another authority or a voluntary organisation, whether or not the area authority have agreed to supervise the placement.

4.43. While authorities should clearly not hesitate to use these powers when they are needed to safeguard a child, the aim should be to bring placements to a planned conclusion, discussing the plans with the child and foster parents and parents and involving them in the preparation of the child. There may be circumstance where the authority have decided that the placement must be brought to an end but removal may be delayed without disadvantage to the child. Authorities should as far as possible avoid removals which appear hasty and arbitrary.

4.44. Children need help in coping with disrupted placements and reassurance that they are not responsible for the placement coming to an end where this is not the case. Disrupted placements should also be considered with the foster parents in a positive and forward looking way, where possible without apportioning blame, but with the aim of understanding and learning (on the part of the authority as well as the foster parents) for the benefit of the child and of future placements.

INTER AGENCY WORKING

4.45. Regulation 8 sets out the circumstances in which a local authority may make arrangements with a voluntary organisation for a child, for whom the local authority is responsible, to be placed by the organisation. Under such arrangements a voluntary organisation undertakes all the duties on behalf of the local authority under the Regulations in respect of the placement. The local authority must be satisfied as to the capacity of the organisation to discharge these duties and that such an arrangement is the most suitable way of discharging the duties. The local authority and the voluntary organisation must enter into a written agreement about the arrangements, which must include provision for consultation and for exchange of information and reports. The local authority continue to carry primary responsibility for the child's care and welfare and for decisions affecting the child's welfare.

4.46. There should similarly be a clear agreement, covering exchange of information, reports, consultation and decision-making, where a local authority arranges for another local authority to supervise a placement made in that other authority's area by the first authority.

4.47. There is no specific provision for a local authority to arrange for a placement to be made by a private or "independent" fostering agency; or for a responsible authority's duties under the Regulations to be discharged by such an agency. Some local authorities have chosen to use the services of such agencies; some agencies may offer a valuable means of supporting and providing services to foster parents. But a responsible authority can make a placement only with a foster parent who has been approved in accordance with the Regulations; and can only make arrangement with another local authority or with a voluntary organisation (in accordance with Regulation 8) for the discharge of the authority's duties under the Regulations. Where they choose to use a private agency the authority remain responsible for ensuring that there is compliance with all aspects of the Regulations.

4.48. Particular care is needed where a child is placed outside the area of the local authority. This applies whether arrangements are made with another local authority or with a voluntary organisation, or whether the authority decide themselves to undertake the supervisory duties. Placements at a distance should only be made on the understanding that supervision and support can be provided to the level required by the placement and the child's welfare, including preparation for independent living and after care.

RECORDS

4.49. The Arrangements for Placement of Children (General) Regulations contain requirements for a register of all children placed in a local authority area and for children's case records. The guidance in volume 2 advises on the keeping of these records; on the general principles of good record keeping; and on access to records.

4.50. Regulation 12 requires each local authority to keep a register of all foster parents in their area, who are currently approved and persons not being an approved foster parent with whom a child is placed in their area pursuant to Regulation 11, whether by themselves or another approving authority. The register should serve as an index to the local authority's own fostering resources, and enable the authority to respond to enquiries from other authorities who are considering approval of foster parents in the area or placement with foster parents.

4.51. Regulation 13 requires approving authorities to keep a case record for each foster parent whom they have approved and each person not being an approved foster parent with whom a child is placed by them pursuant to Regulation 11. A record should also be kept for each prospective foster parent who after assessment, has been issued with notice that he cannot be approved. Authorities should continue to use their discretion in retaining information on applications which do not reach the stage of approval or otherwise, in case of future application or enquiry from another agency.

4.52. The documents and information to be retained in the case record are set out in Regulation 13. These include copies of foster care agreements but not copies of individual foster placement agreements. The general principle is to avoid keeping personal details of the child and family on the foster parent's case record and personal details of the foster parent on the child's case record.

Safekeeping and retention of records

4.53. Regulation 14 provides for foster parents' case records to be kept for at least ten years from the date approval is terminated, or until death of the foster parent if earlier. This should be regarded as a minimum rather than an inflexible rule. Retention for a longer period can be desirable in some cases, for example, where there is a possibility that the foster parents may seek to foster children again and there is information which should be known in the event of a further application.

4.54. Most placements made under the Regulations by voluntary organisations are made by arrangement with local authorities. Voluntary organisations can, however, place children under the Regulations by direct arrangements with parents, or, with a child who is sixteen or over. Section 62 of the Act and Regulations 15 and 16 set out the duties of local authorities in respect of such placements. Section 62 requires local authorities to satisfy themselves that any voluntary organisation providing accommodation for a child is satisfactorily safeguarding and promoting the welfare of the child.

4.55. The requirement in respect of individual children placed by arrangement with a local authority is largely met, through observance of Regulation 8, by the authority which made the arrangement with the voluntary organisation. This does not, however, absolve a local authority from the need to know of the activities of any voluntary organisation placing children in their area under these Regulations, even if the organisation is placing children only by arrangement with a local authority. If an area authority are not satisfied that a voluntary organisation is satisfactorily safeguarding and promoting the welfare of the children they have placed, the authority should inform the responsible authority. In order to satisfy themselves in respect of the welfare of individual children, an authority should be satisfied that the voluntary organisation has the capacity, the resources and the arrangements in place to carry out effectively all their responsibilities in connection with the placement of a child. Their responsibilities are set out in the Act and under the Arrangements for Placement of Children (General) Regulations, the Review of Children's Cases Regulations and the Representations Procedure (Children) Regulations and the Foster Placement Regulations and accompanying guidance. Local authorities will judge the nature and extent of the general enquiries and investigations needed in order to satisfy themselves. The activities, managers and reputation of many voluntary organisations will be well known to local authorities. Some organisations, however, may be less well known and more detailed enquiries may be necessary.

Local Authority Visits

4.56. Visits to individual children and observation of the standard of care will provide important opportunities to determine whether a child's welfare is being satisfactorily safeguarded and promoted. Regulation 15 sets out minimum requirements for visits to children placed by a voluntary organisation *excluding* children who are placed by an arrangement with a local authority. The children to whom this Regulation applies will therefore be children placed by direct agreement with a parent or child. Visits are to be made:

● within 28 days of placement;

● within 14 days of any representations from the voluntary organisation, foster parent or child of circumstances requiring a visit;

● within 7 days of receiving any information that a child's welfare may not be satisfactorily safeguarded and promoted; and

● at intervals of not more than six months, provided the authority is satisfied following a visit as to the welfare of the child.

These intervals are the minimum permissible intervals. Where a local authority has reason to believe that circumstances require an immediate visit, there should be no delay.

4.57. Visits to a child placed by a voluntary organisation by arrangement with another local authority are required from time to time under section 62(2). Consultation between local authorities on the frequency and circumstances of visits is recommended. However, the requirements of section 62 should not be used to delegate responsibility from a responsible authority to a area authority outside the framework of an arrangement in accordance with the guidance in paragraphs 4.45–4.48 above. Section 62(6), (7), (8) and (9) are intended to ensure that social workers can carry out their duties.

4.58. A local authority which are not satisfied that the welfare of a child placed by a voluntary organisation is being satisfactorily safeguarded or promoted are required by section 62(5) to take such steps as are reasonably practicable to secure that the child's care and accommodation is taken over by a parent or relative or a person who has parental responsibility. The authority must also consider the extent to which (if at all) they should exercise any of their functions with respect to the child. This could include, for example, providing accommodation or seeking a court order. The two requirements are not mutually exclusive. Depending on the circumstances an authority could take steps to return the child to the care of a parent or relative and arrange for the provision of services to the child or family. Where a child who is the subject of concern is placed by arrangement with a local authority, it will fall to the responsible authority to discharge these responsibilities and to make fresh arrangements for the child.

CHAPTER 5 — PLACEMENT OF CHILDREN IN CARE WITH PARENTS

5.1. Under the Act, a care order will only have been made if the court is satisfied that the child is suffering or is likely to suffer significant harm, and that this is attributable to the care given to him or likely to be given to not being what it would be reasonable to expect a parent to give or being beyond parental control. It is therefore important to be especially careful when such children are placed with their parents. The Placement of Children with parents etc Regulations 1991 replace the Accommodation of Children (Charge and Control) Regulations 1988. The new Regulations reflect the philosophy of the Children Act that children in need can be assisted most effectively if the local authority works in partnership with the child's parents and that for most children the best place for him to be brought up is in his own family. These regulations are made under section 23(5) of the Children Act 1989 and provide for the welfare and protection of children who are in compulsory care and were placed under the charge and control of a parent or guardian before the Children Act came into force (paragraph 17 of Schedule 14 to the Act (transitional provisions)) and to children who are in compulsory care and placed in accommodation with a parent, other person with parental responsibility or a person in whose favour a residence order was in force before the care order was made, after the Children Act is implemented.

5.2. The Regulations and this guidance seek to provide a framework for good professional practice in relation to such placements. Local authorities should consider carefully whether a placement under these Regulations is the only way to achieve placing the child with a parent or person who has or had parental responsibility. Where it is decided that a child's best interests will be met by such a placement the local authority should look again at why it is considered that the care order is still required. It may be that an arrangement can be negotiated between the parent and the local authority (involving the child and other significant individuals) that would enable the local authority to agree that application to discharge the care order is appropriate. Such an arrangement would need to include agreement on both the level of support and supervision by the local authority and cooperation by the parent, with commitment from all involved to working together in the child's best interests. If such agreement can be reached and the court agrees to discharge of the care order then these Regulations will not apply.

5.3. In many cases where it is decided that a placement under these regulations is the right approach, it will be as part of the progress towards discharge of the care order. The management of the placement should aim to enhance the parent's role and support the family relationship with that aim in mind. Even in those cases where the discharge of the care order is not a foreseeable option, the possibility should be constantly reviewed and the aim should be to build a genuine working partnership with the parent. It is difficult to envisage a successful placement where this is not achieved.

5.4. Principal changes from the 1988 Regulations are:

(a) These regulations do not govern placements of children with relatives or friends unless these persons have parental responsibility for the child by virtue of guardianship or had such responsibility under a residence order immediately before the care order was made.

(b) Only Regulations 4, 5, 10 and 11 of these regulations applies to children aged 16 or over.

(c) Any placement by a local authority of a child in compulsory care with a parent is governed by these regulations. This includes a stay of 24 hours or more for the purposes of contact or otherwise (paragraph 12(2) of Schedule 16 of the Courts and Legal Services Act 1990 inserted a new Section 23(5A) of the Children Act 1989 reversing the effect of the Newham decision in the context of the Children Act (R V Newham London Borough council Ex Parte re "P" (1990)2 All ER19 (4 December 1989) – LACs (90)6 and (90)15 refer). This confirms the amendment to the old Charge and Control Regulations.

(d) The concept of charge and control no longer appears in the regulations. Regulations and guidance are drafted to reflect the new position after a care order is granted whereby the parents do not lose parental responsibility although a local authority acquires it and the power to limit the parents' exercise of their responsibility.

(e) Children on remand and accommodated by a local authority are not in the care of the local authority. In consequence, new placements of such children will not be governed by these regulations.

(f) More flexibility in arrangements for the delegation of the Director of Social Service's decision-making responsibility.

SCOPE

Who is covered

5.5. These Regulations will always apply when a child in care is placed for more than 24 hours with a parent, other person with parental responsibility (not being a parent such as a guardian) or a person in whose favour a residence order was in force immediately before the care order was made (see section 23(5)(A) of the Children Act 1989 as inserted by paragraph 12(2) of Schedule 16 to the Court and Legal Services Act 1990). A parent includes a mother and father of the child whether or not married. A person with parental responsibility not being a parent is a guardian appointed in accordance with the provisions of section 5 of the Children Act 1989. It should be kept in mind that a care order under the Children Act 1989 does not extinguish such parental responsibility (Section 33).

5.6. A child who is placed under these Regulations will be subject to an interim or full care order made under the Children Act 1989 (sections 38 and 31 respectively) or under transitional arrangements made under the Act. This interim or full care order could have been made in any "family proceedings" (defined in section 8(3) of the 1989 Act) such as matrimonial or adoption proceedings, not just proceedings which started out as an application for a care order.

5.7. The Regulations also apply to children committed under the pre-Children Act 1989 Law to local authority care under a court order made in matrimonial, guardianship, custodianship or wardship proceedings (where care is subject to the courts' direction) as these committals are deemed to be care orders (paragraph 15 of Schedule 14 to the Children Act 1989). However, where any direction to this effect was included in the original order, a placement under these Regulations would require judicial approval as the court direction-making power is preserved (see paragraph 16 of Schedule 14). If the local authority decides, in a case where care is subject to the court's direction, that it would be in the child's interest for him to be placed with a parent or other person with parental responsibility or a person in whose favour a residence order was in force immediately before the care order was made, the authority in seeking the court's approval should draw the court's attention to these Regulations.

Who is not covered

5.8. Children who are looked after by a local authority but are not in their care by virtue of a care order are outside the scope of these Regulations.

Placement of children looked after by local authorities with relatives or friends whether or not they are in care under an order will be subject to the Foster Placement Regulations 1991. Children subject to emergency protection orders (EPO) under section 44 of the Children Act 1989 are not in care and they will not be subject to these Regulations.

PLACEMENTS OF CHILDREN AGED 16 OR OVER

5.9. The Children Act places new emphasis on the right of children to be involved in decision-making affecting their welfare and requires their involvement in local authority planning for their future, subject only to the understanding of the child (section 22(4) and (5)). In every day life, the older child increasingly accepts responsibility for his own decisions and parents gradually relinquish their control accordingly. For these reasons, the placement of children aged 16 or over, although subject to these Regulations, are only covered by the provisions of Regulations 4, 5, 10 and 11. However, local authorities will wish to consider how far to apply the principles of the other Regulations in their arrangements for such cases, depending on the maturity of the child and the individual circumstances.

CIRCUMSTANCES COVERED

5.10. The Regulations will apply to the placement of children who have entered care for a variety of reasons. For example, to a young person who has previously been in long term residential or foster care or to a child who has spent a very short time away from home before placement with a parent, other person with parental responsibility or a person in whose favour a residence order was in force immediately before the care order was made. Alternatively a child may have remained at home pending court proceedings and remain there after the granting of a care order or a child could be returned home directly after a court appearance. In all such cases these Regulations will apply and all the requirements of these Regulations must be complied with *before* a placement is made except in the circumstances outlined in this paragraph and paragraphs 5.9 and 5.11. However Regulation 2(3) allows a child to remain in an existing placement while investigations are made under Regulation 3 prior to a decision under Regulation 5 and action under Regulation 6. A short absence from home, such as a period of removal under an emergency protection order prior to the granting of an interim care order, will not prevent the local authority's in all cases from deciding that to all intents and purposes the child is already living with the person with whom he may be placed under these Regulations. This involves questions of fact and law and the local authority's legal advisers should be asked specifically for their advice in any particular case. In the last resort it is a matter for the courts to determine.

IMMEDIATE PLACEMENTS

5.11. In some cases, the local authority will recognise that it is in the best interest of the child to make an immediate placement under these Regulations. For example, in the unforeseen breakdown of a foster placement requiring the child's immediate removal, the least traumatic move for the child may be to a parent. When an immediate placement is made all these Regulations will apply but Regulation 6 provides that only the following basic checks have to be carried out before the placement:

(i)   Interviewing the parent;

(ii) Inspecting the accommodation;

(iii) Obtaining information about other persons living in the household.

The decision to place the child must be made by the Director or nominated person(s) (Regulation 5). The other provisions of the Regulations concerning matters which should be investigated in other cases before a placement is made should be carried out as soon as possible after the placement where there has been an immediate placement. It is the Department's view that the remaining enquiries should be completed within 6 weeks of the immediate placement. All remaining provisions of the Regulations are as relevant to the immediate placements as to other placements. Where the application of all the Regulations indicates that the placement is not in the best interest of the child, the provisions of Regulations 11(1) and the guidance in paragraphs 5.57–5.60 will apply.

SHORT TERM PLACEMENTS

5.12. Regulation 13 allows for a series of short, pre-planned placements under these regulations with the same carer to be treated *as a single placement*. Typically, these placements may be for regular staying contact or to allow the carer or the child to have a break. The other Regulations will apply as for a single longer-term placement. The conditions that such a series of placements has to meet to be treated as a single placement for the purposes of these regulations are:

"(a) all the placements occur within a period which does not exceed one year;

(b) no single placement is for a duration of more than four weeks; and

(c) the total duration of the placements does not exceed 90 days."

PLACEMENTS OF SHORT DURATION

5.13. Relevant placements of more than 24 hours are subject to these Regulations. This includes short-term placements for purposes of contact. In planning and arranging such placements account must be taken of any directions by the court in respect of contact. The provisions of Regulation 7 and the guidance on contact elsewhere in this volume may be relevant in setting up such arrangements in some circumstances. This reflects best practice, which recognises that proper planning and protection for a child is necessary for a placement of short duration as for a long-term placement. The action required by these Regulations should need to be taken only once in respect of an established arrangement such as a weekly, weekend placement if the conditions of Regulation 13 are met (see paragraph 5.12). If these conditions are met but there is any significant change in circumstances, the local authority should consider re-applying afresh the requirements of the Regulations as appropriate.

COURT DIRECTIONS

5.14. When a court gives directions about contact in making a care order or an order under section 34 the local authority should draw the court's attention to these Regulations (Regulation 2(4)). Court directions will override these Regulations in any case of incompatibility. There would then be no need for a Director's or nominated person's decision under Regulation 5, but there would be a need for notification, for support and supervision of placement (subject to directions in these respects from the court).

OVERLAP OF REGULATIONS

5.15. It is possible that both these Regulations and the Foster Placement Regulations will operate in tandem. For example, a child may be accommodated with a foster parent from Monday to Friday and return to the home of a parent Friday evening to Monday morning each week. However when a child placed with foster parents under the Foster Placement Regulations, stays for a short period in another household not being that of a parent, other person with parental responsibility or a person in whose favour a residence order was in force immediately before the care order was made, neither the Foster Placement Regulations nor the Placement of Children with Parents etc Regulations will apply. An example of this is a stay at a school friend's home or with friends of the foster family.

PARENTAL RESPONSIBILITY

5.16. The local authority should negotiate with the parent with whom the child is placed under these Regulations the most appropriate arrangements for exercising their respective parental responsibility. The older child, parents and others with parental responsibility will need to be involved in the discussions about the exercising of that responsibility. It needs to be borne in mind that the local authority can still control the exercise of parental responsibility by others (section 33 (3)(a) of the Children Act 1989) to promote and safeguard the welfare of the child and it is essential they (the local authority) define clearly in the placement agreement to what degree the parent should exercise his parental responsibility without reference back to the local authority.

5.17. Where the proposed carer is the unmarried father who has not acquired parental responsibility by agreement with the child's mother or a court order, the local authority may wish to draw his attention to the Children Act's provisions for obtaining it. If he does not wish to or is unable to obtain parental responsibility, the placement should be agreed on the basis of delegated rather than shared responsibility. A non-parent in whose favour a residence order was in force immediately before the care order was made does not have parental responsibility after the care order is made. A placement with such a person would also be on the basis of delegated responsibility in accordance with section 2(9) of the Act. However, the need to discuss and agree the terms of the placement apply equally to these carers as they do to those with parental responsibility.

5.18. Financial responsibility for the maintenance of the child is recognised in the eligibility of the carer to apply for Social Security benefits. Local authorities should in planning such placements ensure that the entitlement to benefits is considered.

AIMS AND OBJECTIVES OF PLACEMENT

5.19. The consideration of a placement under these regulations should arise as part of the overall planning for the welfare of the child. The reasons for considering such a placement will vary in the light of a child's particular needs and circumstances at any given time. Placement may be seen as short-term in order to increase the degree of responsibility taken by the parent, to foster independence and lead to the child's discharge from care. This will not always be the case. While reunification of the family will often be the motive for the placement, this will not always be possible. For example, a placement may be subject to the requirements of these regulations even though the long-term plan envisages that the child goes to a boarding school, returning home only for holidays throughout his childhood. The purpose of the placement will be to enable the child to maintain links with his family, even though his particular needs require attendance at a residential school.

5.20. It is important that the purpose of the placement is clearly identified and discussed with all concerned during consideration of the placement and that the aims and objectives are understood by the child, the proposed carer, and others prior to the placement (see section 22(4) of the 1989 Act and paragraphs 5.30–5.34 below on consultation). The arrangements for and the aims and objectives of the placement should form part of the plan for the child. This plan should form the basis of the placement agreement with the carer. Arrangements, aims and objectives may change during a placement in the light of unforeseen events or in the course of review meetings while the child is in the placement. New aims and objectives will require discussion between all concerned and any new tasks for the carer will need to be specifically agreed. Some placements will be within specific time limits; others may be open ended and in these placements a careful review of the aims and objectives will avoid drift. Any changes to the plan should be recorded in writing and reflected in the placement agreement.

5.21. The welfare duty contained in section 22(3) of the 1989 Act applies to all decisions made by a local authority in relation to a placement of a child under these Regulations. In deciding whether such a placement is the best way of meeting their welfare duty to the child a local authority will need to assess the various needs of the child and take account of all the circumstances in the case. Each individual child will have particular needs which may change over time. It has to be remembered also that some older children may well be employed or coping with the problems of seeking employment or being unemployed. The reasons for the care proceedings will indicate the degree of supervision and type of support the placement will require. Where an abused child who has been in care for some time is being returned to the home where the abuse took place, the needs of the child and the protection required will vary according to the type of abuse involved and who the abuser was, if known. Thus, every placement will need to be well thought out, appropriately supported and supervised with clearly stated short and long-term objectives which are reviewed.

5.22. General guidance on assessment in planning the placement of children is to be found in the chapters dealing with Arrangements for Placement of Children and Review of Children's Cases respectively. Factors which need to be taken into account in assessing a child's needs and the suitability of a placement include:

(a) **contact with family:** including with a parent who is not the carer, siblings and other relatives; the requirements of section 34 and paragraph 15 of Schedule 2 to the Children Act 1989 should be borne in mind. Where the placement address is not within easy reach, the authority should consider what advice and assistance can be given under paragraph 16 of Schedule 2 of the 1989 Act; where the carer is not the parent, is from a different racial or cultural group to that of the child, provision should be made to maintain close links with the child's cultural heritage;

(b) **health care needs:** as for all children in care the plan should include arrangements for health care based on an assessment of the child's health care needs. Children with disabilities may have been receiving medical services from specialist units while in care and special arrangements may be necessary to ensure continuity of specialist care and treatment. The carer may need to acquire knowledge and skills to cope with a child's medical condition;

(c) **education:** remaining at the same school offers not only continuity of education but continuity in an important part of a child's daily life. Friendships and involvement with community activities (clubs etc) will be particularly important to the child. Where a placement is expected to be short-term or during the settling in period of a longer term placement, the authority should consider whether it would be advantageous to provide transport so that the child can continue at the same school. This is especially important if a child is at a critical stage of education, in the two years working for GCSE, for example. Where a child has special educational needs, the location of suitable schools may be a significant factor;

(d) **religion:** the importance of religion in the lives of some families and children must be recognised (see section 22(5)(c) of the Children Act 1989). Where religion is important it should not be assumed that both parents, or other carers will be of the same religion or, even if that is the case, that religious practices will be the same. Placement with one parent or other carer of a different religion or practice may be more acceptable to the other parent (who retains his parental responsibility for the child) if others of that parent's religion are able to play a part in the child's religious upbringing;

(e) **race, culture and linguistic needs:** religion is often an element in culture and to some parents and children may be a dominant factor. In seeking to understand fully a child's needs and considering the suitability of a placement, social workers need to be aware of differences between minority groups and the significance of religion and culture in relation to racial origin, and to guard against simplistic assumptions of similarity. Such an understanding is also essential where the child has parents of different races and is to live with one parent only. Choice will be influenced by the child's previous family experience and by the child's wishes. As an important principle, children should be given opportunities and encouragement to enjoy and take a pride in their racial and cultural heritage. Linguistic needs should be considered also where appropriate. For example, the child's first language may not be the same as the carer. This might be the case when a child who has been placed with foster parents since birth returns to live with his parents.

(f) **needs of siblings:** the needs and relationships of siblings should always be considered, even though not all may be in care. However, the needs of the individual child should not be subordinated to the needs of the group.

(g) **packages of support:** the practical help which the carer and the child may need if the placement is to be successful should be assessed and an appropriate package of services provided (section 17 of the Act refers). As an example, this may involve support in the form of a family aide, day care or the provision of essential household items. In some cases the provision of a single service may be all that is required. Voluntary organisations may be able to provide appropriate support services on behalf of the local authority and if so representatives of the voluntary organisation should be consulted as the local authority draws up its plan and subsequent agreement.

ENQUIRIES PRIOR TO PLACEMENT

5.23. Enquiries prior to placement required by the Regulations are set out in Regulation 3 and Schedule 1 of the Regulations. Regulations are framed in terms of a single carer but under the rules of interpretation references to the singular include the plural. Whenever responsibility for a placement of the child is to be shared equally by two people in the same household both should be involved in the preparation of the placement, accept the requirements placed upon them, be subject to the necessary checks on their suitability etc and sign the placement agreement.

5.24. Regulations require local authorities to assess the suitability of the proposed carer(s) and where relevant a cohabitee, and to obtain information on and to consider the range of factors set out in Schedule 1. Much of the information to be obtained in the pre-placement enquiries may well be in the local authority's case records. Relationships between parents when only one is to be the carer or between a parent and others with parental responsibility need to be carefully assessed and taken into account. The aim should be to identify all the factors which contribute to a general picture of the carer, his family and way of life. Local authorities should check their own records in respect of the carers and other members of the household, and seek the views of any other authority or agency to which they have applied to foster or adopt, and of the local authority in whose area the carer lives.

5.25. The police should be asked to check, with the proposed carer's permission, whether she has been convicted of any relevant offence unless the information is already available. The permission of other members of the household should be sought for the local authority to ask the police to check whether they have any relevant convictions recorded against them. Attention should be drawn to the Rehabilitation of Offenders Act 1974 (Exceptions) Order 1975 as amended by the Rehabilitation of Offenders Act 1974 (Exceptions) (Amendment) Order 1986. This allows for convictions which are spent under the terms of the 1974 Act to be disclosed by the police.

5.26. In checking health matters it is for the local authority to determine the extent of the enquiries needed in each case. The most satisfactory source of health information will usually be a medical report. The need for the carer or adult members of the household to be asked to undergo a medical examination as part of the pre-placement enquiries is a matter for the local authority to decide in the light of medical advice and the circumstances of each individual case. The costs of providing information should be met by health authorities under the collaborative arrangements.

5.27. The social worker should visit on at least one occasion at a time when it is possible to meet the entire household and explore the relationships of all the members (particularly where the carer is co-habiting with another adult who does not have parental responsibility for the child); the extent to which other members of the household may participate in the care and daily life of the child who may be placed in the household; and the demands which are made on the carer by other members of the household, such as elderly relatives requiring care. Such visits should be arranged so as to minimise inconvenience to members of the household. The social worker should make a point of communicating with the other children of the family and learning about their feelings on the proposed placement. The impact on family and social life should be carefully discussed and considered with the carer. Views should be formed about the proposed carer's current attitudes and expectations in relation to child rearing, discipline, understanding and perception of the placement proposed. These attitudes and expectations will need to be assessed in the light of the child's case history, the child's current needs and wishes and the views of any other person with parental responsibility.

5.28. As well as assessing the suitability of the proposed carers and the other members of the household, the social worker should inspect the proposed accommodation for the child. This inspection should include living, sleeping and washing facilities. Where a child is to share a bedroom with another member of the household, particular attention should be given to ensuring that the arrangements are in the child's best interest.

5.29. After a breakdown of a placement, the social worker will need to reconsider and check again all the relevant factors that formed part of the initial assessment when making another placement under these Regulations to ensure that there are no significant changes in circumstances. Equally, some factors will need to be checked again if a person joins or leaves the household. If complete and up to date information is held there will be no need to obtain all the same information again. However at the very least there will be a need to confirm that there have been no significant changes in circumstances and that no new relevant information is available for consideration.

WHOM TO CONSULT

5.30. It is essential when planning a placement to involve all those concerned with the child from the outset. The local authority need to co-ordinate the involvement of all relevant agencies and all the individuals who are significant in the child's life and the child. There is no regulation in the Placement of Children with Parents etc Regulations requiring consultation going beyond the requirement to consult in sections 22(4) and (5) of the Act itself.

5.31. Section 22(4) of the Children Act 1989 states that before making any decision with respect to a child whom they are looking after or propose to look after, the local authority should so far as is reasonably practicable obtain and take account of the wishes and feelings of –

(a) the child;

(b) his parents;

(c) any person who is not a parent of his but who has parental responsibility for him; and

(d) any other person whose wishes and feelings the authority consider to be relevant.

5.32. Local authorities are advised to use their discretion under section 22(4)(d) of the Act to consult the relevant statutory and voluntary agencies which are and have been previously involved with the child and his family. In most circumstances these will include the district health authority community services including the senior nurse manager (community), the local education authority (who will need to consult the child's school before offering advice and inform the school of decisions taken) the child's GP, and on occasion the probation service and the police. When, for example, a child who is not being returned to the home in which abuse took place is to be placed with a carer other than the abuser, or there has been no previous involvement of the Police in a case, it may not be appropriate to involve the Police except in relation to the checking of criminal convictions (see paragraph 1(k) Schedule 1 to these Regulations and paragraph 5.25). Local authorities should seek to identify and make contact with specific officers in other agencies who will be contacted when pre-placement enquiries are made and who will consult colleagues in the field involved with the child and report back. Existing carers, including foster parents, a head of community home, etc should already be involved in planning for the child but a specific opportunity to contribute to considerations of a placement under those regulations should be arranged.

5.33. The child's family, parents, grandparents and other relatives involved with the child should be invited to participate actively in planning such a placement and to make their views known. The Children Act 1989 requires that parents should be involved in all planning for their children, and should be kept informed of significant changes and developments in the plan for the child. Such sharing of information and participation in decision-making should be the norm subject only to the overriding best interests of the child.

5.34. In cases of child protection, DH guidance **Working Together** recommends that the views of a child abuse case conference should be sought when the local authority is considering major changes in the plan for the child. A placement under these Regulations is regarded as a major change on which a case conference would expect to comment and make a recommendation to the Director or nominated person who will make the placement decision. Views should be sought in writing so far as it is practicable from all those identified above. The outcome of consultations should be recorded, including a note of verbal responses and failure to respond.

THE CHILD

5.35. The child's views should be sought in discussion with the child, subject to the child's understanding (see section 22(4)(a) and (5) of the Children Act). The child will usually attend meetings to review his case. When this does not happen it will always be necessary for the child's views as expressed to be discussed and given due consideration at every review meeting and at case conferences and for those views to be taken into account when a placement decision is made. The social worker should be aware and acknowledge that there may be good reasons why the child's views are different from those of his parents and those of the local authority. The more mature the child, the more fully he will be able to enter into discussion about plans and proposals and participate in the decision-making process. With young children too, the social worker should make efforts to communicate with the child and discover his real feelings. All children need to be given information and appropriate explanations so that they are in a position to develop views and make choices. Providing children with reassurance and helping them with their anxieties about a placement is essential to the success of a placement. Children should feel that they have been properly consulted, that their views have been properly considered and that they have participated as partners in the decision making process. However, they should not be made to feel that the burden of decision-making has fallen totally upon them. Children should not be forced to participate in meetings if they choose not to do so. But their reasons should be explored in case a change in arrangements would enable them to come to a different decision.

5.36. Where the child has communication difficulties appropriate provision will need to be made so that it is possible for the child to express his views and for those views to be considered. Such provision could include someone with the appropriate communication skills such as a sign language interpreter. In the case of a child whose first language is not English, an interpreter should be provided if necessary.

WHOM TO NOTIFY

5.37. It is essential that those involved in the decision-making process are notified of the decision (see Regulation 8) so that they may have an opportunity to make any necessary arrangements for their involvement in the placement or to make their views on the placement decision known. The people to be notified are those specified in section 22(4) and Regulation 8(4):

- the child;
- his parents;
- any person who is not a parent, but who has parental responsibility for the child;
- any other person whose wishes and feelings, the local authority consider to be relevant;
- the district health authority for the district in which the child is living;
- the local education authority;
- the child's general registered medical practitioner;
- the area authority (see definition in Regulation 1(2));
- a person, not being an officer of a local authority, who has been caring for the child immediately before the placement, (eg a foster parent who was looking after a child before the placement decision was made); and
- where there was a residence order in force with respect to the child immediately before the care order was made, the person in whose favour the residence order was made.

5.38. The local authority will need to identify others who were not involved in the decision-making process but who will be involved with the child and have a need to know of the placement arrangements. Consideration should be given, in the light of circumstances of an individual case of the need to notify people who have been involved in the child's life but who are not specified in Regulation 8, such as a relative or friend.

5.39. Local authorities should notify the specific officer in other agencies already identified and consulted about these placements (see paragraph 5.32). These officers should be asked to disseminate the information where appropriate to their colleagues in the field who are or will be involved with the child. In those cases where a child abuse case conference has been consulted, the members of the case conference will need to be notified of the outcome of their recommendation.

THE DECISION

5.40. Local authorities in carrying out their duties have to satisfy themselves that this is the most suitable way of performing their general duty under section 22(3) of that Act. Regulation 5 requires that the Director of the Social Services Department or his nominee(s) makes the decision on these placements because of the importance of the decision for the child and the need for an oversight of the decision. This marks a change from the position under the Accommodation of Children (Charge and Control) Regulations 1988 in the light of the monitoring of their implementation. The Director may now designate more than one officer to take placement decisions on his behalf, where the size and structure of the local authority so require. Where a Director designates another officer as decision maker the nomination should reflect the serious nature of the decision and this nomination should rest at third tier level ie assistant chief officer, area director or area manager or an equivalent senior level. Nominees will need good knowledge of child care practice in order to provide a considered opinion. The nominations of the senior officers can only be made by the Director and should be in writing (Regulation 5(2)).

AGREEMENTS

5.41. During the consideration of a placement, the local authority and the person with whom the placement is to be made should draw up a placement agreement under Regulation 7 of these Regulations. The placement agreement will be based on the plan required by the Arrangements for Placement of Children (General) Regulations. The plan and the agreement should be reviewed and amended as necessary. Other than in the cases of children aged 16 and over and immediate placements (see paragraphs 5.9 and 5.11) the local authority and the parent will need to reach agreement on the terms of this document *before* a placement commences. There is no requirement that the agreement be signed, but drawing up and signing the agreement together will demonstrate the carer's and the local authority's commitment to the placement and recognise their respective roles. The matters to be included in the agreement are specified in Schedule 2 and include the support the local authority will provide. Regulation 7 states that agreement should be reached on all matters specified in Schedule 2 "so far as is practicable". This means that not all particulars will apply to all cases. It does not mean that certain particulars can be overlooked for convenience. If agreement is not reached and the local authority still consider placement to be in the child's best interest, they will need to work with the carer to renegotiate the plan and placement agreement. Placement cannot be made until agreement is reached. A copy of the agreement should always be given to the carer and to the child, subject to his age and understanding. Where two prospective carers are in the household in which the child will live, both should agree the terms of the placement agreement (see Regulation 7 and Schedule 2) and sign the document before the placement is made. Children should not usually sign agreements but on placement of an older child, a signed agreement may be a useful way to record the young person's understanding of the aims of the placement and the degree of responsibility taken on by the carer.

5.42. Agreements will need to be amended whenever a significant change in the placement arrangements is agreed. The parent and the child should be confident that they may seek an amendment if a change in circumstances makes this sensible or if a particular problem is causing difficulty. It is likely that the need to make changes to the agreement will crop up from time to time as part of the process of placement supervision. Some changes may best be dealt with in the review process. But some decisions should not wait. In these cases, changes will need to be agreed after the social worker has discussed the situation with his supervising officer and the persons actually involved.

INVOLVEMENT OF PARENTS WHEN THEY ARE NOT CARERS

5.43. Parental participation is one of the key provisions of the Children Act 1989 and a parent with whom the child is not living should be kept informed about changes in circumstances and of any changes to the placement arrangements unless this is contrary to the child's best interests. Proposals and decisions arising out of supervision and review of the placement should be discussed with parents and their views taken into account along with the views of the child (where he is of sufficient understanding) so far as this is practicable and in the best interests of the child. The nature of the contact between parents (where they are not the carers) and the child and their involvement with the carer will be a crucial part of the placement agreement and will require careful monitoring.

PREPARATION FOR PLACEMENT

5.44. The fact that the child is to be placed with an adult known to the child and the agency does not make proper preparation for the placement less necessary. Preparation should include the assessment of the child's needs in the placement; an assessment of any risk attached to the proposed placement; early discussions with the existing carer and parents and the child of the objectives of the placement and the basis for and terms upon which the placement is made; visits to the proposed placement; identification of the type and level of support required (including social work, therapeutic and/or remedial services and finances or practical help). The establishment of clear aims and objectives of the placement are essential parts of the placement plan and subsequent placement agreement.

5.45. A child's planned return to his family after a placement with another carer will need careful preparation, and child and family will need support over the settling in period until the child is re-integrated into the family. A period of gradual re-introduction may be needed, depending on the length of time the child has been away from the family and the changes which have occurred there. Children may return to different addresses, new babies in the family, new step parents and step brothers and sisters. Sometimes a child must change schools (though this should be avoided if possible) and leave behind friends and interests acquired. Contacts with friends and previous carers should be maintained if this is in the child's best interests. Parents, too, need to be prepared for changes in the child's habits, interests and routines; and for the possibility of disturbed behaviour while the child is settling in. The local authority should asess the support needed to achieve a successful placement and should provide any assistance or services they consider appropriate.

SUPPORT, SUPERVISION, AND MONITORING OF PLACEMENT

5.46. The pre-determined objectives of the placement together with regular reviews will provide the best guide to the specific requirements and arrangements for support, supervision, monitoring and termination of each placement. Regulation 9 sets out the minimum requirement concerning supervision of placements by the local authority. There will be a need to give attention also to the needs of the carer and to other persons in the household, both in the interests of the child and in recognition that there may be separate needs which need to be addressed, not all of which will be directly related to the child's care. It should be recognised that supervision and monitoring of the placement may lead to a change in the level of support for the placement and/ or revision of the agreement. The identification of a difficulty should lead to discussion of the need for different or increased support rather than automatic termination of the placement. Any major change may require further consultation. The plan for the child and the agreement should be amended to reflect this revision. Such amendments should be properly recorded and a note of the amendment given to the carer and others in writing.

SUPPORT FOR THE CHILD

5.47. Each child placed under these Regulations should have a social worker allocated for his support and supervision. In most cases this will be the same officer who provides support for the carer. There may be occasions however, when circumstances indicate that the child should have "his own" social worker separate from his carer's worker. The intention of support for the child is in keeping with the authority's general duty under section 22 of the Act, to safeguard and maintain the child's welfare. Typically this will be achieved by a pattern of visits to the child in his home as required in these Regulations. Additionally office visits and other meetings may be necessary. A record of face to face meetings must be maintained as a contribution towards the process of planning and review. As part of this process social workers will need to consider regular contact with other professionals and significant adults concerned with the care, health, education and training of the child in order to monitor his progress and development. Not the least important, again in keeping with the principles of the Act, are opportunities to discuss with the child his wishes and feelings in relation to the placement and future decisions.

SUPPORT TO THE CARER

5.48. The carer will have agreed to co-operate with such supervision as has been arranged as a condition of the placement and as set out in the agreement at the commencement of the placement. In most cases there will be an agreed package of support. The aim should be to enhance the carer's ability to cope, and to build upon the strengths within the family and to minimise weaknesses. The supervising social worker should ensure that appropriate support, advice and assistance are discussed with and provided to the carer and other family members as required. In some cases it may be necessary for the carer to be allocated a social worker; or in other cases a family aide or links with a family centre might be alternatives which can provide the carer with support at a time when the placement is under stress. Other examples of support include an emergency telephone number, respite care arrangements, baby-sitting or child-minding to provide a break and financial help. The power to make such provision for the child's family or any member of that family is provided by section 17(3) of the Act.

5.49. The supervising social worker will need to be aware of the delicate balance to be achieved in recognising and supporting the needs of the carer, without undermining ability to cope. The social worker's role is to support the carer in the exercise of parental responsibility to the extent that has been agreed. This will particularly apply where a placement is under strain because of the child's behaviour or involvement with another parent. With older children the child's and carer's attitude to choice of girl or boy friends, school attendance, house rules, bedtimes, late nights, spending money, attitude to work, choice of clothes etc may test commitments made by carer and child. The social worker will wish to foster the independence of the older child and move towards working with the child as with an adult. However, it is important that the supervising social worker does not get involved in decisions that can be construed as collusion with either the child or the carer.

5.50. It is equally important that the true carer is recognised when other adults are in the household; the supervisor should ensure that it is the carer with whom contact is made to discuss the progress of the placement so that others do not take over the carer's role. This is particularly important when the carer is not the head of the household and others may seek to deny the supervisor access to the carer or child. Other adults in the household may be involved in discussions about the child or the placement but the carer's role and responsibility should never be lost sight of by the carer, the supervisor or by others.

SUPERVISION OF THE PLACEMENT

5.51. Regulation 9 provides a framework of requirements for the social worker's task of supervision of the placement and working with the child and carer towards achieving the objectives of the plan for the child (see paragraphs 5.52–5.65 for guidance on supervision by an area local authority or by a voluntary organisation on behalf of the local authority). The social worker who is the supervisor of the placement should have knowledge of the child before placement and the child should know the particular social worker.

The supervisor will, except in exceptional circumstances, have been involved in consideration of the plan for the placement. It is sometimes the case that if a child has been taken into care by a particular social worker, he is reluctant to trust her. In these circumstances, it may be desirable for support and supervision of the placement to be undertaken by a new social worker. When a new supervisor takes over it is essential that the reasons are explained to the carer and child. So far as is practicable, a planned handover should take place and whenever possible the new supervisor should be introduced to all the significant individuals in the child's life, including other agencies' workers as well as to the child.

VISITS

5.52. Visits should take place as often as the circumstances of the individual child and placement require, but at the very least, as specified in Regulation 9(1)(b): within one week of the beginning of the placement, then at intervals of not more than six weeks during the first year and at intervals of three months thereafter or when reasonably requested by the child or the person with whom the child is placed as circumstances may require. The Regulations require that on each visit, so far as is reasonably practicable the child should be seen alone. Visits to the child afford an opportunity for independent observation and direct contact with the child. If a child is not seen, or cannot be seen alone then a further visit must be arranged at short notice to see the child. In some cases this may result in a planned, notified visit followed immediately by an unnotified visit. If a child is said to be elsewhere this must be checked out and confirmed by the supervisor as soon as possible. The minimum requirement for visiting a child in a series of short-term placements is once during the first placement in the series and on one other occasion during the series while the child is in the placement (Regulation 13(3)). The frequency of such visits will depend on the individual circumstances of the case and may need to be increased to ensure that the child's welfare is safeguarded and promoted.

5.53. It will also be important for the supervisor to study the interaction between a child, carer and family and to provide to all those people (including, if of sufficient age and understanding, the child or young person) a clear message of expectations and feedback on the supervisor's observations. Depending on the age of the child he may be seen at home, at the other parent's home, on contact visits, at school, in the supervisor's office, at a previous care establishment, or less formally, at a cafe, for example or other setting where the child feels at ease. Contacts may be through any combination of these venues but it is as important to see the child with his carer as it is to see him separately. Even with a teenager the supervisor should avoid a regular pattern of contacts which excludes visits to him in the placement and in the presence of the carer. Contacts with the carer should be either in her own home or at the social services' office. Whilst contacts elsewhere may occur fortuitously and be recorded they should not be seen as substitutes for "visits".

5.54. It will be necessary to check the perceptions of the child and carer in relation to the aims of the placement plan and the ways these may be or are being achieved. The social worker will need to feed back to the child and the carer the social worker's own perceptions of the way the placement is developing over time in relation to changes in circumstances. He should acknowledge attainment of an aim or the failure to do so. The child and the carer should have a sense of stability and security to allow them to build up trust in each other. Thorough and perceptive social work supervision and monitoring will help to develop this, but it should avoid undermining parenting skills and the authority of the carers. It will be helpful in this context to discuss the support provided to the child and the carer and to explore with child and carer whether a change in support is needed.

Others in the Placement Household

5.55. In order to monitor the suitability of the placement environment the supervisor will need to assess the attitudes of others in the household to the child and the placement and to be aware of significant changes in their attitude or circumstances. Social workers will need to be aware of how the accommodation is utilised and any changes in its use during the placement. This means that there is need to see the child's room which will have to be handled sensitively if the room is shared with another young person. The supervisor will need to be alert to other sensitive issues of privacy which may arise.

Reports of Visits

5.56. After each visit, the local authority is required to ensure that the social worker who made the visit produces a written report (Regulation 9(2)). The report should indicate that the child was seen and if not why not, and if the child was seen alone. The report should also comment on the child's welfare and the success of the placement including any comments made by the child or the carer. Any matter for concern or difficulties should be highlighted so that the need for any necessary action can be discussed with the social worker's supervisor.

TERMINATION OF THE PLACEMENT

5.57. Termination will arise from a variety of situations. It is essential that the social worker recognises when the placement is no longer in the best interests of the child. Evidence of failure to thrive, a suspicion of abuse, a lack of co-operation by the carer or an inability to cope should be seen and recorded as indicators that the placement should be reviewed in light of the child's needs. The social worker should be alert also to less obvious or unstated problems; a child may not make a direct request for removal but may make an increasing number of seemingly unrelated complaints or behave in an unexpected or uncharacteristic fashion.

5.58. It will be possible in most cases to plan for removal and so minimise stress to the child and counteract a sense of failue in the carer or child. However, immediate action will be necessary on occasion and in such cases the social worker will need considerable support from her team leader. Under the placement agreement to which the carer is a party the local authority's duty to remove the child at any time is acknowledged. Regulation 11(1) places upon local authorities a duty to remove a child if the local authority considers that to leave the child in the placement would be contrary to the child's interests (section 22(3), Children Act 1989).

5.59. Different degrees of planning will be possible for each of these situations ranging from a carefully prepared planned move to immediate action in an emergency. Wherever possible and if this is in the child's best interest, a placement with the child's wider family, or family friends should be considered taking into account the child's wishes and views and those of his parents. This is in accordance with the local authority's duty under section 23(6) of the Act. It will be necessary to consider who will need to be informed and consulted about the new considerations and decisions. Informing may or may not involve giving explanations which raise issues of confidentiality and care and will be needed to avoid contributing to tensions within the family circle. It will be necessary to give explanations to the child and to the carer when they have not made the request to terminate the arrangement and to the other parent or guardian. There will also be a need to consider the effect on any other children, who may not be in care but who are part of the household. Equally there will be times when a placement involves more than one child of a family yet only one child is to be removed. Both the child removed and those left in the household will need explanations and increased support. The local authority should ensure that all those involved with the child and who need to know of the termination or proposed termination of a placement are informed in writing as soon as is practicable. This will include the carer, parents who are not carers, and those mentioned in paragraphs 5.37–5.39.

5.60. The child's need for balance and stability is equally critical at the end of a placement as at the beginning. Where the child has taken the initiative over leaving it will be important that he is helped to articulate his reasons where possible and handle the change in the least damaging way as part of his own learning. In other situations the child will need reassurance; the supervisor will need to give the child opportunities to discuss anxieties about the future and feelings the child may have.

INTER-AGENCY ARRANGEMENTS IN ENGLAND AND WALES

5.61. Where a child is placed by a local authority (the responsible authority) under these Regulations in the area of another local authority (the area authority) the responsible authority should inform the area authority of the placement and provide sufficient information for the area authority to be able to complete their register in accordance with the Arrangements for Placement of Children (General) Regulations. The responsible authority should notify also the other relevant authorities such as the district health authority, the local education authority etc of the placement and arrangements for supervision etc (Regulation 8(1)).

5.62. A local authority with responsibility for the care of a child may arrange for any or all of the supervisory duties under these Regulations to be performed by another local authority (section 101 of the Local Government Act 1972 refers). In such cases, the responsible local authority should provide the area authority with all the information which is needed to discharge the responsible local authority's duties in accordance with the arrangements and with the Regulations. The area authority should keep the responsible local authority informed of the progress of the child and, in particular, make reports to the responsible local authority following each visit to the placement and each occasion on which the child is seen and following each review. The local authorities are required to consider together as necessary and at least after each review what action, if any, is needed (Regulation 12 of the Arrangements for Placements of Children (General) Regulations).

5.63. When, prior to placement under these regulations, a child has been cared for or supervised by a voluntary organisation on behalf of a local authority, a local authority may decide in the child's best interests to ask that voluntary organisation to undertake supervision of the placement on their behalf. In such cases the statutory duties remain with the local authority and the local authority is responsible for ensuring that the supervising voluntary organisation keeps the local authority informed in the same way that another local authority is required in such circumstances to keep the responsible local authority informed.

5.64. Whatever the arrangements, the responsible authority remains responsible for the child. Wherever it is practicable and appropriate, arrangements should be made to combine the reviews under section 26 of the Act and other assessments and reviews.

PLACEMENT OUTSIDE ENGLAND AND WALES

5.65. A local authority with responsibility for the care of a child should not arrange a placement outside England and Wales unless they are satisfied that all the requirements of these placement Regulations can be met, so far as is reasonably practicable. In addition the effect of such a placement on parental contact should be considered. Section 23(7) of the Children Act 1989 requires a local authority to place a child near his home, so far as is reasonably practicable. Such a placement decision is subject to the welfare duty (section 22 (3)).

5.66. No placement of a child in care outside England and Wales is permitted unless the local authority have obtained the approval of a court (paragraph 19 of Schedule 2 to the 1989 Act). This is because a long term placement under these Regulations may in fact be properly regarded and handled as an emigration or may in time change its nature so that it becomes emigration. Where such a placement is authorised, the local authority should ensure, so far as reasonably practicable, that there is compliance with the Placement of Children with Parents etc Regulations. Where the child is moving to another jurisdiction within the British Islands (ie the United Kingdom, Channel Islands and the Isle of Man) the effect of the care order may be transferred to the relevant public authority under regulations to be made by virtue of section 101 of the Act.

CHAPTER 6　CONTACT

6.1. The new legislative framework of the Children Act remedies the acknowledged defects in previous legislation which prevented parents and others from seeking the court's view in disputes about contact. The Children Act imposes a new duty to promote contact between a child who is being looked after and those connected with him. This applies whether a child is accommodated by voluntary arrangement or as a result of a court order. The Children Act empowers the courts to make orders regarding contact in all circumstances where a child is in care. This is unlike the previous legislation which provided for the courts to make orders in respect of a child in care only when access by specific persons had been refused or terminated.

LEGISLATIVE FRAMEWORK AND GENERAL PRINCIPLES

6.2. Section 34 of the Children Act 1989 requires the court to consider the proposed arrangements for contact between a child who is the subject of care proceedings and the child's parents and other involved relatives. The court may make directions about the kind or amount of contact which should be allowed. When preparing an application for a care order, an outline of the proposed contact arrangements should be drawn up, so that the court can give consideration to the local authority's proposals and the submissions of others about the proposals. Local authorities will be expected to provide details of the proposals for contact when applying for an interim or full care order.

6.3. The Contact with Children Regulations, made under section 34(8) of the Act, impose requirements on local authorities in relation to refusal of contact, departure from the terms of an order made under section 34 and notification of variation or supervision of contact arrangements made otherwise than under a section 34 order (see Annex D).

6.4. The guidance that follows builds upon that provided by the **Code of Practice – Access to Children in Care** which it replaces. This guidance, unlike the code, covers all children looked after (the code did not apply in most respects to children received into care). Policies, procedures and practice will need revision to take account of that and of the new legal position of parents upon the making of a court order; that is the sharing of their parental responsibility with the local authority rather than loss of that responsibility. Equally the emphasis on participation in local authority decision-making by children and parents will require changes in approach, where this has not been the policy and practice prior to the implementation of the Children Act. For instance, many foster parents have played a crucial part in promoting contact with the child's family, and this needs to be reflected in the involvement of foster parents in the decision-making process. Others will need more training and support to enable them to work under the new approach.

CONTACT WITH CHILDREN IN CARE

6.5. Where a child is in care, the local authority must allow reasonable contact with a child's parents, any guardian and any other person with whom he was living under a court order immediately before the care order was made (section 34(1)). The court order may be a residence order or an order under the inherent jurisdiction of the High Court. The power to make orders concerning contact are set out in section 34(2), (4), (5), (6) and (7). In the event of a dispute about contact when a child is not in care, a section 8 order may be made on the application of the child, a parent or other person, if the matter cannot be resolved by agreement, or the representations procedure has not provided a solution. The Contact with Children Regulations require local authorities to notify those affected about proposals to change arrangements for contact in relation to a child in care. If those arrangements are defined in a court order, Regulation 3 provides for the terms of the order to be departed from with the agreement of the person named in the order in specified circumstances. In these cases, notification should also be given to the child's parents (if not the person with whom the agreement has been made), a guardian, a person in whose favour a residence order was in force immediately before the care order was made; and if the child is in care, any person who had care of the child by virtue of a wardship order and any other person whose wishes and feelings the authority consider to be relevant (Regulation 2).

6.6 Subject to any order of the court, it is for the local authority to make decisions about contact arrangements in an individual case where a child is in care. As stated already, the Children Act imposes a new duty to promote contact between a child who is being looked after (whether or not the child is in compulsory care) and those who are connected with him (paragraph 15(1) of Schedule 2). These people include the child's parents, any one else with parental responsibility for him and any relative or friend of the child, unless it is not reasonably practicable or consistent with the child's welfare to do so. To support the new duty, the local authority are required to take reasonable steps to inform the child's parents and any other person who has parental responsibility for the child of the child's address (paragraph 15(2) of Schedule 2). However, information need not be given if the child is subject to a care order and it would prejudice the child's welfare to give it (paragraph 15(4) of Schedule 2). Equally, a parent or other person with parental responsibility for the child in care must inform the local authority of his address (paragraph 15(2)(b) of Schedule 2).

CONTACT WITH CHILDREN LOOKED AFTER BY VOLUNTARY AGREEMENT

6.7. Arrangements for contact with children looked after by voluntary agreement are a matter for negotiation and agreement between the local authority, the older child, parents and others seeking contact. The local authority should ensure that parents and others know where to seek advice about negotiations over contact.

PROMOTION OF CONTACT WITH CHILDREN NOT LOOKED AFTER

6.8. Where a child in the area of the local authority and in need is living apart from his family, but is not looked after by that local authority, paragraph 10(b) of Schedule 2 requires the local authority to promote contact between the child and his family. For example, in the case of a child living in a long-stay health authority establishment, the local authority could decide to provide services to the child or family under Part III of the Act to promote contact.

IMPORTANCE OF CONTACT

6.9. For the majority of children there will be no doubt that their interests will be best served by efforts to sustain or create links with their natural families. Contact in the sense of personal meetings and visits will generally be the most common and, for both families and children, the most satisfactory way of maintaining their relationship. But other means which can help to keep family bonds alive should be borne in mind: letters, telephone calls, exchange of photographs. Contacts, however occasional, may continue to have a value for the child even when there is no question of returning to his family. These contacts can keep alive for a child a sense of his origins and may keep open options for family relationships in later life.

6.10. The first weeks, during which the child is looked after by the local authority, are likely to be particularly crucial to the success of the relationship between the parent, the social worker and the child's carers and to the level of future contact between parent and child. It is at this time that patterns are set which it may be difficult to change, whether the child is looked after by a voluntary arrangement or as a result of a care order. Parents should be involved in the assessment and planning prior to placement wherever possible. Emergency admissions require special care if parents are to be reassured from the outset that they have a continuing role in their child's life and to minimise distress for the child. Early visits and meetings should be encouraged, even though parents may need help to enable them to cope with the child's distress and their own. These considerations, subject to whatever safeguards are necessary for the child's protection, are equally important where children are subject to emergency protection orders.

CONTACT AND CHILD PROTECTION ORDERS

Child Assessment Order

6.11. If in making a child assessment order, the court directs that the child may be kept away from home, it must also give directions as it thinks fit about contact between the child and other persons during this period. A temporary overnight stay cannot be equated with being placed in care, but the court may well be guided on contact by the presumption of reasonable contact between a child in care and his parents, guardian and certain other persons established by section 34. The court would also want to consider requests to be allowed contact from other persons who have to be notified of the hearing. As for all questions affecting the child that arise under the Act, the court must give paramount consideration to the child's welfare when considering contact (section 1(1)).

Emergency Protection Order

6.12. Where the court makes an emergency protection order (EPO) it has the discretion to give directions as appropriate with regard to contact which is or is not to be allowed between the child and any named person (section 44(6)(a)). The court direction may impose conditions (section 44(8)). However, subject to any of these directions, there is a general duty on the applicant to allow the child reasonable contact with a range of persons. These are his parents, any person who is not a parent but has parental responsibility, any person with whom he was living before the order was made, any person in whose favour a contact order (a section 8 order) is in force with respect to the child, any person who is allowed contact by virtue of an order under section 34 (see guidance in volume 1 in this series) or anyone acting on behalf of any of these people. The court may give directions regarding contact not only when the EPO is made, but also at any time while it is in force. The court may also vary the directions at any time.

Contact with a Child in Police Protection

6.13. While a child is in police protection under section 46, the designated officer must allow such contact (if any) as he considers is reasonable and in the child's best interests with the following categories of persons:

(a) the child's parents;

(b) any person who is not a parent of the child but who has parental responsibility for him;

(c) any person with whom the child was living immediately before he was taken into police protection;

(d) any person in whose favour a section 8 contact order is in force with respect to the child;

(e) any person who is allowed to have contact with the child by virtue of a section 8 order;

(f) any person acting on behalf of any of those persons.

If the child in police protection is accommodated by the local authority for the area in which the child usually lives, the local authority are required by section 46(11) to afford such contact to these people.

PLANNING AND CONTACT

6.14. The responsible authority must make plans for the child (see guidance on planning contained in Chapter 2 – Arrangements for Placement). Consideration of contact is an essential element in the planning process. So far as is reasonably practicable, the views of the child, if he is old enough, the parents and the child's carers must be ascertained before a decision about contact arrangements is made (section 22(4), 61(2) and 64(2) of the Act). The value and purpose of contact should be clearly understood and agreed so far as possible by all concerned. There should be a clear understanding from the outset about all the arrangements and what is expected of the parents, the responsible authority and the child's carers in connection with the arrangements.

6.15. The contact arrangements should include those made in respect of relatives, siblings, grandparents and unmarried fathers; all those people with whom the child's contact should be preserved. In some cases it may be appropriate to identify relatives, who may include a parent, with whom contact has lapsed and to follow up the prospects of re-estabishing contact. Care will clearly be needed where there is family or marital conflict, but responsible authorities should be ready to explore possibilities of preserving, establishing or promoting contact which could be beneficial to the child. In doing so they should not overlook problems which may arise when a child is placed with a person who may be reluctant to provide contact with, for example, an unmarried father, relatives or friends of the child. Carers and the child may need support to cope with these situations.

SECTION 34 ORDERS FOR CONTACT

6.16. When an order for contact under section 34 is in force, the local authority remains responsible for the child's welfare. Subject to the terms of the order in relation to decisions about contact, the local authority must continue to plan and care for the child in accordance with their general duty under section 22(3)(a) of the Children Act. In handling decisions about contact within the terms of the order, local authorities should continue to apply the principles set out in this guidance.

PLACEMENT AND CONTACT

6.17. The implications for contact are among the factors which should be considered when deciding where to place a child. In the case of children looked after by local authorities, section 20(7)(a) of the Children Act specifically requires local authorities to place a child near his home, so far as practicable, subject to his welfare being safeguarded. The effect on parental contact should always be considered when it is proposed to seek the court's consent to the emigration of a child in care (paragraph 19 of Schedule 2 to the Act).

THE SETTING FOR VISITS

6.18. Visits by the parents to the child in his foster home, residential home or in the family home are the most usual forms of contact. They can provide continuity for the child in that setting and opportunities for the parents and carers to meet. If family reunification is the plan, visits should be in the family home at the earliest possible stage. Such visits also have the advantage of maintaining links with the neighbourhood to which the child will be returning. However, other venues may have advantages for some children and in some circumstances. Outings are one example. Whatever the venue, the aim should be to ensure that privacy and a welcoming and congenial setting are available. If possible, parents should be encouraged to participate in some way in the child's daily life, by preparing tea, for example, or shopping for clothes or putting a young child to bed.

FOSTER CARE

6.19. Foster parents can play an invaluable role in promoting both successful contact and reunification. But the extent to which they will be able to do this, in practice, depends on the recruitment, training and support which are available to them. There must always be a clear understanding with the foster parents from the outset about the child's continuing relationship with his parents and other family members; about proposals for and the purpose of contact; and about arrangements for review of the plan for the child including contact.

6.20. Visiting a child in a foster home can be a source of severe stress for all concerned, especially where there has been insufficient preparation. Foster parents will need preparation and continuing support to help them cope with difficulties. Parents also need help to cope with the stress of seeing their child in someone else's home, living as part of someone else's family. Usually the parents will have been involved in discussions between the foster parents and social worker about the plan for the child's placement. The social worker should bring the parents to meet the foster parent and discuss the needs of the child before the placement is made. This may not always be possible when an immediate placement is made, but parents should not be left to make their own way to a placement for the first time and to introduce themselves to a foster parent. A social worker should always accompany the parents to help with introductions and the discussion of practical aspects of the contact arrangements and the child's care as soon after placement as possible if not before. Sometimes visits to the foster home can be so stressful for one or more of the parties that the tensions cannot be quickly resolved. If the placement is nonetheless considered to be in the child's best interest, an alternative venue for meetings may be better, at least for the time being.

RESIDENTIAL CARE

6.21 Residential care staff also need training and preparation to make a positive contribution to the success of contact arrangements and to deal with tensions and difficulties which can arise. The potential influence of the establishment's regime should not be overlooked, in particular for children who have been placed in secure accommodation. In every establishment care is needed to ensure that the importance of the contact arrangements is recognised, that the internal organisation and timetable do not make visiting difficult and that arrangements for visiting are sufficiently flexible.

6.22 Regulations preclude the use of sanctions which could affect agreed arrangements for contact between the child and his parents or other relatives as a form of control of the child (see also paragraphs 6.25–6.26 below). More detailed guidance on specific issues in respect of residential placements will be found in the volume on residential care in this series.

TRAVELLING ARRANGEMENTS AND EXPENSES

6.23 Parents and others having contact may need advice and help with travelling arrangements. Local authorities have power under paragraph 16 of Schedule 2 to help with the cost of visiting looked after children where there would otherwise be undue financial hardship. The power is not limited to assistance with travelling expenses, but can be used to meet all reasonable costs associated with visiting. Parents may also need advice about benefits which may be payable during a child's extended visits home.

THE CHILD'S WISHES

6.24. The local authority have a duty to give due consideration to the child's wishes and feelings, having regard to his understanding in relation to decision-making by the authority (section 22(5)(a)). Generally children want to see their parents, other members of their family and family friends. However, sometimes children are openly unwilling to see some or all of their family or have ambivalent feelings about contact which make them reluctant to see their parents or experience persistent distress at the prospect. The social worker, with the help of the carers and any other adults in whom the child may have confided, must attempt to understand the source of these feelings. They may arise from factors which can be changed or which the child can be helped to understand. The social worker and carers should also make real efforts to help the child to understand what is likely to be of greatest benefit to him both for the short and long-term.

6.25. Where the difficulties cannot be resolved the local authority may conclude that a child's reasons for not wanting contact are valid. A child should not be forced to persist unwillingly or unhappily with seeing a parent or other person. In such a case local authorities will need to obtain legal advice. A child in care has a right to make an application to the court to authorise the local authority to refuse to allow contact between the child and a named person (section 34(4)). It may be that the local authority will decide that it is in the child's best interest to initiate such proceedings if the child so wishes. The child's feelings may change as he develops and in the future he may be more ready to see his parents. The fact that the child or the local authority has obtained an order ending contact does not preclude the need to reconsider issues of contact.

RESTRICTIONS OF CONTACT WITH CHILDREN IN CARE

6.26. Planning will generally be based on the assumption that contact will be beneficial to the child unless there are clear indications to the contrary. There are sometimes reasons why, to safeguard the child's welfare, contact must be supervised, restricted or suspended. A child may be committed to care in circumstances which call for a decision to refuse contact from the beginning. Where there are special circumstances which mean that no contact arrangements – including short-term arrangements or supervised arrangements – can be offered to a parent while a decision about contact is under consideration, local authorities must bear in mind section 34(1) of the Children Act 1989 and any order under section 34(3). Section 34(6) of the Act provides for local authorities to refuse to allow contact that would otherwise be required under section 34(1) or by a section 34 order if:

"(a) they are satisfied that it is necessary to do so in order to safeguard or promote the child's welfare; and

(b) the refusal –

(i) is decided upon as a matter of urgency; and

(ii) does not last for more than seven days."

6.27. Regulation 2 of the Contact with Children Regulations requires local authorities which have decided to refuse contact under section 34(6) to notify in writing as soon as a decision to refuse contact has been made:

"(a) the child, if he is of sufficient understanding;

(b) the child's parents;

(c) any guardian of his;

(d) where there was a residence order in force with respect to the child immediately before the care order was made, the person in whose favour the order was made;

(e) where immediately before the care order was made, a person had care of the child by virtue of an order made in the exercise of the High Court's inherent jurisdiction with respect to children, that person; and

(f) any other person whose wishes and feelings the authority consider to be relevant."

It will be important to inform the child in a manner appropriate to his understanding and to explain the reasons for the action.

6.28. The notification should contain as much of the information referred to in the Schedule to the Regulations as the local authority decides is necessary. The information referred to in the Schedule includes:

- local authority's decision;
- date of the decision;
- reasons for the decision;
- duration (if applicable);
- remedies in case of dissatisfaction.

6.29. Local authorities must have a clear understanding of what is being considered and why. Local authorities should always obtain legal advice about provisions concerning contact under section 34, which generally require court authority, unless all parties are in agreement. Local authorities should consider making applications to the court for decisions under section 34 in advance of the implementation of the Act on 14 October 1991, if they wish to maintain a restricted contact regime on or after that date, in cases where the presumption under section 34(1) applies.

6.30. Local authorities should also bear in mind that the Act urges that there should be no avoidable delay in decisions relating to children, because of the unintended and generally undesirable effects of delay on the plans for the child's future (sections 1(2) and 32). A child's experience of the passage of time varies according to age and to his general stage of development. Even temporary breaks in contact can have especially damaging effects on the relationship between parents and very young children. Older children will be more able to benefit from help from the social worker and from their carers in understanding the reasons for any necessary limitation or disruption of contact. These considerations apply equally whether decisions are being made when a child begins to be looked after or after he has been in care for a lengthy period. Whatever the decisions made about contact at any stage in a local authority's involvement with a child, it will be necessary to review the decisions in the light of current circumstances at each review.

DEPARTURE FROM TERMS OF COURT ORDER ON CONTACT UNDER SECTION 34

6.31. Regulation 3 of the Contact with Children Regulations provides for a local authority to depart from the terms of any order for contact under section 34. The circumstances in which this may be done are as follows:

- there is agreement between the local authority and the person in relation to whom the order is made;
- the child, if of sufficient understanding, also agrees;
- written notification of the agreement is provided within seven days to all the persons listed in Regulation 2. This notification should be on a need to know basis.

This provision allows for flexibility and partnership in contact arrangements, obviating the need to go back to the court when all concerned agree a new arrangement.

VARIATION OR SUSPENSION OF CONTACT ARRANGEMENTS NOT GOVERNED BY A SECTION 34 ORDER

6.32. When a local authority decide to vary or suspend an arrangement for contact between one person and the child in care with a view to affording another person contact with that child, they are required to notify those persons specified in Regulation 2 of the Contact with Children Regulations. This requirement is set out in Regulation 4 which states that the notification should be given as soon as the decision to vary or suspend contact is made. The information provided in the notification should be on a need to know basis.

COMMUNICATING DECISIONS ABOUT CONTACT

6.33. Subject to what is said in paragraphs 6.27–6.32 above, all decisions about contact should be explained to parents and discussed with them. Local authorities should also confirm in writing to the parents all decisions and agreements about contact arrangements and any changes to the arrangements and the outcome of all formal and informal reviews of contact. Where limitations or control on contact have been imposed, these should be clearly stated. Similarly, any postponement of contact should be confirmed in writing together with the reasons. Unless the child is subject to a court order, limitations, controls and postponements of contact should be agreed by all those involved.

6.34. Simple but informative leaflets about care and the law can be helpful, especially when a child begins to be looked after whether on a voluntary basis or by order of a court. They can help parents to understand their position and that of their child in relation to the authority and can reassure them about their continuing place in their child's life. Similarly, descriptive leaflets produced by community homes with information about visiting and public transport can help and reassure parents. Local authorities may prefer to design their own leaflets or to use publications available from other agencies and organisations. Leaflets should be couched in terms which are simple and clearly understood, avoiding professional terminology and jargon. Local authorities should produce leaflets in languages other than English where there is a local need and produce information in a format accessible to people with communication difficulties. Leaflets should never be used in place of personal letters confirming decisions and agreements about the individual child.

6.35. It is equally important that there should be clear and full communication and understanding of all contact decisions and arrangements among all those who are involved with the child's care, including foster parents and officers in charge of residential homes. Where children are cared for by other agencies, there should be effective liaison and clear agreements with the agency about all matters relating to contact.

DISAGREEMENT WITH PARENTS

6.36. Local authorities should ensure that they have clear arrangements to inform parents and others about how to pursue complaints about contact and ask for decisions to be reviewed. Responsible authorities should ensure that the representations procedure recognises the need to accept complaints from people, other than parents, who have contact with children who are being looked after.

6.37. Arrangements should be made for parents to discuss their anxieties and dissatisfactions with senior officers if they feel they have reached an impasse with their social worker. Those arrangements should not be used to prevent or hinder use of the representations procedure required by the Act. All parents and, where appropriate according to the child's understanding, the child should be informed of these procedures. (See guidance in Chapter 10 on the operation of the representations procedure). When a disagreement persists, parents of a child subject to a care order should be advised to seek a legal opinion on the most appropriate action open to them.

REVIEWING CONTACT

6.38. Contact arrangements, whichever responsible authority is involved, should be kept under review, and not necessarily just as part of reviews. Contact should be monitored to check whether the arrangements are working as intended and to identify any problems which have arisen and any changes which are needed: whether, for example, the arrangements are unnecessarily restrictive. Difficulties should be discussed openly with the parents and with the child's carers so that solutions can be explored and help given. It cannot be in the interests of the child and is no service to parents to allow them to drift to the periphery of a child's life, without reminding them of the possible implications of this course to the plan for their child and his relationship with them.

6.39. Some children will be cared for by other agencies, for example, in voluntary homes, special schools, Youth Treatment Centres or by another local authority. Wherever the child is placed, the stautory responsibility for his welfare lies with the local authority. They should continue, in co-operation with any other agency which is involved, to keep under review the child's contacts with his family and the progress of contact arrangements.

6.40. When an order for contact is made under section 34, the local authority will need to review the plan for the child. Contact should continue to be monitored. The local authority will need to consider whether it would be appropriate to apply to the court for variation of the order, including variation of any of the conditions attached to the order.

RECORD KEEPING

6.41. Full and clear records are essential to the effective monitoring of contact. They will provide a basis for a clear understanding, when social workers or carers change, of the decisions about contact which have been made and the reasons for them. Records about contact should form part of the child's case record required by the Arrangements for Placement Regulations.

CHAPTER 7 **INDEPENDENT VISITORS**

7.1. This Chapter gives guidance on the statutory framework in paragraph 17 of Schedule 2 to the Children Act 1989 governing the appointment, role and function of independent visitors. The categories of persons who are not to be considered as independent are set out in the Definition of Independent Visitors (Children) Regulations 1991. Throughout the guidance the child is referred to as he/him and the independent visitor as she/her for convenience to distinguish the two.

DUTY TO APPOINT AN INDEPENDENT VISITOR

7.2. Paragraph 17 of Schedule 2 to the Children Act places a duty on a local authority to appoint an independent visitor in respect of any child they are looking after if they believe that it would be in a child's best interest and certain conditions are satisfied. The need for such an appointment arises where communication between the child and his parent or a person who is not a parent but who has parental responsibility has been infrequent, or where he has not visited or been visited by his parents or a person who is not a parent but who has parental responsibility during the preceding 12 months.

7.3. Under the old law the appointment of visitors was restricted to children who were accommodated in community homes which provided education (section 11 of the Child Care Act 1980), and then only in respect of children in compulsory care. The Children Act extends the requirement to include all children who are being looked after by a local authority. A child is being looked after by a local authority if he is in care or if he is not in care but is provided with accommodation by the authority (section 22(1)).

7.4. The appointment of an independent visitor is not a duty falling to a local authority with respect to any child not being looked after by them. The provisions do not extend to children accommodated by health authorities or children accommodated in residential care, nursing or mental nursing homes unless the child is being looked after by a local authority which has placed the child (who may perhaps be disabled) in any of the above type of facility under their general accommodation and maintenance duties (section 23(2)).

DEFINITION OF INDEPENDENT VISITORS

7.5. Paragraph 17(7) of Schedule 2 to the Children Act empowers the Secretary of State to make regulations as to the circumstances in which a person appointed as a visitor is to be regarded as independent of the local authority appointing her.

7.6. The regulations provide that a person is not to be regarded as independent if she is a member of the local authority or of its committees or sub-committees whether elected or co-opted or is an officer of the social services department of the authority or is the spouse of any of these. Additionally, where the child is being accommodated by an organisation other than the local authority, eg in a voluntary or registered children's home, a person who is a member or a patron or trustee of the organisation, or who is employed by the organisation whether paid or not, or who is the spouse of any such person is not to be regarded as independent.

7.7. Local authorities should consider in this connection whether it would be appropriate to treat people who are in a stable cohabitation relationship as spouses.

IDENTIFICATION OF CHILDREN FOR WHOM AN INDEPENDENT VISITOR SHOULD BE APPOINTED

7.8. Regulation 5 of the Review of Children's Cases Regulations 1991 places a duty on a local authority to consider at reviews whether an independent visitor should be appointed in respect of a child looked after by them. It is likely to be at a review that consideration is first given to the appointment of an independent visitor. However, in some cases the question may arise when the local authority first draws up a plan for a child whom they are looking after (Regulation 4 of the Arrangements for Placement of Children (General) Regulations 1991.

7.9. If either of the two following criteria is satisfied the local authority may be required to appoint an independent visitor:

(i) where it appears to a local authority in relation to any child whom they are looking after that communication between the child and a parent of his, or any person who is not a parent of his but who has parental responsibility for him, has been infrequent;

(ii) where any child whom they are looking after has not visited or been visited by (or lived with) a parent of his, or any person who is not a parent of his but who has parental responsibility for him, during the preceding twelve months (paragraph 17(1) of Schedule 2).

7.10. If either of these threshold criteria is satisfied, the authority has to assess whether it would be in the child's best interests for an independent visitor to be appointed (paragraph 17(1) of Schedule 2). In reaching their decision, the local authority has to have regard to the general duty in relation to children whom they are looking after (section 22(4)) to ascertain as far as is reasonably practicable the wishes and feelings of a range of persons, including the child. The wishes of the child are of particular importance. The authority must also take into consideration in reaching the decision not only the wishes and feelings of these persons but also the child's religious persuasion, racial origin and cultural and linguistic background (section 22(5)). The local authority may not appoint an independent visitor for a child if the child objects to it and the authority are satisfied he has sufficient understanding to make an informed decision.

7.11. It is possible that, in certain circumstances, although the threshold criteria for appointing an independent visitor set out above exist, the local authority may decide that such an appointment is unnecessary and therefore not in the child's best interests. For example, a child (at the time the Children Act came into force) may be well settled in a permanent placement with foster carers and already have sufficient contacts, friends and – if necessary – opportunities to seek advice. In some cases members of his family other than his parents may be in regular contact making the appointment of an independent visitor unnecessary.

SELECTION OF AN INDEPENDENT VISITOR FOR A PARTICULAR CHILD

7.12. In matching a particular visitor with a particular child the authority, as they did in the question of whether or not to appoint a visitor, will need to have regard to the wishes of the child, his parents or those with parental responsibility and any other persons whose wishes and feelings are relevant. If the child objects to the authority's choice they may not make the appointment.

7.13. The child's social worker will have been involved in the process whereby the authority decided that an independent visitor was necessary and her advice in the matching of a potential visitor to the child is crucial.

7.14. The personal qualities required of an independent visitor will include an ability to relate to children generally and more specifically in a manner appropriate to the age and circumstances of the child for whom she is to be appointed.

7.15. A child's views about whom he would like as an independent visitor and the reasons why will vary greatly. The child in his teens may prefer an independent visitor to be more like an elder sibling than a parent in age and role. Other children and circumstances may suggest that a much older person, perhaps resembling a grandparent, would be the preferred choice. Some children will appreciate having an independent visitor who has herself been in care. The local authority will need to take into account the child's wishes and feelings and these may also include whether the independent visitor should share his religion, culture, language and racial background. Where it has not proved possible to make a placement which entirely reflects the child's race and culture the independent visitor could be a link with the child's racial and cultural background.

7.16. There will be a need for introductory meetings to provide an opportunity for mutual assessment and to enable the child to decide whether he wishes the appointment to be made. If the child does not, the local authority should consider whether the appointment of another person might be possible and appropriate.

7.17. In a very limited number of cases there may be a relative who would be appropriate to fulfil the role of independent visitor and this arrangement might be the child's preferred option. Local authorities will need to distinguish between the small minority of cases where the designation of a relative or friend as the child's visitor is appropriate and the more common situation where the child properly has ongoing contact with relatives and friends. In the latter situation the local authority should encourage such contacts and may pay expenses without the necessity of changing the status to that of independent visitor (paragraphs 15(1) and 16(2) of Schedule 2).

RECRUITMENT

7.18. The local authority will need to devise a strategy for the recruitment of appropriate persons to act as independent visitors. It may be helpful to consult with community groups, voluntary bodies and other organisations with an interest in children. Imaginative and energetic recruiting measures may have to be devised to ensure that the needs of the child can be met in terms of his religious persuasion, racial origin, cultural and linguistic background. Particular requirements may also arise in the case of children with disabilities. It may be acceptable in some circumstances for an independent visitor to fulfil that role for more than one child.

7.19. For a child in his early teens and likely to remain in care, the relationship with the independent visitor might last four or five years. A variety of factors will determine the length of the relationship, but since it has the potential to be long-term, there are clearly strong arguments for recruiting as independent visitors people who are able to make a long-term commitment to the role. However, recruitment procedures should not preclude those potential independent visitors who, although able only to offer their services for shorter periods, may have valuable qualities and could well be needed and play a valuable role.

7.20. Local authorities may wish to consider recruiting a pool of persons to act as independent visitors. This should allow the selection of an individual visitor for a particular child to take place more quickly than would be possible if the complete recruitment and appointment process had to be undertaken from the beginning. However, even if there is a pool of visitors with a variety of backgrounds and ages, there may still be situations where the local authority and the child identify specific requirements which cannot be met by those visitors who have already been recruited. Moreover, there are disadvantages to the pool approach. Individual independent visitors may become frustrated and disillusioned by over-long waiting periods between appointment to the pool and introductions to a child.

Training and Support

7.21 The recruitment, assessment and support of independent visitors requires the deployment of administrative and professional skills which have similarities to those needed to assess foster and adoptive parents. For this reason authorities may wish to consider locating the responsibility for the independent visitor service with such a specialist team. There are alternative settings such as the local authority's volunteer sector or an independent inspection unit.

7.22. The effectiveness of the independent visitor will depend principally on her personal qualities, ability to communicate with children, commitment and interest in children's welfare. These are pre-requisites. However, such qualities will be enhanced by the provision of an induction programme which will need to cover not only the formal aspects of their role and functions but also the duties and procedures of the local authority and the relevant aspects of the legislation. Some familiarity with the principles and practice of inter-agency working in child abuse matters would be helpful. It is not intended that independent visitors should be required to undertake intensive training beyond the induction phase but there may be occasions when, because of the circumstances of an individual child, the independent visitor would benefit from some additional training.

7.23. Induction training will also allow the opportunity to set expectations in respect of access to file information concerning the child and the extent to which the independent visitor herself keeps any record, over and above that required to claim expenses. On appointment of the independent visitor, the local authority will have to decide the amount of information to be given to her in the circumstances of the child's current situation and history. The general approach is likely to be based on "the need to know" principle but there will always be some situations where it would be judged preferable to give the independent visitor the maximum information possible. The child himself should be involved in deciding what information is made available to her. It should be noted that the independent visitor, although appointed by the local authority, has no formal right to inspect the child's case files.

7.24. In most situations it will neither be necessary nor appropriate for the independent visitor to keep detailed records of her discussions with the child. However, she may well wish to keep a note as an *aide memoire;* for example, the names of relatives who the child mentions or birthdays. The independent visitor may also feel it appropriate to note the decisions of meetings such as reviews she has attended with the local authority. Induction training should stress the importance of ensuring that such confidential information is safely stored, in the context of wider discussion about general confidentiality issues. Furthermore, there should be a clear understanding that such records would be destroyed on termination of her appointment.

7.25. Independent visitors and local authorities should discuss at an early stage how to deal with any anxieties which the child's carers might understandably feel about the appointment of an independent visitor. Local authorities should arrange for the preparation of carers and provide any support or explanations to them and the child about the independent visitor's functions. Explanation should not be left to the independent visitor. She will of course require to be sensitive in all her dealings with the child and his carers particularly where the child is in a family placement and she is visiting the family's home.

7.26. Independent visitors do not require supervision or day to day management – indeed such an approach might seriously prejudice their independence. However, they will require support. Many of the children whom they seek to befriend will have had a history of breakdowns of relationships. In these cases the independent visitor may have to overcome a barrier of cynicism and distrust before they can forge and maintain a good relationship with the child. They may welcome opportunities to discuss in a confidential setting individual situations or wider dilemmas perhaps being faced by a number of independent visitors. The task of the independent visitor may at times be stressful. Local authorities should recognise this and, in considering the overall organisation of the independent visitor service, should consider how best to provide appropriate support for them.

Appointment

7.27. Local authorities will need to take steps to avoid the risk that unsuitable persons who pose a serious threat to children's safety are inadvertently recruited. Appointment procedures need to be rigorous and formal. Applicants will need to submit detailed background information and provide the names of two personal references. Police references should always be sought under the terms of Circular LAC(88)19 (WO Circular 45/88) and a check made of the Department of Health Consultancy Service. Attention should be drawn to the Rehabilitation of Offenders Act 1974 (Exceptions) Order 1975 as amended by the Rehabilitation of Offenders Act 1974 (Exceptions) (Amendment) Order 1986, which allows convictions which are spent under the terms of the 1974 Act to be disclosed by the police and to be taken into account in deciding whether to appoint the applicant. The applicant therefore may properly be requested to list all convictions and cautions. The applicant must give her permission in writing for a police check to be carried out. Where appointments are made the independent visitor should be provided with a letter of authority and arrangements should also be made for the provision of authenticated photographs for identification purposes. These will need to be withdrawn when the appointment is terminated.

REVIEW AND TERMINATION OF APPOINTMENT

7.28. Local authorities will need to consider at each review under the Review of Children's Cases Regulations 1991 the appropriateness of the continuing appointment of the particular independent visitor and indeed of any independent visitor. The child's views will be highly relevant. The local authority will need to consider the most appropriate way of ascertaining the child's wishes about the continuation of an appointment which has been made. The older child should be given the opportunity from time to time to express his views about the value of the appointment. If he objects to it continuing and the authority are satisfied that he has sufficient understanding to make an informed decision, the authority must terminate the independent visitor's appointment in respect of that particular child (paragraph 17(6) of Schedule 2). They should then consider whether it would be appropriate to appoint another independent visitor.

7.29. The independent visitor ceases to be appointed if she gives notice in writing to the authority who appointed her that she resigns the appointment or the authority give her notice in writing that they have terminated it (paragraph 17(3) of Schedule 2). Such a termination is in respect of a visitor's appointment to an individual child but may also signal that the local authority does not wish the independent visitor to be appointed again for any child. However, where an independent visitor is acting in respect of a number of children, termination of appointment in respect of one of them does not terminate appointment in respect of the others. Each case should be considered separately.

7.30. The local authority must act with the greatest care to avoid any suggestion that the termination of an independent visitor's appointment is a consequence of that visitor acting with appropriate independence and, for example, challenging the validity of the authority's care planning or standards of service in respect of a particular child.

7.31. Where the independent visitor disagrees with the local authority's action regarding termination she may wish to make a formal representation and complaint. The local authority has discretion to decide whether the independent visitor is a person with sufficient interest in the child's welfare to warrant his representations being considered under section 26(3)(e). The situation may also arise where, notwithstanding the local authority's wish to terminate the appointment, the child wishes it to continue on a friendship basis. The local authority in considering the child's wishes may conclude on balance that acceptance of such a position is preferable to official opposition provided the child's welfare is not endangered.

7.32. There may be exceptional circumstances where the behaviour of the independent visitor, whilst falling short of criminal activity, is nevertheless totally inappropriate and constitutes a serious risk to the child's welfare. Failure to terminate the independent visitor's appointment would amount to a breach of the local authority's duty to safeguard and promote the welfare of the child. In these circumstances the local authority should review any other current and all previous appointments of that person as an independent visitor and carry out such investigations as are necessary. Authorities should place that person's particulars on the Department of Health Consultancy Services Register (see paragraph 7.27 above). The child may well and need particular help and support. Consideration will have to be given to implementing child protection procedures.

THE ROLE AND FUNCTION OF THE INDEPENDENT VISITOR

7.33. The functions of the independent visitor comprise visiting, advising and befriending the child. These are specific duties set out in paragraph 17(2) of Schedule 2. It is recognised, that in some instances, independent visitors may have qualities, skills, experience and qualifications which in other settings entitle them to undertake work in a professional capacity with children. In general, however, the role is envisaged as being undertaken by volunteers from a lay perspective. This section of the guidance discusses further the role of the independent visitor and also a range of specific functions which, depending on the individual child and his circumstances, may have greater or lesser prominence.

7.34. How the independent visitor pursues her role in terms of a plan and timetable of more specific activities will vary depending on the circumstances. She will need to form her own judgements about how best to proceed. Taking into account the local authority's view of the child's needs, the child's wishes and her developing relationship with him, the independent visitor must reach her own conclusions as to how, in this particular situation, her activities might best be focused. Whatever she does should be directed at contributing to the welfare of the child, and this includes promoting the child's developmental, social, emotional, educational, religious and cultural needs. It may also require her to encourage the child to exercise his rights and to participate in decisions which will affect him. It will also include (unless she feels that there is clear evidence to act differently) supporting the care plan for the child and his carers, such as foster parents or residential workers who have day to day care for the child.

7.35. The independent visitor's role and functions can also be described in terms of what she is not intended to do. She is not to be anything other than child-focused, however sympathetic she may be to other points of view. Her functions are not that of a substitute parent or carer but she should aim, as far as possible, to complement their activities. In bringing the lay perspective, she must not allow her personal prejudices to determine her actions. She is not expected to accept unquestioningly what those responsible for the child tell her is in his interests, but should remain open-minded and even sceptical.

Visiting

7.36. Face to face contact with the child is an important aspect of the independent visitor's role. The frequency and length of such visits will depend on the circumstances of each situation and may change in the course of the relationship between the child and independent visitor. A child may have often experienced the disappointment of the cancellation of an arranged visit from a parent or relative and the independent visitor will need to be particularly sensitive and reliable in this regard. The independent visitor will need to make arrangements in advance about visiting with the child's carers as well as the child himself.

7.37. As the relationship develops it may well be appropriate for the independent visitor and child to got out somewhere. The type of outing will depend on the child's interests and the range of facilities in the area. The independent visitor will need to be sensitive to avoid being regarded and treated as the person who simply provides 'treats'. It is not intended that the independent visitor should provide compensating leisure experiences which ought more appropriately be the responsibility of the child's carers. However, such outings can afford privacy, ease communication and develop the relationship between independent visitor and child through a shared activity. There may be activities which the carers cannot provide, perhaps for example connected to the cultural background or religion of the child. The fact of the child being of a different culture or religion from that of the residential carers or foster parents may not only influence the selection of an independent visitor but also her choice of the type of activity in which she involves the child. She may be able to promote contacts in the area relevant to the child's cultural development.

7.38. In exceptional circumstances it may be appropriate if the relationship with the child has developed, for the independent visitor to invite the child to her own home. Again, such a step must be seen within the overall care plans for the child and agreed with the authority and carers with due sensitivity. This is not an area suited to spontaneous gestures. There are obvious dangers that the child's hopes for the future may be unrealistically aroused and carefully laid plans distorted. However, there is also a general principle that children in care should experience normal activities and they will know that other children in their class at school, for example, will often visit friends at their homes.

7.39. Similar arguments will apply, again in exceptional circumstances, where the independent visitor, child and local authority agree that an overnight stay or short holiday (perhaps with the independent visitor's own family, if she has one) would be appropriate. Although the independent visitor has been the subject of formal checks on appointment (see paragraph 7.27), the local authority will have to make further checks before such an arrangements is agreed.

Advising

7.40. There will be a range of issues about which an independent visitor might offer the child advice. Some of these may be quite straightforward such as where to find or who to ask for particular information. The advising role becomes more complex where it overlaps with counselling and the responsibilities of other professionals involved with the child. It is not intended that the independent visitor should engage the child in intensive counselling. Independent visitors need to recognise that it is not their role to counsel or advise the child in complex situations. They should rather encourage and support the child to seek and accept help from his social worker in the first instance.

Befriending

7.41. Whoever is appointed will need to try to establish with the child a sense of trust in the relationship which must form one of the basic elements in the befriending role. The independent visitor must also be prepared for the process of establishing trust to be a slow one and for there to be setbacks. For some of these children earlier relationships with adults have ended in disappointment and disillusionment. They may be reluctant or find it very difficult to establish rapport with adults and to place any trust in them.

Meetings with the Local Authority or Other Agencies

7.42. The possible involvement of the independent visitor in meetings or consultation processes arises in some circumstances as a legal requirement and in others is on a discretionary basis.

7.43. The mandatory involvement is in respect of a child who has an independent visitor and who is in secure accommodation. Where the local authority intends to make an application to court to keep the child in that accommodation, the authority has to inform a range of persons, including the child's independent visitor if one has been appointed, of the intention (Regulation 15 of the Secure Accommodation Regulations 1991). If the placement of the child in secure accommodation continues, Regulations 16 and 17 require reviews to take place and, if practicable, the wishes and feelings of a range of persons to be taken into account. The independent visitor is included here and may be able to give her views in person, in writing or both. The independent visitor is also entitled to know the outcome of the review (Regulation 17(3)).

7.44. The independent visitor will have the opportunity to provide contributions to the review of a child's case either in writing or at meetings where the child's case is to be discussed and to which she has been invited because she has something relevant to contribute or because the child has requested that she attend with him. The independent visitor may wish to put views to the meeting as a friend of the child. The independent visitor will have to take care to distinguish between repeating what the child has asked her to say on his behalf, interpreting such information and offering her own view as to what is best for the child.

7.45. The child may wish the independent visitor to speak as a friend on his behalf in order to help resolve a particular issue or difficulty. This may involve the independent visitor's attendance at a meeting; perhaps a review meeting, or an oral hearing of a complaint being made under the representations procedure. Independent visitors do not constitute the independent element of the representations procedure, but the child might wish the independent visitor to accompany him in the capacity of a friend to an oral hearing convened under the representations procedure (see Chapter 10).

7.46. The Children Act also offers the opportunity for an independent visitor to contribute views outside the formal review arrangements. The child may be involved in family proceedings where the court has requested a welfare report (section 7). Another possibility in relation to court proceedings is that a guardian ad litem has been appointed (section 41). The views of the independent visitor about the child may well be of relevance to such proceedings and the independent visitor may need to take the initiative in seeking out the relevant person in order to convey her views. She will wish to consult with the child before taking such action.

ADVOCACY

7.47. In some situations, the position of the child may be an unhappy one. The child may be dissatisfied with the current arrangements for his care or the absence of progress in achieving a plan for the future. He may dislike and distrust his carers and those in the authority who have responsibility for him. He may feel that his views are ignored or never sought and that he has no realistic opportunity to complain or challenge the validity of the legal processes which affect him. He may disclose that he is being abused by his carers. In such a bleak scenario the child has an urgent need for skilled advocacy. This is not a role the independent visitor is expected to play.

7.48. Instead, the independent visitor must be able to recognise the needs of the child in such serious situations and with the child's agreement draw their concerns to the attention of the child's social worker or, if necessary, a more senior officer in the social services department. In certain cases it may be appropriate to refer the matter to one of the voluntary organisations which specialises in advocacy.

Expenses

7.49. The independent visitor is entitled to recover from the authority who appointed her reasonable expenses incurred by her for the purpose of her functions in visiting, advising and befriending the child (paragraph 17(2)(b) of Schedule 2). The term 'expenses' is meant to cover travel and out of pocket payments but is not meant to equate to a regular payment or salary for undertaking the role of independent visitor. Whether anticipated expenditure may form a pattern or be a one-off amount, the local authority and independent visitor will need to reach some prior agreement about normal spending limits and authorisation for additional expenditure. The independent visitor will also need to keep records for the purpose of submitting expenses claims.

When a Child ceases to be looked after

7.50. The need for an independent visitor to continue his relationship with a young person once he ceases to be looked after by the local authority, where the young person seeks this, should not be overlooked. Such continuing arrangements would be on an informal basis but the local authority should consider whether it would be appropriate to continue to meet the cost of reasonable expenses associated with this continued role until such time as its own after-care responsibilities expire.

CHAPTER 8   <u>REVIEW OF CHILDREN'S CASES</u>

INTRODUCTION

8.1. Chapter 2 dealt with planning of arrangements for children who are looked after by a local authority or accommodated by a voluntary organisation or a registered children's home. This chapter deals with the review of children who are looked after by a local authority or accommodated by a voluntary organisation or a registered children's home. Reviews form part of a continuous planning process – reviewing decisions to date and planning future work. The purpose of the review is to ensure that the child's welfare is safeguarded and promoted in the most effective way throughout the period he is looked after or accommodated. Progress in safeguarding and providing for the child's welfare should be examined and monitored at every review and the plan for the child amended as necessary to reflect any significant change.

8.2. The Review of Children's Cases Regulations (like the Arrangements for Placement of Children (General) Regulations) apply to local authorities which are looking after children and to voluntary organisations and registered children's homes which accommodate children not looked after by the local authority. For the purpose of this guidance, 'review' means review under the Review of Children's Cases Regulations. 'Responsible authority' means local authority, voluntary organisation or person carrying on a registered children's home. Where guidance deals with a matter which is not equally applicable to all groups, this is made clear.

WHAT IS A REVIEW?

8.3. The concept of review as governed by the Reviews of Children's Cases Regulations and discussed in this guidance is a continuous process of planning and reconsideration of the plan for the child. Review will include a number of components leading to meetings held to discuss the plan which has been drawn up for a child who is being looked after or accommodated by a responsible authority. This will require consultation and the gathering of information on an ongoing basis, discussing that information and making decisions to amend the plan as necessary. The agenda for meetings should include consideration of progress in implementing the plan, need for changes in approach on service provision, a possible reallocation of tasks or a change in the status of the child (need for care proceedings or discharge of a care order, for example). Any meeting which is convened for the purpose of considering the child's case in connection with any aspect of the review of that case falls within the scope of these Regulations. Whether such a meeting is called a planning meeting or a review or review meeting will not determine whether it is in fact part of a review. This will depend on the purpose for which the meeting is convened.

8.4. A review is not a reconsideration after a complaint or a part of line management supervision of a decision although either could indicate the need for a review of the child's circumstances. Neither is it a case review as described in "Working Together". A review is different from a case conference, although case conferences could well provide information to be considered in a review (a case conference is a multi-disciplinary meeting usually called to formulate advice on a specific issue). But where the discussion at a case conference combines consideration of wider issues affecting the plan for the child, it constitutes part of a review and falls within these Regulations. It also differs from a case discussion as part of line management as that is an exercise whereby managers, amongst other matters, review the performance of their staff. Guidance on a review of a decision in the light of a complaint is dealt with in Chapter 10 on representations procedures. See also **Working Together** Part 7 re case conferences and case reviews. A review of an individual child's case is held solely to make plans in the interests of safeguarding and promoting that child's welfare.

REQUIREMENT TO REVIEW AND FREQUENCY

8.5. Regulation 2 places a specific statutory duty on the responsible authority to review the case of a child who is looked after or accommodated, in accordance with these Regulations. Regulation 3 sets out the maximum intervals that may separate reviews. The first review should take place no later than four weeks after the date on which the child begins to be looked after or is provided with accommodation. In the case of a child looked after by a local authority this will bring together the assessment and planning that has been taking place since the child was indentified as being in need of the local authority's services. The second review should take place not more than three months after the date of the first review. Thereafter, subsequent reviews should take place at intervals of not more than six months after the date of the previous review.

8.6. The frequency of reviews required by the Regulations is the minimum standard and a review of the child's case should take place as often as the circumstances of the individual case requires. If the need arises for substantial changes to the plan, then the date of the next review should be brought forward. Parents and children should be consulted about the need for additional reviews on a regular basis. Any request for an additional review from a parent or a child should be given serious consideration.

SHORT-TERM PLACEMENTS

8.7. Regulation 11 allows for a defined series of short pre-planned placements (eg for respite care or staying contact) to be treated as a *single placement* for the application of these Regulations and those relating to specific placements. All the requirements of the Review Regulations apply, but need not be repeated for each episode of accommodation so as long as the conditions in Regulation 11 are met. The conditions in Regulation 11 are:

"(a) all the periods are included within a period which does not exceed one year;

(b) no single period is for a duration of more than four weeks; and

(c) the total duration of the periods does not exceed 90 days."

All the placements should take place with the same carer for a family placement and at the same establishment for a residential placement ("at the same place"). Similar provision is made for short-term placements in the Regulations relating to specific placements.

A SYSTEM FOR REVIEWS

8.8. Each responsible authority will wish to revise their present arrangements to ensure that they provide a system for review of children's cases which will satisfy the requirements of the Children Act and Regulations 4, 8, 9 and 10 as described below. In revising existing arrangements or establishing new procedures responsible authorities should ensure that their review system provides for:

● the full participation of both children and parents in the decision-making process;

● a structured, coordinated approach to the planning of child care work in individual cases; and

● a monitoring system for checking the operation of the review process.

8.9. Regulation 4 sets out the manner in which cases are to be reviewed and requires that the arrangements should be in writing and made known to children, parents, other persons with parental responsibility, other persons whose views the responsible authority consider relevant and those involved in conducting reviews of children's cases (Regulation 4(1)). The responsible authority is required by Regulation 4(2) to co-ordinate review action and by Regulation 4(3) to appoint an officer to achieve that coordination. The responsible authority need not make a special appointment to deal with these duties. For example in the case of local authorities, it is suggested that senior officers are designated to fulfil this role in each management area of the authority. These officers could combine this role with their other duties.

Preparations for the Review

8.10. Before the review is arranged the field social worker responsible for the case, in discussion with his line manager, should identify who should be invited. Only in exceptional cases should a parent or a child not be invited to a review meeting. The first review meeting is the occasion on which the planning process is most clearly illustrated as being inseparable from the review process. It is the first opportunity to confirm formally that the plan is meeting the child's needs. Those to be invited should include those who have been consulted (including the child and his parents) in drawing up the initial plan and who may need to contribute to the review.

Consultation

8.11. As with planning, it is essential that there is full consultation with all the relevant individuals before the review meeting is held. There should also be a written record kept on the child's case record of the results of the consultation exercise before each review meeting. Appropriate provision should be made for children and parents with communication difficulties or whose first language is not English. Sections 22(4), 61 and 64 of the Children Act state that before making any decision with respect to a child looked after or accommodated by a responsible authority, the responsible authority should obtain and take account of the wishes and feelings of:

(a) The child (subject to his age and understanding and so far as this is in his best interests);

(b) His parents;

(c) Any person who is not a parent of his but who has parental responsibility for him;

(d) Any other person whom they consider ought to be notified.

Any other person may include:

(i)   His current carer (foster parent or residential social worker);

(ii)   The independent visitor (if one has been appointed);

(iii)   The relevant health care professionals of the district health authority;

(iv)   The child's general medical practitioner (GP);

(v)   The appropriate local authority where it is proposed (or it is the case already) that the child will be looked after in their area;

(vi)   The local education authority;

(vii) The child's teacher (in relevant cases);

(viii) Any other person whose views the responsible authority consider should be sought (for example, a representative from a voluntary agency, police child protection liaison officer, housing officer or community leader).

(See paragraphs 2.45–2.53 which contain guidance on consultation in relation to the Arrangements for Placement of Children (General) Regulations which is equally applicable to the Review of Children's Cases Regulations.)

8.12. Where it is considered that written views or reports will be adequate these should be sought and obtained in time for the review. Any relevant information which needs to be circulated before the meeting should be sent out with the agenda (see paragraph 8.14 below). A process should already be in place to ensure the continuous collection of information as part of the planning system rather than as a separate one-off exercise for a review. Consultation about the initial plan for the child, amendments to that plan as time passes and subsequent reviews will inform the planning process and will be relevant material for discussion at all review meetings.

Who Chairs a Review?

8.13. A meeting to review a child's case should be chaired by an officer of the responsible authority at a more senior level than the case social worker. The field social worker responsible for the child's case and that person's supervisor should be in attendance. The intention is that the role of the chairperson will bring a degree of oversight and objectivity to the monitoring of the responsible authority's practice and decision-making in relation to the plan for the child.

Agenda

8.14. It will be useful to have a checklist or agenda of the issues for discussion at a review meeting which is circulated in advance to those attending including the parent and the child. Items for the agenda will arise out of the considerations for discussion in paragraphs 8.19–8.20 below. This will help to ensure that no issues are overlooked and that the people attending the meeting are prepared to discuss and consider the relevant issues. Use of such a list or agenda should not become exclusive or inhibiting; those present should be free to raise issues they consider to be important.

Who Should Attend?

8.15. Regulation 7(2) requires that the responsible authority, where they consider it appropriate, should involve the child and his parents in review meetings. The involvement of the child will be subject to his understanding and welfare. The possibility of a child being accompanied to a review meeting by a person who is able to provide friendly support should be considered. Where a child's welfare would be prejudiced by his parent's attendance at the same time as the child, separate attendance may be arranged. The attendance of the child and his parents at meetings to review the child's case will be the norm rather than the exception (subject to the reservations already expressed). It is expected that the parents and the child (if he is of sufficient understanding) will be present at the whole of the review, but this will depend on the circumstances of each individual case. The involvement of the parents and the child in review meetings is in line with the basic philosophy of the Children Act in relation to the participation and wishes and feelings of the child and his parents, and the spirit of partnership between the local authority and parents.

8.16. The flexibility given to responsible authorities in the Regulations regarding the attendance of the child and parents at review meetings recognises the fact that in a few cases their attendance will not be appropriate or practicable. This may be the case if there is a clear conflict of interests which might militate against the attendance of either or both the child and parents. However, the fears or inhibitions of professionals should not be the reason for excluding a child or his parent from a review. Alternative arrangements should be considered. Any decision to exclude the child or the parents from a meeting (or part of a meeting) should be discussed and agreed with the chairperson. If a parent or child is excluded from a review, a written explanation should be given with a copy placed on the child's case record on other arrangements made for their involvement in the review.

8.17. In addition to the parent and child, the child's carer should be invited. Other people with a legitimate interest in the child should also be invited if they have a contribution to make which indicates that they should take part in the discussions at the review meeting. This may apply, for example, to the child's GP, the child's community health doctor, health visitor, child psychologist, school teacher, foster parent, residential care social worker, independent visitor (if appointed) or ethnic minority representative. The attendance of such people should always be discussed with the child before invitations are made and his views on their attendance obtained. It may be appropriate where the contribution from such people is strictly factual for the information to be provided in writing. Where a long-term plan has been set in place, a small group (those consistently and constantly involved with the child) should be identified as essential attenders at the next and subsequent review meetings. In the majority of cases, the group will consist of the social worker, the child, parents, the chairperson and the carer (if different from the parent). This will vary according to the circumstances of the individual case.

Venue for A Review Meeting

8.18. Separate, but equally important considerations apply in deciding where to hold a meeting to review a child's case. The child should always be asked for his views about the venue. Meetings should be arranged at a place (and time) which will be the most likely to provide a setting and atmosphere conducive to the relaxed participation of all those attending. Particular regard should be paid to the needs of the child. Arrangements should be made to secure the attendance of those identified as necessary to the particular review and allow serious discussion and planning to take place. Consideration should be given to assisting parents with travelling costs or the provision of other support, such as a child-minder, if there would otherwise be difficulty for a parent in attending a review (paragraph 16 of Schedule 2 to the Act may be relevant).

Matters for consideration in the the Review

8.19. The primary matter for consideration at the review is the plan for the welfare of the child (under the general welfare duties placed on authorities by sections 22, 61 and 64 of the Children Act). At the first review this will be done by examining and confirming the plan, with or without amendments. Subsequent reviews will be occasions for monitoring the progress of the plan and making decisions to amend the plan as necessary in the light of changed knowledge and circumstances. As the reason for planning and review is to safeguard and promote the welfare of the child the matters for consideration when planning and reviewing a case are nearly identical. After the first review, a review should always include consideration of progress made since the previous review – whether the goals and tasks set have been achieved; and if not, why not and what action is needed.

8.20. Schedule 2 provides a checklist of matters for consideration at the review which is not comprehensive or exclusive but sets the minimum requirements. In addition, the review must consider matters specified in the Act relating to the welfare of the child. Other matters will arise in individual cases which it is not possible to cover in a list of general application. The matters covered by Schedule 2 and the relevant statutory provisions are:

(a) an examination of the responsible authority's plan for the child in relation to the wishes and feelings of the child and having regard to his understanding;

(b) an examination of the responsible authority's plan for the child in relation to the wishes and feelings of the parents;

(c) whether the plan fulfils the responsible authority's duty under sections 22(3), 61(1) or 64(1) of the Act to safeguard and promote the child's welfare.

Paragraph (c) above includes the following:

● where the child is in the care of a local authority, whether or not the care order can be discharged or varied to a lesser order;

● whether the placement continues to be appropriate;

● the views of the child's carer;

- whether the plan makes necessary provision for the child's religious persuasion, racial origin and cultural and linguistic background;

- where a child is looked after, whether the plan takes account of the duty under section 23(6) to enable the child to live with a parent, other person with parental responsibility, relative, friend; and where the child is in care, a person in whose favour a residence order was in force immediately before the care order was made, or other person with a legitimate interest in the child;

- the arrangements made for contact and where the child is looked after by a local authority with regard to the duty on the local authority in paragraph 15 of Schedule 2 to the Act to promote and maintain contact between the child and his family;

- where a child is looked after, the views of an independent visitor if one has been appointed, and if not whether to appoint one;

- whether the plan takes account of any particular needs the child may have, eg if the child has a disability;

- the arrangements made for the child's health (including consent to examination or treatment);

- the arrangements made for the child's education;

- the arrangements, if any, for financial support of the placement;

- where the child is provided with accommodation by voluntary agreement, whether or not the arrangements for the involvement of the parents in the child's life are appropriate; whether the social worker needs to encourage greater exercise of the parents continuing responsibility to the child; whether or not there is still a need for accommodation or whether another sort of service would be more appropriate, or whether there is a need (for a local authority) to take care proceedings;

- reunification of the child with his parents and family;

- where a child has been in an agreed placement (not in care) for some time, whether the existing plan ensures that the child and the carer have an adequate sense of stability. Whether the carer should seek a residence order, for example; and

- where appropriate, arrangements for aftercare.

Report of Review

8.21. Regulation 10 requires that a written record of each review is drawn up and put on the child's case record for further reference. The record of the review should have attached to it the results of the consultation exercise, including any written reports submitted. It should also include the agenda with a note of the discussion under each item, what was decided and who is responsible for implementing particular decisions. It should be clearly noted whether the child and his parents were invited to the review, if they were not, the reason why not, whether they attended and what views they expressed on each of the agenda items. Any dissenting opinion should be recorded with an explanation of the rationale of decisions taken. The chairperson should check the record of the review to ensure that an accurate, comprehensive record is placed on file and, in particular, that any necessary action has been correctly identified and tasks allocated.

Notification

8.22. Regulation 7(3) requires that the child, his parent, others with parental responsibility and other persons considered appropriate are notified of the result of the review and decisions taken in consequence of the review. It may be necessary to notify third parties of the result of the review, because they need to know about a decision. Care should be taken to provide only that information which the third party needs to know.

8.23. The notification of the result of each review meeting should be a written summary of the main points of the written report of the review which makes clear who is responsible for implementing decisions arising from the review and the relevant time-scales. The field social worker responsible for the case should supplement this written notification by explaining in advance wherever possible to the parents and the child the decisions taken at the review meeting and the reasons for these decisions, even if the parents and child were present for all or part of the meeting. Where they were not present, it will be particularly important to do this. It is recommended that this notification is sent no later than 14 days after the review has been held. The notification should indicate whom the child or parent should contact if there is disagreement about any of the decisions taken.

Implementing Decisions

8.24. As part of the review system each responsible authority will need to set in place arrangements for implementing decisions made in the course of a review of a child's case (Regulation 8). Health authorities, local education authorities, local housing authorities and other social services departments have a duty under section 27 of the Children Act to comply with a request from a social services department for help in the exercise of their functions under Part III of the Act. Consultation in child protection work is provided for in Section 47(9) and (11) of the Act. Section 28 imposes new duties on local authorities to consult the appropriate local education authority before they accommodate a child in an establishment which provides education. All responsible authorities will need to make specific arrangements to secure the cooperation of all others who have a role to play in implementing the plan for the child.

Disagreements

8.25. Where disagreements arise in the course of the review process between the child and parents, the child and the responsible authority or the parents and the responsible authority, the responsible authority should make every effort to resolve these by explaining fully the reasons for their decisions. When a disagreement cannot be resolved, the responsible authority should ensure that the child (where he is of sufficient understanding), parents, carers and others involved with the child are aware of the representations procedure required by section 26(3) of the Children Act 1989 and are given advice and assistance as necessary (see Chapter 10).

MONITORING THE SYSTEM

8.26. Responsible authorities are required by Regulation 9 to set in place a system for monitoring of the operation of the review system. While the review of an individual case and the implementation of decisions will involve sharing information and action with others the monitoring of responsible authority's review system will be a matter for that responsible authority alone. The purpose of the monitoring exercise will be to assess how far the system has achieved the objective of ensuring good management of individual cases, to provide an indication of the quality of practice, how far practice reflects the authority's policies and service priorities and to afford an overview of effectiveness in decision making and social work practice. In some local authorities an officer with a title like Principal Assistant (Child Care in General) is appointed to be concerned with policy rather than line management and to concentrate on deployment of resources and service monitoring. Where such posts exist it would be appropriate for such a person to conduct the oversight of the review system. Local authorities may wish to consider this in connection with other quality assurance measures being set in place.

CHAPTER 9 AFTER-CARE: ADVICE AND ASSISTANCE

SUMMARY

9.1. This guidance describes the statutory framework in section 24 of the Children Act 1989, dealing with the duty of local authorities to prepare young people they are looking after for the time when they cease to be so looked after and the powers and duties of local authorities to provide after-care advice and assistance to such young people and certain other defined young people who were accommodated by other bodies. The guidance also deals with the preparation of children accommodated by or on behalf of voluntary organisations (section 61(1)(c)) and those accommodated in registered children's homes (section 64(1)(c)).

9.2. For the purpose of simplicity the guidance describes young people as being 'cared for' or 'leaving care'. This is intended to refer to the concept of caring rather than the young person's legal status: it encompasses all the young people referred to in the previous paragraph and it does so whether they are being cared for under voluntary arrangements or on a compulsory basis. Young people who are privately fostered are covered by the arrangements.

INTRODUCTION

9.3. The successful re-integration of a young person with his family or other responsible person, or the establishment of the ability in the young person to become as self-supporting as possible, where this is necessary, is the culmination of a young person's experience in being cared for by a local authority, private foster parents, a voluntary organisation or in a registered children's home.

9.4. It Is of vital importance that young people are properly prepared for this step and are given access to support afterwards. Young people coming towards this stage will do so from a wide variety of backgrounds and in a wide variety of circumstances, at various ages and with various levels of support available to them from families and friends. All of this implies the need for a very flexible service to meet such a wide range of potentially differing experiences and needs. The quality of preparation for leaving care, and of the after care subsequently provided, may profoundly affect the rest of a young person's life.

9.5. Whether or not the local authority has parental responsibility (under a care order) it adopts, in effect, part of the role of the parent of a young person it is looking after and may provide subsequent advice and assistance. The Act lays powers and, in certain cases, duties, on each local authority to provide this help until a young person reaches the age of 21. (Note: in certain cases, help given to meet expenses concerned with education or training may continue beyond a young person's 21st birthday – see sections 24(8) and (9) of the Act).

9.6. In acting in this way, a local authority will wish to work in partnership with the young person's parents if possible. (It may not, of course, always be possible; for example, they may have died, or they may have rejected the young person or have been rejected by him). Similarly, if a young person has been fostered, the local authority will also need to work in partnership with the foster-parents.

9.7. These responsibilities are laid on local authorities as corporate bodies. The social services department (SSD) is likely to play a leading role in discharging them, but it will need to liaise with many other agencies, both internally and externally. For example, with housing and education departments, health authorities, careers advice and social security offices. This does not, of course, mean that the SSD should take on duties more properly performed by these other agencies.

9.8. The Act recognises the need for inter-agency liaison, and section 27 gives a local authority (in effect the SSD) the right to request help in its discharge of these functions from any other local authority, any local education authority, any local housing authority, any health authority and "any person authorised by the Secretary of State". Any such request is bound to be complied with "if it is compatible with (the other agency's) own statutory or other duties and obligations and does not unduly prejudice the discharge of any of their functions". With this reservation, therefore, any such request must be complied with as far as possible.

THE LEGAL FRAMEWORK

9.9. The powers and duties of local authorities to prepare young people they are looking after for the time when they cease to be so looked after, and the provision of after-care advice and assistance, are described in section 24 of the Act. These are more clearly defined and comprehensive than those formerly in sections 27–29 of the Child Care Act 1980 and the *duty* to prepare young people for this change in their circumstances is new. A comparable new duty to prepare young people for the time when they are no longer cared for is also placed on voluntary organisations (section 61(1)(c)) and those carrying on registered children's homes (section 64(1)(c)). All of these powers and duties need to be carried out in the light of the general child care principles on which the Act is based.

SECTION 24: LOCAL AUTHORITY POWERS AND DUTIES

9.10. Broadly speaking, the powers and duties of local authorities in section 24 of the Act cover all young people leaving a variety of forms of care when aged 16 or over; and they continue until each young person reaches the age of 21.

Section 24(1): If a young person of any age is being looked after by a local authority, it is the duty of the authority to advise, assist and befriend him so as to promote his welfare when he ceases to be looked after by it. Although this has always been a matter of good practice, it is now a duty.

Section 24(2): In addition, a local authority has responsibilities to advise and befriend any young person who "qualifies for advice and assistance". This applies to any young person aged under 21 who ceases, after reaching the age of 16, to be:

(a) looked after by a local authority,

(b) accommodated by or on behalf of a voluntary organisation,

(c) accommodated in a registered children's home,

(d) accommodated by any health authority, NHS trust or local education authority, or in any residential care home, nursing home or mental nursing home, (provided that he was accommodated for at least 3 months), or

(e) privately fostered.

Section 24(3): section 24(2)(d) applies even if the 3 month period began before the young person reached the age of 16.

These responsibilities may be a duty or a power, according to the form of care that the young person has left (see sections 24(4) and (5) below).

Sections 24(4) and (5): Where a local authority knows that a person described in section 24(2) is in their area, they have:

(a) a duty to advise and befriend him if he was formerly looked after by a local authority or accommodated by or on behalf of a voluntary organisation; and

(b) a power to advise and befriend him in all other cases provided that:

  - the young person has asked for such help; and
  - the authority considers that he needs to be advised and befriended; and
  - the person who formerly looked after him (if not the local authority) does not have the necessary facilities for advising and befriending him.

Sections 24(6) and (7): If a local authority has a duty or a power to advise and befriend someone, they may also give him assistance. This assistance may be in kind or, in exceptional circumstances, in cash.

Section 24(8): A local authority also has a power to give assistance to anyone who "qualifies for advice and assistance" and who was formerly looked after by the local authority (section 24(2)(a)) in the following ways:

- by contributing to expenses incurred by him in living near the place where he is, or will be, employed, or seeking employment, or in receipt of education or training;
- by making a grant to enable him to meet expenses connected with his education or training.

Section 24(9): If a local authority is making a contribution or grant under section 24(8) to meet expenses connected with education or training, it may continue to do so until the end of the course, even if the young person reaches the age of 21 before the end of the course. It may also disregard any interruption in his attendance on the course if he resumes it as soon as is reasonably practicable.

Section 24(10): Assistance given by a local authority under section 24 may be given unconditionally or may be repayable in part or in whole. However, no-one shall be liable to repay any assistance at any time when in receipt of income support or family credit. Before giving any assistance or imposing any conditions about repayment, the local authority shall take into account the means of the young person concerned and of each of his parents. (Note: these conditions do not apply to assistance given under section 24(8), which is always unconditional and not repayable).

Section 24(11): If a local authority has been advising and befriending a young person under section 24 and becomes aware that he proposes to live, or does live, in the area of another local authority, it must inform the other local authority.

Section 24(12): If a young person ceases, after reaching the age of 16, to be accommodated:

(a) by a voluntary organisation or in a registered children's home; or

(b) by any health authority, NHS trust or local education authority; or

(c) in any residential care home, nursing home or mental nursing home;

– then the organisation, authority or person carrying on the home (as appropriate) must inform the local authority in whose area the young person proposes to live.

Section 24(13): sections 24(12)(b) and (c) only apply if the accommodation has been provided for a consecutive period of at least 3 months.

The Courts and Legal Services Act 1990 inserts two more subsections into section 24 of the Children Act. These are as follows:

Section 24(14): "Every local authority shall establish a procedure for considering any representations (including any complaint) made to them by a person qualifying for advice and assistance about the discharge of their functions under this Part (of the Act) in relation to him".

This will (*inter alia*) allow young people to complain if they consider that the local authority has not given them adequate preparation for leaving care, or adequate aftercare. It will enable them to make a complaint even if they have left the care of the local authority or another agency. (The general complaints procedure specified at section 26(3) of the Act only applies to a young person who is a 'child', ie under 18 years of age).

Section 24(15): This will enable the Secretary of State to make Regulations governing the way in which local authorities consider any representation made under section 24(14).

9.11. Transitional Arrangements: These are set out in paragraph 22 of schedule 14 to the Act. Under these arrangements, a local authority's powers and duties under section 24 of the Act extend to any young person who:

(i)   left voluntary or compulsory care or ceased to be subject to a criminal care order before the Act came into force (see paragraphs 15(1)(a) to (g), 20(1) and 36 of Schedule 14 to the Act);

(ii) was at least 16 when he left care; and

(iii) is not yet 21.

These transitional arrangements will be in force for five years, ie until anyone qualifying for advice and assistance under these arrangements has reached his 21st birthday.

SECTION 61(1)(c): DUTIES OF VOLUNTARY ORGANISATIONS

9.12. Section 61(1)(c) of the Act stipulates that where a young person of any age is accommodated by or on behalf of a voluntary organisation, it is the duty of that organisation "to advise, assist and befriend him with a view to promoting his welfare when he ceases to be so accommodated". The voluntary organisation does not have a statutory duty to provide aftercare for the young person once he has ceased to be accommodated by the organisation or on its behalf. However, it is desirable to link the provision of care with that of aftercare. As a matter of good practice, the voluntary organisation should consider the provision of appropriate aftercare services for any young person ceasing to be accommodated by it, or on its behalf, after reaching the age of 16. Social services departments of local authorities should therefore encourage the provision of such services by all voluntary child care organisations within their local authority areas.

9.13. In addition, a voluntary organisation has a duty under section 24(12) of the Act (see paragraph 9.10) to inform the local authority if it is ceasing to accommodate a young person aged 16 or more. The local authority so informed will be the authority in whose area the young person proposes to live after ceasing to be accommodated by the voluntary organisation.

9.14. The voluntary organisation will need to inform the local authority as early as possible, ie as soon as it is known on what date the young person will cease to be accommodated by the organisation or on its behalf.

This will alert the local authority to the fact that it may have a responsibility to provide aftercare for the young person under section 24 of the Act (see section 24(5)(b)). The voluntary organisation should also keep the young person informed at all stages, by telling him as early as possible when he is likely to cease to be accommodated by the organisation and by letting him know what provision for aftercare will be made and by which agency.

SECTION 64(1)(c): DUTIES OF REGISTERED CHILDREN'S HOMES

9.15. Section 64(1)(c) of the Act stipulates that where a young person is accommodated in a registered children's home, it is the duty of the person carrying on the home (ie the owner) to "advise, assist and befriend him with a view to promoting his welfare when he ceases to be so accommodated". The person carrying on the home does not have any duty to provide aftercare once the young person has ceased to be accommodated in the home. Again, however, it is desirable to link the provision of care with that of aftercare. As a matter of good practice, the person carrying on the home should consider the provision of appropriate aftercare services for any young person ceasing to be accommodated in the home after reaching the age of 16. Social services departments of local authorities should therefore encourage the provision of such services by all registered children's homes within their local authority areas.

9.16. In addition, the person carrying on the home has a duty under section 24(12) of the Act (see paragraph 9.10) to notify the local authority if the home is ceasing to accommodate a young person aged 16 or more. The local authority so informed will be the local authority in whose area the young person proposes to live after ceasing to be accommodated in the registered children's home.

9.17. The person carrying on the home will need to inform the local authority as early as possible, ie as soon as it is known on what date the young person will cease to be accommodated by the home. This will alert the local authority to the fact that it may have a responsibility to provide aftercare for the young person under section 24 of the Act (see section 24(5)(b)). The person carrying on the home should also keep the young person informed at all stages, by telling him as early as possible when he is likely to cease to be accommodated in the home, and by letting him know what provision for aftercare will be made and by which agency.

PRINCIPLES UNDERLYING PREPARATION FOR LEAVING CARE

9.18. The principles underlying preparation for leaving care should reflect good child care practice generally, following the principles of the 1989 Act:

- Services for young people must take account of the lengthy process of transition from childhood to adulthood, to reflect the gradual transition of a young person from dependence to independence. The support provided should be, broadly, the support that a good parent might be expected to give.

- Young people should be fully involved in discussions and plans for their future. Well before a young person leaves care, a continuing care plan should be formulated with him. This should specify the type of help the young person will be receiving and from whom. This plan should incorporate contingency arrangements in the event of a breakdown in the young person's living arrangements after he has left care since such breakdowns in arrangements are not uncommon. Such arrangements might include, for example, the possibility of a return to a community home or to foster care.

- Parents should be invited to help formulate the plan (if they are not estranged from the young person). So, too, should foster parents if the young person is leaving a foster placement (whether local authority or private).

- Preparation for leaving care should help develop a young person's capacity to make satisfactory relationships, develop his self-esteem and enable him to acquire the necessary practical skills for independent living.

- In helping young people to develop socially and culturally, carers must be prepared to take some risks and to take responsibility for doing so; to let young people take some risks, eg in attempting relationships that do not work; and to take responsibility for supporting young people through breakdowns in relationships.

- All preparation for leaving care and provision of aftercare must take account of the religious persuasion, racial origin, cultural and linguistic background and other needs of a young person (section 22(5)(c)).

- Preparation for leaving care and the provision of aftercare must be planned in conjunction with all other interested agencies, eg education and housing authorities, health authorities and, where appropriate, other local authorities. These agencies should be invited to contribute to a young person's continuing care plan.

LOCAL AUTHORITY WRITTEN POLICIES ON LEAVING CARE

9.19. Each local authority should take the above principles into account in developing leaving care and aftercare policies and in applying those policies to the needs of individual young people.

9.20. To help ensure this, each SSD should provide a written statement of its philosophy and practice on the preparation of young people for leaving care and the provision of aftercare support. It is a requirement of paragraph 1(2) of schedule 2 that each local authority must publish information about services provided by them under section 24 and take such steps as are reasonably practicable to ensure that those who might benefit from the services receive the relevant information. The statement should be comprehensive, acknowledging the different leaving care and aftercare needs of different young people, according to their age, sex and maturity. It should take into account the special needs of certain groups of young people, eg young people with disabilities and those with a statement of special educational needs (see paragraphs 9.28 to 9.42 below), pregnant girls and girls with young babies and young people from a range of cultural, racial and linguistic backgrounds. The statement should be revised periodically by the local authority to ensure that it remains up-to-date. It is suggested that 3-yearly revisions would be appropriate.

9.21. The statement should also cover the role of other agencies, who should be asked to provide contributions to the statement on the part they play in the preparation of young people leaving care and the provision of aftercare. They should be invited to revise their contributions to the statement when the statement itself is being revised by the local authority (see paragraph 9.20). The roles of other agencies are considered below, in more detail, at paragraphs 9.28 to 9.42 and 9.75 to 9.102.

9.22. The statement should be informed by the views of young people who are, or have been, cared for in those ways referred to in section 24(2) (paragraph 9.10). There should be a formal means of ensuring that the local authority continues to take their views into account, both when the statement of policy is being revised and at other times. One way of doing this might be to encourage young people who are being, or have been, cared for, to set up their own groups. Such groups would also enable these young people to meet each other and discuss matters of common interest; and they would help to overcome the common problem of loneliness felt by many young people who have left care. The local authority might also consider establishing a newsletter or other means of communication to inform young people who are being, or have been, cared for and to seek their views on matters such as these.

9.23. It would also be desirable for the statement to be informed by the views of the parents of these young people and by those of foster parents where a young person is fostered privately or by the local authority. There may be no formal mechanism for seeking these views, particularly since a local authority may have responsibility for providing aftercare for a young person whom they did not look after. However, a local authority may wish to consider obtaining a sample of views from parents and foster parents whenever a statement is prepared or revised. This might be done by sending copies of the statement to the parents and foster parents of at least some of the young people looked after by the local authority itself and seeking their comments on it.

9.24. The statement should be drafted so as to be easily comprehensible to young people and to their parents and foster parents. The local authority will need to provide translations of the policy statement in relevant ethnic minority languages. It will also need to consider how to provide the statement in versions that can be understood by young people with communication difficulties: for example a sign language video version might be particularly helpful for hearing-impaired young people whose preferred choice of communication is in sign language.

9.25. In addition, each SSD should provide an easy to read guide to its services for young people when they leave care. Like the policy statement, this should include a brief guide to services available from other agencies, based on information provided by those other agencies. The guide should be informed by the views of young people who are being, or have been, cared for, and their parents and foster parents. The local authority will need to provide translations of the guide in relevant ethnic minority languages. It will also need to consider how to provide the guide in a form that can be understood by young people with communication problems. For instance, a large print, braille or tape version may be helpful for blind or visually-impaired young people. A sign language video of the guide may be appropriate for hearing-impaired young people, or advice and information could be provided by workers trained in the needs of, and communication with, hearing-impaired young people.

9.26. The guide should include the following information:

● The advice and befriending services available to young people who have left care, under section 24(2) of the Act;

● The local authority's policy and practice on making payments in cash or in kind, under sections 24(6) and (8) of the Act, to young people who have left care;

● The nature of the help, including financial advice, that other agencies can give in preparing young people for leaving care and supporting them when they have left care; and the ways in which young people can obtain this help;

● Details of youth counselling services run by the local authority or the voluntary sector;

● The local authority's policy on giving young people access to their social services records;

● The local authority's complaints procedure, under sections 24(14) and 26(3) in case any young person considers that he is being denied appropriate advice and assistance (for further guidance see Chapter 10 of this volume);

● The name, address and telephone number of a contact point in each of the agencies mentioned in the guide.

9.27. Each local authority should nominate a designated officer in the social services department, of sufficiently senior rank, to ensure that the authority fulfils the responsibilities set out in paragraphs 8.19 to 8.27 above. In fulfilling his responsibilities, the designated officer may need to persuade the authority that it is legitimate to use staff time both to carry out aftercare work and to train staff to carry out this work properly. It may be useful if the designated officer is also the local authority's 'Appropriate Officer' for the purpose of the Disabled Persons (Services, Consultation and Representation) Act 1986.

YOUNG PEOPLE WITH DISABILITIES: PARTICULAR NEEDS

9.28. Young people with disabilities are, for the purpose of this guidance, young people who are "blind, deaf, or dumb, or (suffer) from mental disorder of any kind or (are) substantially and permanently handicapped by illness, injury or congenital deformity. . . ." (section 17(11) of the Children Act).

9.29. Young people with disabilities may well have particular needs over and above the needs of other young people who are being cared for. It is essential to ensure that these needs are met when preparing these young people for leaving care and subsequently, providing aftercare. At the same time, care must be taken to ensure that these young people do not fail to achieve their full potential as a result of under-expectation on the part of those caring for them.

9.30. The following paragraphs refer specifically to the responsibilities of local authorities (particularly SSDs). However, apart from paragraphs 9.34 to 9.39, they also apply to voluntary organisations and registered children's homes, who have a duty to prepare young people whom they are caring for, for the time when they leave care, and who may also provide aftercare for these young people.

9.31. SSDs should ensure that they have access to information on special resources and services necessary to meet the needs of young people with disabilities who are leaving care. They will also need to liaise closely with education departments and health authorities to ensure that the particular needs of these young people are met at all times. And they will need to take any steps necessary to ensure that the views of these young people about their needs, and the ways in which these can be met, are taken into account. This may necessitate the use of skilled appropriate communicators to enable better communication to take place between young people with disabilities and the various agencies.

9.32. Local authorities will need to note, in addition, that they have a duty to assist local education authorities with the provision of services for any young person who is subject to a statement of special educational needs (section 27(4) of the Children Act).

9.33. SSDs will also need to liaise with housing authorities over the housing needs of young people with disabilities. They should ask the relevant housing authority to consider the particular needs of any young person with a disability who is leaving care.

9.34. In discharging these responsibilities, local authorities will need to take account of their powers and duties under other Acts of Parliament, as set out below. These powers and duties are not, of course, limited to young people who are being looked after by local authorities. Voluntary organisations and registered childrens homes may therefore consider what help the local authority can give, under these Acts, to young people whom they themselves are preparing for leaving care or providing with aftercare.

9.35. Section 2(1) of the Chronically Sick and Disabled Persons Act 1970 lays on each local authority a duty to provide various welfare services to any person living within its area if this is necessary in order to meet the needs of that person.

9.36. Sections 5 and 6 of the Disabled Persons (Services, Consultation and Representation) Act 1986 are also relevant since they are designed to ensure a smooth transition from full-time education to adult life for a young person who is subject to a "statement of special educational needs". Their effect is to require the relevant education department to obtain the view of the SSD as to whether such a young person is disabled. This is done at the first annual review of the statement of special educational needs, or the first reassessment of the young person's educational needs, following the young person's 14th birthday. If the SSD does consider that the young person is disabled, it must assess his needs, before he leaves full-time education, to decide what welfare services it has a duty to provide him with. (See the relevant sections of the 1986 Act for details).

9.37. Local authorities should, as a matter of good practice, also provide communication support for all young people who require it. This could take the form, for instance, of text telephones or interpreters.

9.38. When a child is being looked after by a local authority and placed in accommodation which provides education on the premises, the local authority is required to inform the appropriate education department when the child leaves that accommodation (section 28(3)).

9.39. In deciding the young person's future needs, the SSD should continue to liaise with the education department, which is responsible for providing "adequate facilities for further education" and which needs to "have regard to the requirements of persons over compulsory school age who have learning difficulties" (section 41 of the Education Act 1944 as substituted by section 120(2) of the Education Reform Act 1988).

9.40. More generally, local authorities will wish to note that some disabilities inhibit natural maturity and may delay learning processes and this must be taken account of in preparing a young person for leaving care and in providing aftercare.

9.41. Specific health requirements may also continue into adulthood. The transition from child to adult health services is not always easily made by a young person, who may well require help and support from the local authority, acting as a "good parent". In providing this help and support, local authorities should, of course, liaise closely with health authorities.

9.42. The particular needs of young people with disabilities will – as mentioned above – need to be taken into account in preparing them for leaving care and also in providing the necessary aftercare. It is important to note that the needs of young people with disabilities will not suddenly and fundamentally cease when they do leave care. Liaison between the various agencies concerned with a young person's welfare should continue after he has left care.

THE NATURE OF PREPARATION FOR LEAVING CARE

9.43. Sections 24(1), 61(1)(c) and 64(1)(c) make it clear that preparation for leaving care must start well before a young person ceases to be looked after or accommodated and is likely to continue until well after he has done so. Preparation for this process should be incorporated in the care plan for the young person as soon as he starts to be looked after, accommodated or privately fostered. The relevant SSD, voluntary organisation or registered children's home will play a leading role in preparing young people for the time when they leave care, but other agencies will need to be involved. Schools and the Careers Service, for instance, will need to be consulted about the long-term educational and training needs of a young person; and the relevant health authority may need to be involved if the young person is disabled.

9.44. Thus, preparation should be regarded as an integral part of the care process. A stable care relationship is, in its turn, an important basis on which to plan the preparation of a young person for leaving care.

9.45. There are three broad aspects to preparation for leaving care:
- enabling young people to build and maintain relationships with others, (both general and sexual relationships);
- enabling young people to develop their self-esteem;
- teaching practical and financial skills and knowledge.

Each of these is considered in more detail below. SSDs, voluntary organisations and registered children's homes should ensure that social workers, residential staff and foster parents are trained so that they can help young people to be properly prepared for leaving care.

9.46. The capacity to form satisfying relationships and achieve inter-dependence with others is crucial to the future well-being of the young person. With such a capacity, he is much more likely to cope with the transition to adulthood and the special difficulties associated with leaving care. It is crucial, therefore, that the experience of being cared for provides both the opportunity for such personal development and the attention that is required when special help is needed. This experience should be planned so as to cover the following points:

● Changes in care placements should be kept to the minimum consistent with the young person's welfare. This will provide continuity of care and of relationships, thereby showing young people how to relate to others.

● Social workers, residential staff and foster parents, as well as other young people who are being cared for, will therefore be able to help a young person to relate to other people.

● However, a young person's friends should not all come from the care system since, if they do, he may be very lonely when he leaves care.

● It is therefore well worth encouraging young people who are being cared for to make friends with young people outside the care system, eg through school or local youth clubs.

● Young people who are being cared for should also be encouraged to develop friendships with suitable adults outside the care system who can provide role models. Volunteer adult befrienders who have been carefully vetted through a volunteer befriending scheme and who can stay in touch with a young person after he has left care can play a very important role here. The befriender will need to be 'matched' with the young person, eg he should preferably be from the same cultural, linguistic, racial and religious background. It is desirable for the young person to decide who is to act as his befriender. The befriender should be prepared to give time to his task; should be remunerated if appropriate; and should be allowed to make contributions to reviews and on other occasions, if the young person so wishes. (See also Chapter 7 – "Independent Visitors").

● The foster parents of a fostered young person can also be encouraged to continue to take an interest in him even when the fostering placement has ended.

● A young person's parents (and his relatives generally) should also be encouraged to stay in touch with him unless this would not be in his best interests.

● Young people from ethnic minorities will need to have contact with adults and young people from their own cultural background and may find it helpful to be put in touch with youth clubs or other voluntary organisations set up for people from their cultures.

● Young people with disabilities may have particular needs, and it may be useful to refer them to suitable materials, and to voluntary organisations of and for people with disabilities, to support them in finding friends and developing social skills.

The process of preparation should ensure that when a young person does leave care, he has a supportive network of friends, many of whom will be from outside the care system; and that he is well equipped to enter into relationships with others.

9.47. A local authority, in preparing a young person for leaving care, should also take account, where appropriate, of the need to enable the young person to relate better to his own family. Indeed, the local authority has a duty to make arrangements to enable a young person whom it is looking after to live with parents, relatives or friends "unless that would not be reasonably practicable or consistent with his welfare" (section 23(6)). Even if it is proved to be impracticable or undesirable to make such arrangements, any improvement in relationships between a young person and his family that can be achieved is usually to be welcomed and will contribute to the young person's capacity to cope in adult life. Similarly, general contact with family and friends should be promoted where consistent with a young person's welfare (paragraph 15 of schedule 2). Similar responsibilities are reflected in the duties of voluntary organisations and persons carrying on registered children's homes under Regulation 6 of the Arrangements for Placement of Children Regulations (see Chapter 3).

Enabling Young People to Build and Maintain Relationships with Others: Sexual Relationships

9.48. The experience of being cared for should also include the sexual education of the young person. This may, of course, be provided by the young person's school, but if it is not, the SSD or other caring agency responsible for the young person should provide sexual education for him. This is absolutely vital since sexuality will be one of the most potent forces affecting any young person in the transition from childhood to adulthood.

9.49. Sexual education will need to cover practical issues such as contraception, particularly in view of the spread of AIDS. However, it must also cover the emotional aspects of sexuality, such as the part that sexuality plays in the young person's sense of identity; the emotional implications of entering into a sexual relationship with another person; and the need to treat sexual partners with consideration and not as objects to be used. The emotional and practical implications of becoming a parent also need to be explained in some detail.

9.50. Those responsible for the sexual education of young people will need to bear in mind the particular needs of different young people: the fact that young people with mental or physical disabilities have sexual needs should be acknowledged, for instance. And young people who have been abused, or have been in touch with abused young people, may need special counselling if they are not to regard sexual feelings as a matter for shame or to regard sexual relationships as impersonal and exploitive. The needs and concerns of gay young men and women must also be recognised and approached sympathetically.

Enabling Young People to Develop Their Self-esteem

9.51. Many young people who are being, or have been, cared for, have described feelings of shame about being cared for. These are frequently compounded by misunderstandings on the part of others, eg that most young people being cared for have committed criminal offences, or that there is something wrong with them, or that their parents are inadequate and unable to cope. It is therefore all the more necessary to encourage young people, from the day they begin to be cared for, to value themselves; to regard their experience of being cared for without embarrassment; and to be able to explain calmly to other people why they are being cared for and how they feel about it.

9.52. In doing this, it is particularly helpful if young people are told as much as possible about their family background and about all aspects of their cultural and individual identity, eg race, language, culture, sex, gender, religion and any physical or mental disability. It is also helpful for young people to understand how they came to be cared for. A young person's individual identity and his cultural background should be presented to him in a positive light and not as something about which he should feel defensive. The use of life-story books may be helpful in achieving this end, but local authorities and other caring agencies will need to note that young people should be enabled to accept themselves emotionally and not simply intellectually.

9.53. Some young people may need considerable counselling before they do come to accept themselves. Young people who have been rejected by their parents may need a lot of help before they can accept, emotionally, that this is no reflection on their own worth. Young people with disabilities may also require a lot of counselling to enable them to accept themselves and to develop a sense of self-esteem. Gay young men and women may require very sympathetic carers to enable them to accept their sexuality and to develop their own self-esteem. And young people from ethnic minorities may need help—preferably from someone with the same background—to enable them to take a pride in their racial, cultural, linguistic and religious background.

9.54. If necessary the local authority or other caring agency may also act as an advocate for all young people leaving care in dealing with departments, organisations and people who may display prejudice.

Practical and Financial Skills and Knowledge

9.55. Many young people leave care without adequate preparation in practical and financial skills and knowledge. These include:

- How to shop for, prepare and cook food.
- Eating a balanced diet.
- Laundry, sewing and mending and other housekeeping skills.
- How to carry out basic household jobs such as mending fuses (which will involve basic electrical and other knowledge).
- Safety in the home and first aid.
- The cost of living.
- Household budgeting, including the matching of expenditure to income, the regular payment of bills and avoidance of the excessive use of credit.
- Health education, including personal hygiene.
- Sexual education, including contraception and preparation for parenthood. (This is particularly vital given the spread of AIDS).
- Applying for, and being interviewed for, a job.
- The rights and responsibilities of being an employee.
- Applying for a course of education or training.
- Applying for social security benefits.
- Applying for housing and locating and maintaining it.
- Registering with a doctor and dentist.
- Knowledge of emergency services (fire, police, ambulance).
- Finding and using community services and resources.
- Contacting the social services department and other caring agencies.
- Contacting organisations and groups set up to help young people who are, or have been, in care.
- The role of agencies such as the Citizens Advice Bureau, local councillors and MPs.
- How to write a letter (a) of complaint; (b) to obtain advice.

9.56. Some young people who are being cared for, particularly those in children's homes, do not have any opportunity of learning such skills. It may therefore be necessary to change the regime at the homes concerned to give them that opportunity. Young people who are being cared for should—like any other young people—start to learn these skills at a basic level when entering their teens and should be well advanced in them by the time they leave care. Young people with disabilities may need additional specific training and rehabilitation programmes to enable them to acquire these skills and to promote their independence. The nature of the programme will depend on the nature of the disability, eg sight replacement or sight enhancement techniques for visually-impaired young people. In addition, young people with communication difficulties, eg those who are hearing-impaired or speech-impaired, may need interpreters to facilitate their acquisition of these skills through sign language and also to improve their prospects at job interviews.

AFTER LEAVING CARE

9.57. Most young people will continue to need some help after they have left care. The continuing needs of young people may differ widely according to their individual circumstances and they may include any or all of the following examples:

- Advice and information.
- A continued interest in their welfare, possibly from a person specified to advise and befriend the young person.
- Assistance in cash or in kind.
- A return to care, if necessary.
- Education and training (education department).
- Accommodation (housing department: but social services departments have some responsibilities under section 20 of the Act—see paragraph 9.86 below).

The first four of these are social services responsibilities. It is impossible to specify precisely what services each local authority should offer within these broad headings. However, aftercare programmes of some kind should be available to all young people leaving care and should be organised so as to enable them to take control of their own lives. They should be flexible enough to meet the needs of all young people leaving care, including those with particular needs, eg disabled young people, those from religious, racial, cultural or linguistic minorities, young mothers and pregnant young women and gay young men and women. Each programme might be targeted at a particular group of clients, eg one might provide particularly extensive support for young people who are obliged to live independently after leaving care. The views of each young person should be sought on his needs, as he sees them, and the degree to which the local authority is meeting them. The senior officer responsible for ensuring that the local authority prepares young people properly for leaving care might usefully be responsible for ensuring that the local authority also provides a suitable range of aftercare services.

9.58. Aftercare programmes may also be offered by voluntary organisations and other caring agencies.

9.59. The possibility of encouraging young people to form their own groups has already been mentioned (paragraph 9.22). It may also be useful to set up "drop-in" bases where young people who have already left care can call for advice; to talk over any problems; or simply to keep in touch with their social workers and residential care workers. The Youth Service, both statutory and voluntary, may be able to help in developing such facilities. The role that the voluntary Youth Service can play is worth stressing. Many young people will prefer voluntary facilities to statutory ones since they will regard them as particularly able to help them escape from the stigma of being, or having been, cared for. Young people should, of course, also be encouraged to develop a social life outside care circles as well.

9.60. Some young people will also have had independent visitors appointed to visit them during their stay in care because they have infrequent or no contact with their families (paragraph 17 of schedule 2). Even when a young person has left care, he may wish to keep in touch with his independent visitor and the visitor may be a valuable source of advice, support and friendship. (See the detailed guidance on Independent Visitors in Chapter 7 of this volume). If a young person has been fostered, his foster parents may continue to give him advice, support and friendship after the end of the foster placement.

9.61. It is desirable to monitor aftercare schemes and to evaluate them to establish how effective they are. This should be done at regular intervals. The local authority should include in these exercises representatives of the groups set up by young people who are being, or have been, cared for. This will ensure that the views of young people continue to be heard.

9.62. Young people may move to a different part of the country after leaving care and it is important to ensure that they do not fall through the net of local authority support if they require it. The local authority that has been helping them must inform the local authority into whose area they have moved, (section 24(11)) and in doing so should inform the second local authority of any particular needs of the young person. The second local authority will then assume the relevant powers and duties under section 24.

9.63. Furthermore, if a young person leaves certain forms of care other than local authority accommodation, after reaching the age of 16, the organisation or agency formerly accommodating him must inform the local authority in whose area he proposes to live (section 24(12)). The local authority should then consider what powers and duties to invoke in order to provide the young person with the appropriate aftercare.

THE DELIVERY OF SERVICES

9.64. Many local authorities are developing specialist services for young people leaving care. A number of models now exist, but it is probably too early to assess their respective merits. Where authorities have established separate aftercare teams, it is important that the person who has been most closely involved with the young person whilst in care maintains contact and provides continued support directly to him as well as contributing to the team's planned approach. This will necessitate close liaison between the aftercare team and the social services staff responsible for fostering and for residential child care. The principle that preparation for leaving care is to be regarded as an integral part of any care placement from the outset should underpin the development of specialist services. (See principle 16 on page 9 of "The Care of Children: Principles and Practice in Regulations and Guidance" (HMSO, 1990)).

9.65. In discharging the responsibilities outlined above, the 'key' person working with a particular young person will need to liaise closely with any services provided by the local authority and the voluntary sector for young people with special needs, eg those who are disabled.

9.66. It is important that managers provide sufficient time and resources for staff, including staff of residential establishments and also foster parents, to undertake and develop the necessary skills associated with leaving care and continuing support. Local authorities should take account of the need to train staff and foster-parents to do this difficult job properly. The local authority's designated officer (paragraph 9.27) will need to assume responsibility for ensuring that all this is done.

9.67. The guidance given above relates to the local authority's own responsibilities. However, the authority's policy statement on leaving care and aftercare services, and its easy to read guide to those services, needs to refer to the role of other agencies in helping young people who are leaving care. In preparing both documents, and providing services accordingly, the local authority will wish to note the help that it can require from other agencies under section 27 of the Children Act (see paragraph 9.8).

9.68. These other agencies will include those who are caring for young people, who might be encouraged to assume responsibility for preparing the young people they are caring for, for the time when they leave care (voluntary organisations and registered children's homes do, of course, have a duty to do this). Local authorities will also wish to encourage them to provide aftercare for young people who have left their care. (See also paragraphs 9.12 to 9.17 and 9.76).

9.69. The primary income – support role lies with the Department of Social Security. However, local authorities may also give financial assistance to young people leaving care on account of their particular needs over and above those of other young people.

9.70. Where a local authority has either a duty or a power to advise and befriend young people who have left care (section 24(4)) it may also give assistance which may be in kind or, in exceptional circumstances, in cash (sections 24(6) and (7)). Many young people leaving care, particularly those who are required to live independently because they have no family home to return to, can face very severe financial difficulties at this time—both immediately and during their transition to full independence. It is already the policy of many local authorities to provide all young people leaving care with a leaving care grant of sufficient amount to ease this transitional process, and this is to be encouraged. It should, however, be borne in mind that the local authority's power to provide assistance extends until every young person referred to in section 24(2) reaches the age of 21. Where a young person has no parent to turn to for help, or where a parent does not have the capacity to provide assistance, it is to be expected that they will turn to the local authority, which has in many cases been a major influence in their lives, for such help.

9.71. Local authorities are encouraged to be pro-active in advising young people of the circumstances in which assistance can be provided and to take into account the fact that the reference to the provision of financial assistance "in exceptional circumstances" in section 24(7) refers to the individual young person rather than the general policy of the authority. It will be for the authority to decide in each case whether the provision of financial assistance would be appropriate, but the presumption should be that such assistance should be provided where this is necessary to protect the young person's welfare and it cannot be made available by any other agency. Local authorities are encouraged to be flexible in deciding what leaving care grants can be given for; and to consider a young person's wishes about the way in which any grant given should be spent.

9.72. In addition to the general powers to provide assistance under section 24(6) of the Act, local authorities have a specific power to provide financial assistance to young people they formerly looked after where this is connected with the young person's further education, employment or training (section 24(8)). This provision enables an authority to contribute towards the costs of accommodation which enables the young person to live near the place where he is employed, seeking employment, or receiving education or training. It should be noted that the "exceptional circumstances" qualification to the provision of cash assistance in section 24(7) does not apply to assistance given under section 24(8) nor are the provisions of section 17(7)–(9) applied in such cases (section 24(10)). Bearing in mind the serious problems experienced by many young people in obtaining suitable and affordable accommodation, and the importance to be attached to the ability of young people to gain stable employment or further their education, local authorities are encouraged to exercise their powers under section 24(8) flexibly. Provision is also made for local authorities to make grants to young people to help them meet expenses connected with their further education or training (for example the purchase of books, tools or materials). It should be noted that any such financial assistance or grant provided under section 24(8) where this is connected to a course of education or training, may continue even though the young person reaches the age of 21 before completing the course (section 24(9)).

9.73. It is important that young people, residential and field social workers, parents and foster-parents should be aware of the assistance that the local authority can provide. This can be achieved through the provision of a clear statement of policy on financial assistance, which should be incorporated in the published statement of the authority's services under section 24 and in its easy to read guide to those services. Young people with disabilities may be particularly in need of financial assistance, especially if they have communication problems that make it difficult for them to apply to other agencies, such as voluntary organisations, for help.

9.74. It should be noted that financial assistance provided under section 24 is disregarded for the purposes of calculating entitlement to Income Support, Housing Benefit, Community Charge Benefit or Family Credit. It is also disregarded in assessing the maintenance grant of a student on a designated course. It is important to note that a young person does not have to qualify for Income Support before being given financial assistance under section 24.

THE ROLE OF THE VOLUNTARY SECTOR

9.75. There are two separate, but related, aspects to the work of the voluntary sector in preparing young people for leaving their care. Voluntary organisations may accommodate young people in one of their homes. In such a case, the voluntary organisation must assume the responsibility for preparing the young person concerned for leaving its care (section 61(1)(c) – see paragraphs 9.12 to 9.14). The duty of ensuring that this is done should fall to a designated senior member of staff within the voluntary organisation. When a young person ceases to be accommodated by the voluntary organisation and is aged 16 or over, the voluntary organisation must inform the local authority in whose area the young person proposes to live. The notification should be made by the designated member of staff referred to above. The notification is necessary because the local authority will have certain powers and duties to provide aftercare; therefore the voluntary organisation and the local authority must liaise closely in preparing these young people to leave the voluntary organisation's care and in providing aftercare for them. The care and aftercare services should be closely linked to each other (see also paragraph 9.43). Young people aged 16–20 who are being, or have been, cared for by a voluntary organisation, should be made aware by that organisation of the statutory amenities open to them.

9.76. The other aspect of the voluntary sector's role lies in the aftercare services provided by it. Voluntary organisations are not under a duty to provide these services, but local authorities will wish to encourage them to provide them for young people whom the organisations concerned formerly cared for. In some cases, local authorities will also be able to "purchase" aftercare services from voluntary organisations to help young people whose care was not provided by those organisations. Local authorities are therefore encouraged to liaise with voluntary organisations in their areas to make use, where appropriate, of any aftercare services they may offer (see in particular section 17(5)).

9.77. These aftercare services may include: drop-in centres; counselling; advocacy for young care-leavers—both individually and as a group; and various forms of accommodation, eg sheltered and half-way housing, refuges for young people at risk, supported lodgings and continued foster care. The role of housing associations in providing suitable accommodation is particularly important. So, too, is the specialised information and advice that voluntary organisations can give to young people with a wide range of disabilities. It is important for local authorities and other caring agencies to put young people with disabilities in touch with the appropriate voluntary organisations in order to provide them with additional opportunities for involvement with particular self-help or interest groups.

9.78. Local authorities will also wish to bear in mind the help that young people leaving care can obtain from the Homelessness Advice Service. The Service operates through the national network of Citizens' Advice Bureaux. It is particularly concerned with the prevention of homelessness, the provision of advice on the dangers of leaving home without access to accommodation, the provision of access to suitable accommodation and financial counselling.

Specialist and detailed advice is provided by Shelter and SHAC organisations if necessary.

THE ROLE OF THE PROBATION SERVICE

9.79. A minority of young people who are being or have been cared for will have committed criminal offences. Some of these young people will be subject to a probation order or to a supervision order designating the probation service as the supervisor. The probation service are naturally concerned to ensure, as far as possible, that these young people do not re-offend. In trying to achieve their aim, they will concern themselves not only with a young person's offending and its consequences but with his development into a self-reliant adult who has "grown out" of offending. It is therefore important for each local authority to consult the probation service when drawing up its written statement of policies on leaving care and aftercare services and its easy to read guide to those services; and to cover the role of the probation service in both documents. It is also necessary for the SSD or other caring agency to involve the probation service closely when preparing one of these young people for leaving care or providing him with aftercare.

THE ROLE OF THE HOUSING DEPARTMENT

9.80. When a young person leaves care, it may not be possible for him to return to his family: he may have none, or he may be estranged from them. Young people who have left care are over-represented among the single homeless and this emphasises the need to consider the housing needs of young people who are about to leave care. This is particularly necessary if they have disabilities (see paragraph 9.33).

9.81. The primary responsibility for housing lies with the housing department of a local authority. Close liaison between SSDs and housing departments ("housing authorities") is therefore necessary. This may best be achieved through the establishment of formal arrangements, particularly as social services and housing may be provided by different tiers of government; the SSD in a shire county, for instance, will have to deal with several district council housing departments. It is suggested that liaison should take place between the designated senior officer in the SSD and designated colleagues in the housing department(s), whether or not housing and social services are provided by the same tier of government. They should, between them, agree the arrangements for referring young people to the housing departments. At the same time, housing departments can make clear what priority they can give to young people leaving care in general and to those who have disabilities or who are otherwise vulnerable in particular. The housing departments' policies on these issues will, of course, need to be spelt out in their contribution to the local authority's written statement of leaving care and aftercare services and in its easy to read guide to those services – see paragraphs 8.22 and 8.26.

9.82. The priority afforded to providing housing for young people leaving care is a matter for consideration locally. However, local authorities do have a statutory duty (exercised primarily by housing departments) to ensure that accommodation is provided for single homeless people whom they assess as vulnerable. In fulfilling their duties, local authorities must bear in mind the advice contained in the Code of Guidance accompanying the Housing Act 1985. Careful consideration should be given to the vulnerability of homeless young people who have left care and in particular those who are disabled or are at risk of sexual or financial exploitation. Many housing associations provide accommodation specifically for young people. Authorities are strongly encouraged to liaise with housing associations, who may prove receptive to the needs of those young people leaving care who are not judged to be a priority for council housing. (Note: Whether housing is provided by a local authority or another organisation, it should be adapted as soon as possible to the needs of any disabled young people living there).

9.83. The local authority's housing department may provide sheltered or halfway accommodation for young people leaving care and it may also wish to consider reserving some of its stock of conventional accommodation to meet the needs of young people leaving care who are capable of living independently. It may also wish to liaise with the voluntary sector, which may well provide accommodation and advice itself. In all cases (including those in which the local authority is not the caring agency) the SSD should consider well in advance whether a young person is likely to need help with housing when he leaves care. If he is, the SSD will need to discuss his housing needs with the housing department in time to make the necessary arrangements before he leaves care. The housing department may be able to offer accommodation. However, even if they cannot help a particular young person in this way, the SSD will know this in good time and will be able to approach other agencies offering housing, such as housing associations.

9.84. Young people who have left care are over-represented amongst young homeless people, including those who are sleeping rough. Studies suggest that as many as a third or more of young rough sleepers have been in local authority care at some point in their lives. In formulating a policy to meet the housing needs of young people leaving care, the housing and social services departments should consider:

- the ability of the young people to live independently;
- the extent to which some supervision may still be necessary;
- the personal preferences of young people leaving care;
- the possibility of arranging a private interview with a Housing Officer for any young person applying for assistance with accommodation;
- the need to clearly inform any such young person of the decision and advice of the housing department as soon as possible;
- how best to provide advice and assistance on housing;
- the contribution that the voluntary sector can make towards the provision of accommodation;
- how far landlords and landladies can contribute towards getting young people into independent living.

9.85. Housing and social services departments will also wish to consider how best to meet the following needs in providing local authority housing:

- The provision of some sheltered or halfway housing, with appropriate support services;
- The provision of a reasonable quality and range of accommodation (Note: Young people leaving care may move from sheltered accommodation to increasingly independent forms of accommodation);
- The provision, where necessary, of housing adapted to meet the needs of disabled young people;
- Good housing management and maintenance and upkeep of properties;
- A regular and simple system of rent collection;
- A system to select and match the tenants of shared properties;
- Clear tenancy agreements;
- Training for housing personnel in the special needs of young people who have left care, who may well be younger than most local authority tenants and less used to looking after themselves. Training for the staff of sheltered or halfway housing is particularly necessary.

9.86. Local authorities should also note that they have powers under section 20(5) to provide accommodation for young people aged 16–20 in their area if this is necessary to safeguard or promote their welfare. The provision of accommodation under section 20 of the Act may be a desirable course of action if it is not possible to provide suitable accommodation in any other way for a young person who has left care. There is, of course, a duty to provide accommodation if a child is in need and section 20(3) applies.

THE ROLE OF THE YOUTH SERVICE

9.87. Local authorities will wish to note the help that the youth service—both statutory and voluntary—can give to young people who are being, or who used to be, cared for. This help may include advocacy of the interests of individual young people. More particularly, the youth service can offer support to vulnerable young people and give them the opportunity of extending their social network outside the care system. Disabled young people may need advice and help to enable them to integrate into local youth services and they may need to be enabled to choose to use special youth services (eg deaf clubs) if they think these are right for them.

9.88. Young people from ethnic and cultural minorities may also find the youth service particularly helpful in enabling them to meet other young people, and adult youth leaders, from their own ethnic and cultural background. This, in turn, should help them to develop a sense of pride in their cultural identity.

THE ROLE OF THE SCHOOL

9.89. For a variety of reasons, many young people leaving care have few, if any, academic qualifications. It is essential that every effort be made to enable a young person to fulfil his potential and to reduce the degree of disadvantage experienced by many of those leaving care. To this end, SSDs and other caring agencies will need to liaise closely with schools and to support them in promoting the welfare of these young people.

9.90. It is important for schools to be aware of the dangers of under-expectation regarding the academic potential of young people who are being cared for and to ensure that such young people are given every encouragement to obtain academic qualifications and to develop their emotional, social and intellectual potential generally. Young people who are under-achieving at school will need attention to remedy this well before they leave care. The role of the SSD or other caring agency in this is that of a good parent. In exercising parental responsibility the young person's carer should ensure that the school is made fully aware of all relevant information regarding the young person's abilities and interests and that the school receives the support and reinforcement that would be expected from a concerned parent. Such support should include supervising homework and attending meetings at school with teachers, headteachers and careers staff. (Note: under education legislation, 'parent' is defined to include the carer).

9.91. The SSD or other caring agency should also encourage the young person to continue his education beyond the minimum school-leaving age unless he will quite clearly not benefit from this. It is important to note that a lot of disabled people, including many with impaired sight, hearing or speech, are quite capable of benefiting from further education and should be encouraged to undertake it. They may, of course, need special facilities such as interpreters, note takers and readers.

9.92. Where the young person concerned has a statement of special educational needs, the SSD, voluntary organisation or person carrying on a registered children's home will often, in effect, be exercising the responsibilities normally exercised by parents in ensuring that the young person's special educational needs are appropriately identified and met. This will entail close liaison with the education department, including attendance at assessment meetings and at annual reviews and ensuring that the SSD liaises closely with the education department in order to discharge its duties under sections 5 and 6 of the Disabled Persons (Services, Consultation and Representation) Act 1986. (See paragraphs 9.36 and 9.39).

9.93. Like any other young person, a young person who is being cared for will receive careers education and guidance at school. The SSD or other caring agency should ensure that this is received in good time, is appropriate and includes advice on the possibilities of undertaking a course of further education. The young person's carer should be involved in considering such advice and should discuss the available options with the young person, assisting him or her to reach a considered decision in full knowledge of the short and long term advantages and disadvantages of any choice.

TRAINING

9.94. Training and education should not be regarded as distinct and separate activities. However, training is covered separately from education in this guidance in order to explain the role of the different agencies concerned.

9.95. The SSD or other caring agency involved should be ready to inform the young person of the existence of training, eg Youth Training and training schemes geared to a particular occupation. Although it will not be able to advise in detail on such training schemes, it should be able to refer the young person to those best able to advise him. This referral may be to the school careers advisory service, the local Careers Officer (for Youth Training) and the relevant occupational body for schemes geared to a particular occupation. If the young person has a disability, it may be useful to refer him to a Disablement Resettlement Officer at a Job Centre.

THE ROLE OF THE CAREERS SERVICE

9.96. The Careers Service provides the link between the worlds of work and further education. The Service is a prime source of contact for employers, training providers, teachers, those involved in higher and further education and others responsible for helping young people. The Careers Service aims to ensure that young people understand all the options open to them, including both the short-term and the long-term prospects in any particular career, so that they can make informed choices. The Careers Service gives information to young people on employment and training opportunities; it is the main placing agent with Youth Training (YT); and it gives young people information on what YT programmes are available. Careers Officers work closely with careers teachers in schools and generally contact pupils in their 3rd year at school. SSDs and other caring agencies will, as good parents, need to ensure that all young people whom they are caring for do receive this advice from the Careers Service. Young people with disabilities should receive careers advice like other young people in care. It is important to ensure that they are not advised to take up an undemanding job unless their disability really does prevent them from embarking on a challenging career.

RETURNING TO TAKE UP COURSES OF EDUCATION OR TRAINING

9.97. Many young people have left care without qualifications but have effectively returned to school in order to obtain qualifications or training. SSDs may wish to consider advising those who have left school without qualifications that it is not too late for them to remedy this situation and they may wish to provide advice on finance for educational and training courses. If the SSD is still exercising parental responsibility, the carer might support the young person by attending meetings at the school to discuss an appropriate programme of study. The SSD may also need to liaise with the education department, which has responsibility for further education.

LOCAL AUTHORITY ASSISTANCE TO YOUNG PEOPLE RECEIVING EDUCATION OR TRAINING; OR EMPLOYED; OR SEEKING EMPLOYMENT

9.98. SSDs should bear in mind the powers they have to assist young people who left local authority care when aged 16 or over and who are employed, or seeking employment, or in receipt of education or training (section 24(8)). These powers last until a young person reaches the age of 21 and they can therefore be invoked well after the young person has left the local authority's care. (See paragraph 9.72).

SOCIAL SECURITY

9.99. Local authority powers to give assistance in cash or in kind are designed to meet the special needs of young people leaving care over and above the needs of other young people. They are not designed simply to duplicate the social security system, which is why the making of these payments is at the discretion of the local authority.

9.100. However, local authorities should advise young people who are in, or have left, care on the social security benefits they may be entitled to and the way in which they can claim them. This can most easily be done by obtaining the relevant social security leaflets from the local social security office, or material specially prepared for young people by youth organisations, and making them available to the young people concerned as a first step. This material should be made available in ethnic minority languages where appropriate. Regulations for awarding income support to 16 and 17 year olds are very stringent and are linked to the provision of Youth Training (YT) placements. Specialist advice is often required to ensure that young people receive their full entitlement and where advice is not readily available within an SSD, reference to an agency such as the Citizens' Advice Bureau should be considered.

9.101. If a young person has a disability, advice on benefits for disability should be available as a priority. If the local authority has a welfare rights officer, he should be able to give this advice. The services of an interpreter may be necessary if the young person's disability involves problems in communicating.

9.102. Local authorities will wish to note that any payments made to a young person under section 24 are not regarded as a part of his income or capital when calculating his entitlement to Income Support, Housing Benefit, Community Charge Benefit or Family Credit.

CHAPTER 10 REPRESENTATIONS PROCEDURE

10.1. Local authorities, voluntary organisations and registered children's homes (henceforward called 'responsible authorities') are required to have a procedure for considering representations (including complaints) about children's services. This procedure relates to sections 24(15), 26(3)–(8), 59(4), paragraph 10(2)(l) of Schedule 6 and paragraph 6 of Schedule 7 to the Children Act. It should cover all representations about local authorities' actions in meeting their responsibilities to any child in need under Part III of the Act. Voluntary organisations and registered children's homes are also required to set up representations procedures to consider representations – including complaints – made by or on behalf of children accommodated by them but not looked after by the local authority. The primary legislation and the Representations Procedure (Children) Regulations are a common framework on which all the responsible authorities should build to achieve a procedure and approach which best suits their local needs and organisational structure. The Regulations set the minimum standard provision that responsible authorities should establish to meet the requirements of the Children Act 1989.

10.2. This procedure and that required for other local authority social services functions by the Directions made under section 7B of the Local Authority Social Services Act 1970 (inserted by section 50 of the National Health Service and Community Care Act 1990) are broadly compatible. Both procedures have been designed so that local authorities wishing to do so will be able to use common structures for handling representations, including complaints. The main difference between the two procedures is that the Children Act requires the involvement of an independent person at each stage of consideration of a representation or a complaint. The links between the procedures are discussed at other points in the guidance.

10.3. The Children Act envisages a high degree of co-operation between parents and authorities in negotiating and agreeing what form of action will best meet a child's needs and promote his welfare. It also calls for the informed participation of the child and his parents in decision-making about services for the child. Sometimes the required co-operation will not be achieved or will break down or delays will occur. The Act requires that responsible authorities establish a procedure which provides an accessible and effective means of representation or complaint where problems cannot be otherwise resolved. Definitions of representations and complaints are set out in paragraph 10.5 below. It is envisaged that the procedure will be used primarily for handling complaints rather than representations. Accordingly the guidance concentrates on complaints. The procedure will involve independent persons in responsible authorities' considerations and should ensure that the child, his parents and others significantly involved with the child have confidence in their ability to make their views known and to influence decisions made about the child's welfare.

10.4. The responsible authority should aim to develop a procedure which is understood and accepted by all involved: children, parents and their representatives, as well as the responsible authority's staff and the local authority's elected members. Plans for implementing representation procedures should take account of the need for consultation with community groups, voluntary and other organisations with an interest, carers and with staff at all levels. The responsible authority should seek to involve the community in setting up their representations procedures so that the procedure reflects the needs of those who may need to use it. Adherence to the principles of the Race Relations Act 1976 and other equal opportunities legislation requires consultation with community groups reflecting the racial and cultural diversity of the local community.

DEFINITIONS

10.5. For the purpose of this guidance, the following definitions are used:

(a) A 'responsible authority' is a local authority, voluntary organisation or registered children's home;

(b) 'Representations' will include enquiries and statements about such matters as the availability, delivery and nature of services and will not necessarily be critical;

(c) A 'complaint' is a written or oral expression of dissatisfaction or disquiet in relation to an individual child about the local authority's exercise of its functions under Part III and paragraph 4 of Schedule 7 of the Children Act 1989 and matters in relation to children accommodated by voluntary organisations and registered children's homes. A complaint may arise as a result of an unwelcome or disputed decision, concern about the quality or appropriateness of services, delay in decision-making about services or about their delivery or non-delivery (the precise meaning of complaint is a matter for interpretation by the courts);

(d) A 'complainant' is the child or person making the complaint on his behalf;

(e) An 'independent person' is a person, not a member or officer of the authority handling the child's case who is required by section 26(4) to take part in the authority's consideration of a complaint made to them and not excluded by the provisions of Regulation 1(3). The independent person is not an advocate for the child nor an investigator; his role is to provide an objective element in the authority's considerations (see Regulations 6 and 8);

(f) A 'panel' is a group of 3 persons, at least one of whom is independent (as defined in Regulation 1(3) of these Regulations) appointed by the authority to consider complaints reviewed by the responsible authority under the complaints procedure when the complainant remains dissatisfied and to make a recommendation about further action (see Regulations 8 and 9).

(g) The 'procedure' is the representations and complaints procedure which responsible authorities are required to set up by the Children Act;

(h) The 'designated officer' is the officer which the authority is required to appoint to assist in the co-ordination of all aspects of the consideration of complaints (see Regulation 3(1)).

WHO MAY COMPLAIN

10.6. Section 26(3) requires the responsible authority to establish a procedure for considering any representations (including any complaint) made to it by:

"(a) any child who is being looked after by them or who is not being looked after by them but is in need;

(b) a parent of his;

(c) any person who is not a parent of his but who has parental responsibility for him;

(d) any local authority foster parent;

(e) such other person as the authority consider has a sufficient interest in the child's welfare to warrant his representations being considered by them,

about the discharge by the authority of any of their functions under this Part in relation to the child."

10.7. The first person listed is the child. The responsible authority should always check with a child (subject to his understanding) that a complaint submitted on his behalf reflects his views and that he does wish the person submitting the complaint to act on his behalf. Where it is decided that the person submitting the complaint is not acting on the child's behalf, he may still be eligible to have the complaint considered under the procedure. Regulation 4(4) makes it clear that the local authority have discretion to decide in cases where eligibility is not automatic whether or not an individual has sufficient interest in the child's welfare to justify his own representation being considered by them (section 26(3)(e)). The local authority should have a clear policy on this matter that takes account of the Act's emphasis on participation in decision-making of all those persons who are significant to the child or can make a positive contribution to planning for the child's future. A flexible approach to this issue will ensure that such individuals are not overlooked or obliged to use other means to make their views or complaint known.

WHAT MAY BE COMPLAINED ABOUT

10.8. A local authority's procedures must cater for complaints from the people mentioned above about local authority support for families and their children under Part III of the Act. This will include complaints about day care, services to support children within their family home, accommodation of a child, aftercare and decisions relating to the placement of a child or the handling of a child's case. The processes involved in decision-making or the denial of a service must also be covered by the responsible authority's arrangements. In addition to those matters directly related to the provision of services to children in need, other matters fall within the scope of the Regulations and must be covered by the procedure a local authority sets up to meet the requirements of these Regulations. Regulation 12(2) refers to representations about decisions by a local authority in respect of exemptions to the "usual fostering limit" (paragraphs 4–6 of Schedule 7). Such representations should be dealt with in accordance with these Regulations and the guidance below. Regulations 11(1) and (2) require that voluntary organisations and registered children's homes also set up representations procedures in line with these Regulations to consider representations from children accommodated by them and others eligible to make representations.

10.9. The responsible authority should consider what other matters might be appropriate to the procedure set up to meet the requirements of these Regulations. Local authority and private foster parents are not entitled to use the representations procedure on their own behalf except in connection with decisions about the "usual fostering limit" (see also paragraph 10.21 on appeals). The local authority may wish to consider allowing foster parents to make complaints on their own behalf about other matters too. The responsible authority should also allow representations to be made about matters which affect a group of children rather than an individual child to be processed within their Children Act procedure. For example, inappropriate restrictions on the lives of children in foster care or residential care such as preventing children's activities for the convenience of staff, fixing meal times to suit staff rather than to fit in with the normal needs of children or preventing children's normal activities outside the home.

10.10. Representations or complaints about child care matters which fall outside Part III of the Act are not covered by this procedure but by the Complaints Procedure Directions. However, dissatisfaction about a local authority's management or handling of a child's case, even where related to a court order, may be appropriate to the procedure. The inclusion of a child's name on a child protection register is an administrative action not carried out under any statutory provision (even where the decision is linked to a recommendation to seek a court order) but it is part of an inter-agency process for which the local authority is in the lead but does not carry full responsibility. While the requirements of section 26 are confined to the local authority's functions under the Act it would be good practice to provide, with the agreement of the Area Child Protection Committee (ACPC), an appropriate procedure to handle complaints about inter-agency case conferences and their recommendations.

OBJECTIVES

10.11. Children and others making representations including complaints should have access to a procedure which provides them with an opportunity to make representations and complaints about and challenge decisions made in relation to services provided to them direct or via an agency. This is particularly important when no other means of redress is open to them but is valuable even when alternative avenues exist. A well publicised statement of commitment to the representations procedure should encourage the identification and speedy resolution of representations and complaints as they arise. A secondary benefit of the system will be to illustrate for the responsible authority how policies translate into practice and to highlight areas where the responsible authority should be more responsive to the needs of individual clients and the community.

10.12. The statutory requirements and the associated guidance seek to achieve an accessible and effective means of making complaints, close to the point at which the problem arose but with an independent element that will inspire confidence in the procedure. That confidence will not develop unless complaints are acted on in the shortest possible time and an opportunity to challenge the outcome of the considerations is available. For that reason the Regulations require that the responsible authority's arrangements should provide a process which satisfies those criteria. It is not intended that all problems that arise in the day to day handling of child care services should automatically be elevated to the status of a complaint. A matter which is promptly resolved to everyone's complete satisfaction when drawn to the attention of an officer of the responsible authority is not something that requires referral to the procedure.

PROBLEM SOLVING

10.13. Where a problem arises, it will usually be possible to resolve the issue satisfactorily before a complaint is made. Efforts to resolve matters will include discussion and reconsideration as well as explanations of decisions made and actions taken. The aim should be to resolve dissatisfaction as near to the point at which it arose as possible. The responsible authority may wish to consider how they can ensure that advice and support is available to persons expressing dissatisfaction at this stage. Some local authorities have appointed an officer with responsibility to support children and their representatives in participation in decision-making and in voicing their concerns. The appointment of such an officer in the authority or the involvement of people and agencies in the community who can provide independent advice would assist problem-solving and may, therefore, prevent dissatisfaction developing into a matter for complaint. Advocacy as a service to the child as part of child care service provision is not ruled out by these Regulations, nor is it ruled out if a responsible authority wish to provide such a service to support the child in this or other procedures. However, attempts at problem-solving should not be used to divert an eligible person from lodging a complaint under the statutory procedure.

10.14. Staff will need advice on the difficult issue of when an unresolved problem becomes a complaint. This will help to ensure that the problem solving stage is not prolonged beyond any positive period of action, thereby delaying or preventing recourse to the representations procedure, and that problems capable of simple resolution do not become complaints. The responsible authority may wish to consider whether it would be helpful to individuals to know that they are expected to resolve a request for a review of a decision within a specified time limit. Attempts at problem-solving should not end once a complaint has been registered. Rather, there should be continued efforts to resolve the dissatisfaction of service users so that the matter complained of is resolved during consideration of the complaint.

PUBLICITY

10.15. Section 26(8) requires local authorities to publicise their representations procedures. It is recommended that the local authority should publicly announce the setting up of the procedure and invite the participation of service users, community groups and others. The publicity should make clear who is entitled to make use of the procedure and how they may do so, what the procedure covers, to whom a representation or complaint should be addressed, who is available to give advice, the stages in consideration of a representation or complaint and the timescale for each stage. The publicity should be framed in terms that make clear that the procedure is a part of the local authority's commitment to partnership and the informed participation of child and parents in the authority's decision-making about provision of services to safeguard and promote the welfare of a child in need.

10.16. Information should be available in the form of leaflets and posters at social services departments, health service clinics, schools, libraries, family centres, doctors' surgeries, residential homes, Citizens Advice Bureaux and other suitable places. Information leaflets and booklets, using plain language and, where relevant, in other appropriate languages, should be freely available to children where they are of sufficient understanding, parents, foster parents and others who may be eligible to use the procedure. In addition it would be good practice to ensure that the information on the representations procedure forms part of an information pack made available prior to a first review of a child's case or at the time a decision is issued in respect of approval of a foster parent. The local authority may wish to discuss with voluntary organisations and others how best to provide the information in alternative formats such as in large print, braille, on tape or video. All the material should present a positive view of the use of the procedure and seek to diminish fears that invoking the procedure will cause problems for a complainant in their day to day contact with authorities' staff.

MANAGEMENT ISSUES

10.17. A representations procedure will be effective only if the responsible authority demonstrates commitment to it, ensuring, as required by Regulation 3(2), that their policy and the detail of the procedure are known, understood and accepted by elected members, staff, independent persons and clients. Staff may have concerns about workload, their own ability to operate within the procedure or their vulnerability to unfounded complaints. An unequivocal policy statement on the scope and benefits of the procedure, together with recognition of the need for management structures and staff training which reflect the demands of that policy will help to reassure staff. Discussions with staff and their associations will identify areas of concern and afford opportunities for addressing these concerns. Some responsible authorities will have procedures in place that will require little modification to meet the requirements of the Children Act. Where this is the case staff will still need to know of any changes, including the scope of the procedure and an explanation of the effect on the procedure of the Children Act's requirements. Other responsible authorities will be establishing a formal procedure for the first time. Responsible authorities and their staff are more likely to operate the procedure fairly and properly if it is viewed as an aspect of service provision to promote partnership.

REPRESENTATIONS INVOLVING MORE THAN ONE LOCAL AUTHORITY

10.18. If a representation is made which involves more than one local authority, it should be considered by the local authority which is looking after the child. If the child is not being looked after but provided with other services the local authority in whose area the child normally resides should consider the complaint. In such cases, it is suggested that the designated officers of the local authorities involved work together and maintain good liaison.

LINK WITH OTHER PROCEDURES

10.19. The responsible authority should be aware of the need in appropriate cases to identify where a complaint is more appropriate to another procedure or where linked issues require joint consideration. A local authority's procedure for dealing with child care matters will have links with their procedure for hearing other representations and complaints described in "Community Care in the Next Decade and Beyond: Policy Guidance" Chapter 6, "Complaints Procedures" (HMSO 1990). How far the two procedures operate separately or come together will be for individual authorities to decide, bearing in mind the need to safeguard the welfare of the child and to provide appropriate child care expertise. The two procedures are administratively similar and in practice the two procedures might operate together at the point at which the panel becomes involved.

10.20. There will be a need for links with other procedures including those within health authorities and other agencies contributing to child care services. For example, NHS staff may be involved in family support and child protection work. Other agencies apart from health authorities who may be involved in child care services include local education authorities, housing authorities, voluntary and private child care organisations, the probation service and the police. It is essential that arrangements cover both the separating out of representations or complaints appropriate to another procedure and cases where some joint action is appropriate.

OTHER AVENUES OF COMPLAINT

10.21. The procedure required by these Regulations is not an appeals procedure. Separate procedures exist under the Children Act for appeals against the "usual fostering limit" exemption. Appeals against court orders will be to the court. Such court procedures need not exclude the processing of a complaint which is eligible for consideration under the representations procedure, but legal advice should be sought in such cases.

The Commissioner for Local Administration

10.22. The existence of a second stage panel within this complaints procedure does not affect any rights an individual might have under Part III of the Local Government Act 1974. This is because the panel is not a decision-making body. A Local Commissioner may therefore investigate a complaint about local authority maladministration where the complainant is not satisfied with the conduct or outcome of the authority's own investigation.

Elected Members

10.23. Similarly, the complaints procedure should not affect in any way the right of an individual or organisation to approach a local councillor for advice or assistance. The procedure should, however, indicate clearly how complaints made to councillors which cannot be resolved on the spot should be handled.

Children with Disabilities

10.24. Complaints about the discharge by the local authority of any of their functions under Part III of the Children Act 1989 including functions in relation to children with disabilities will be dealt with under this procedure, whether the complaint is about services provided or about decisions on what services are or are not to be provided following an assessment of a child's needs.

10.25. Whenever a complaint is made the implications for other procedures should be considered and addressed. Procedural guidance will need to be clear on the distinction to be made between a complaint, a grievance and the reporting of a matter which is a criminal offence. Staff will wish to be reassured that the establishment of a representations procedure will not lead to the by-passing of existing grievance and disciplinary procedures and clients need to know which procedure is deemed appropriate and why.

10.26. The handling of a complaint may be concurrent with action under the disciplinary procedures or child protection action and on occasion a police investigation. Decisions on how to proceed will be made on the basis of individual cases and local guidance will be necessary on how priorities are identified and decisions made in relation to individual cases. The need to protect a child has to be the first priority and where the complaint is made by a child, the need for child protection action should be considered. If child protection action is appropriate, the inter-agency procedure should be brought into action at the earliest possible stage. The fact that a child is accommodated by or on behalf of the local authority makes this more important, not less (see **Working Together HMSO 1988).**

10.27. Usually a complaint will be a perceived failure of the responsible authority, not the individual and will be clearly a matter for consideration under this procedure. A complaint may be linked to a matter that is being dealt with under the grievance procedure (which concerns staff issues such as conditions of service) or the disciplinary procedure (which applies to actions of staff in relation to failures to comply with instructions, guidance or codes of practice etc. The responsible authority should make clear to staff (and trades unions and professional associations) that consideration of the complaint is separate to any action that may be necesary under the grievance or disciplinary procedures. In such cases staff and trades unions should be kept informed of progress in consideration of the complaint, but they should not be given any details that would breach confidentiality or work against the child's best interests.

SUPPORT OF THOSE USING THE PROCEDURE

10.28. The responsible authority will need to consider what type of support and encouragement it can offer to clients both to make use of the system and to pursue their representation or complaint through the procedure. Information leaflets and open letters to children and parents being provided with services will help to make clients aware of the procedure. However, some parents and most children will need advice and confidential support to make their representation or complaint, to pursue it, to understand the administrative process and to cope with the outcome.

10.29. Regulation 4(1) requires that responsible authorities offer "assistance and guidance on the use of the procedure or give advice . . . " on where this may be obtained. Responsible authorities will wish to consider how this obligation can be fulfilled. Where the responsible authority has made the kind of provision to assist problem-solving outlined in paragraph 10.13, it may wish to extend those arrangements to provide support for complainants. Children accommodated in a residential care setting or a foster placement are likely to need support at every stage if they are to be confident enough to invoke the procedure and to be sure that making a representation will not rebound upon them. This may mean that a person who has no line management or service delivery responsibility or involvement in the child's case should be available to work with the child in the matter of a representation. The responsible authority will wish to consider how this could best be arranged. Where voluntary organisations and registered children's homes are providing accommodation for children in small establishments, they will need to take special care that their arrangements provide the children with appropriate support and the independent element required in the procedure.

10.30. Staff directly involved in a matter complained of or with the child in another context should be informed of a complaint and actions that are taken during the considerations by the authority. Whatever their involvement staff may need increased support and supervision from line managers to help them co-operate with considerations under the procedure and to work positively with the child.

STAFFING

10.31. The Regulations give responsible authorities discretion as to how to decide to use the officer they are required to designate to assist in the co-ordination of all aspects of the consideration of representations. However it is recommended that each responsible authority designate an officer to take day to day responsibility for the co-ordination of the procedure. The post will need to be at a sufficiently senior level to reflect the importance of the task and the responsible authority's commitment to it. The skills required are not specific to any one discipline and it may be that an administrator would best combine the variety of tasks the post will include. The appointment of an administrator, recognisably independent of professional line management, could help demonstrate the separate role of the designated officer. Small responsible authorities such as registered children's homes will need to give careful consideration to how they achieve that objectivity.

10.32 In particular, the designated officer might:

- receive and investigate, or oversee the receipt and investigation of complaints that cannot be resolved informally;
- give advice on the response of the responsible authority to individual complaints;
- ensure the smooth running of the panel arrangements, including the appointment and servicing of panels.

The responsible authority may wish additionally to give responsibility for the overall organisation and effectiveness of the authority's procedure to a senior officer of the authority. This job could include:

- establishing, resourcing and monitoring the procedure;
- directing and overseeing the arrangements made for training and publicity;
- the collation of data on complaints and the dissemination of that data to line managers and to members of the authority.

Either of these posts could combine responsibility for the local authority's Local Authority Social Services Act and Children Act complaints procedures.

INDEPENDENT ELEMENT OF THE PROCEDURE

10.33 The Regulations provide for a two stage procedure with an independent element at each stage. Regulation 5 requires that an independent person be involved from the outset of the considerations and Regulation 8 requires that a panel be convened including at least one independent person where a first stage consideration has not satisfied the complainant. There is nothing in the Regulations which prohibits the independent person involved in the first stage consideration of a case from being a member of the panel, but the responsible authority will wish to consider to what extent the panel can take a fresh look at the case if the same independent person is involved. The responsible authority may wish to draw up a list of independent persons suitable and willing to act as an independent person or to sit on a panel. It would be good practice to consult community groups when drawing up a list. Consortium or reciprocal arrangements between authorities may be one way to facilitate the availablity of independent persons. Local authorities should seek also to draw upon voluntary groups, other agencies and independent professionals to ensure that independence is demonstrably built into their procedure. Responsible authorities will need to look carefully at the independence of a member of a voluntary organisation when contractual arrangements exist between the authority and the organisation.

10.34 Local arrangements will reflect the demand upon the procedure, the different racial and cultural groups in the area and the availability of suitable people willing to serve. In some areas a standing panel appointed for a period (perhaps not exceeding 3 years) might be an effective arrangement. In other areas, it may be more appropriate for a panel to be convened for each occasion. The responsible authority will need to consider what training or other support such as legal advice it might wish to provide for independent persons. This might be appropriately dealt with by joint initiatives to devise appropriate training strategies between responsible authorities.

APPOINTMENT OF INDEPENDENT PERSONS

10.35. The responsible authority will need to appoint independent persons both to consider complaints as individuals at the first stage and as part of a panel at the second stage. Regulation 2(3) states who is excluded from acting as an independent person. In addition, it is recommended that the independent person should not be a spouse of an officer or member of the responsible authority. It is also recommended that co-habitees of those excluded from being independent persons are excluded. The responsible authority will need to make clear to prospective independent persons the nature of the task and the degree of commitment required. The responsible authority will need to be able to identify quickly independent perons with particular skills or knowledge that may be required in a particular case. Independent persons should be given a letter of appointment explaining the duties they will be required to carry out, drawing attention to important issues such as confidentiality, and making clear the working arrangements involved in the consideration of complaints. The letter should also describe the expenses and other payments to which they may be entitled.

SETTING UP THE PROCEDURE

10.36. The complaints procedures established by the responsible authority should be uncomplicated, accessible to those who might wish to use them, understood by all members of staff and should reflect the need for confidentiality at all stages. The responsible authority has discretion to decide how exactly to implement the Regulations and set up the procedure to best suit local needs. However, to meet the minimum requirements of the Regulations and the Act, the responsible authority should:

- designate an officer to assist in the co-ordination of all aspects of the consideration of complaints (Regulation 3(1) and paragraphs 10.31 and 10.32);
- publicise the procedure (section 26(8) and paragraphs 10.15 and 10.16);
- ensure that members of staff of the responsible authority and independent persons are familiar with the procedure (Regulation 3(2) and paragraphs 10.17 and 10.34);
- acknowledge all complaints received by sending the complainant an explanation of the procedure and offer assistance and guidance on it or advice on where assistance and guidance may be obtained (Regulation 4(1) and paragraph 10.37);
- accept and record any oral complaints in writing agreeing them with the complainant (Regulation 4(2) and paragraph 10.38);
- appoint an independent person to consider the complaint with the responsible authority (Regulation 5 and paragraphs 10.33–10.35);
- consider the complaint with the independent person and respond within 28 days of receipt of the complaint (Regulation 6 and paragraph 10.41);
- address their response to the person from whom the complaint was received; and also, where different, to the person on whose behalf the

complaint was made and to any other persons who appear to have a sufficient interest or are otherwise involved or affected. The response should advise the complainant what further options are open should he or she remain dissatisfied (Regulation 8 (1) and paragraph 10.42);

- make arrangements so that where a complainant remains dissatisfied and requests (within 28 days) that his complaint be reviewed, a panel is constituted by the responsible authority to meet within 28 days of the responsible authority's receipt of the complainant's request (Regulation 8(2) and (4) and paragraphs 10.42 and 10.43). (The panel is required by Regulation 8(3) to include at least one independent person). The complainant, the local authority and the independent person appointed under Regulation 5 should be allowed to make oral or written submissions to the panel if he is not a panel member (Regulation 8(5) and paragraph 10.45). The complainant may be accompanied at a panel meeting by another person of his choice who may speak on his behalf (Regulation 8(6) and paragraph 10.45);

- ensure that the panel's recommendation is recorded in writing within 24 hours of the completion of their deliberations (Regulation 9(1)), and is sent (formally) to the responsible authority, to the complainant, to the first stage independent person and to anyone acting on the complainant's behalf (Regulation 9(1) and paragraph 10.47);

- decide on their response to the recommendation of a panel after consideration with an independent person from the panel (section 26(7)(a), Regulation 9(4) and paragraph 10.48) and make their decision known in writing to the person who requested that the complaint be considered by the panel, and where different, the person on whose behalf the request was made, the first stage independent person (if different from the independent person on the panel) and any other persons as appear to have a sufficient interest or are otherwise involved or affected. Notification should be given within 28 days of the date of the recommendation. The letter should explain the responsible authority's decision and the reasons for it and any action they have taken or propose to take (section 26(7)(b));

- keep a record of all complaints received and the outcome in each case; and identify separately those cases where the time limits imposed by the directions have been breached (Regulation 10(1) and paragraph 10.52);

- provide an annual report on the operation of the procedure (Regulation 10(3) and paragraphs 10.54 and 10.55).

Receipt of Complaint

10.37. When a responsible authority receives a complaint about the discharge of any of its functions under Part III of the Act in relation to a child by any of the persons eligible to make a complaint (see paragraph 10.6 above and section 26(3)(a)–(d) of the Act), an acknowledgement of the complaint should be sent to the complainant with a leaflet describing how the representations procedure works and giving the name of the designated officer with responsibility for co-ordinating the handling of complaints under the procedure (see Regulation 3 and paragraphs 10.31 and 10.32). The provision of a clear and easy to understand leaflet is an important part of the local authority's duty to publicise the representations procedure (see section 26(8) of the Act and paragraphs 10.15 and 10.16 for guidance on publicity). It will be good practice for the leaflet to inform the complainant of other avenues by which to puruse their complaint including, in the case of a local authority, the option of complaining directly to the Commissioner for Local Administration.

Oral Complaints

10.38. If a complaint is made orally, the responsible authority is required by Regulation 4(2) to arrange for it to be recorded in writing and agreed with the complainant. The authority will need to consider how to meet the varying needs of children in this respect. This will be particularly important in relation to children from ethnic minorities and whose first language is not English and children with communication difficulties. Similar consideration will also apply in relation to adults from these groups who may be making the complaints. Facilities available for people from these groups should be well publicised including to local voluntary organisations and community or self-help groups.

Determination of Eligibility to Complain

10.39. The responsible authority may also receive complaints in relation to a child from persons other than those covered by the categories who are automatically entitled to complain by virtue of section 26(3)(a)–(d) (see paragraph 10.6 above). The complaint could be made by a relative, friend, teacher, GP or any other person. The responsible authority has to consider whether that person has sufficient interest in the child in order to determine their eligibility. The responsible authority should consider the views of the child where he is of sufficient understanding and of the other people mentioned in section 26(3)(b)–(d) to help them decide whether it is necessary to consider the representation in order to promote and safeguard the welfare of the child.

Notification of Determination of Eligibility

10.40. Once the responsible authority has determined whether the complaint is eligible for handling under the procedure, the complainant should be notified in writing and provided with a copy of the responsible authority's leaflet on their representations procedure. The child should also be notified where he is not the complainant if the authority considers he is of sufficient understanding, whether or not the complaint is deemed to be eligible. The date of receipt of a complaint which required consideration for eligibility will be the day on which the authority makes their decision about eligibility. Where it is decided that an individual is not eligible to pursue a complaint on behalf of a child, the authority should consider whether the substance of the complaint needs to be addressed as if the child had complained.

Consideration with Independent Person

10.41. The basis of the representations procedure is that an independent person should be actively involved in considering the complaint (section 26(4) of the Act). Once appointed by the responsible authority the independent person should take part in all discussions the responsible authority may hold about the complaint. He should be allowed to interview the child, the complainant where this is not the child, parents and other involved persons including relevant members of staff if he considers this necessary in order to form an independent view. He should also be given access to relevant parts of the case record. It is recommended that the independent person should provide written comments to the responsible authority.

Notification of Responsible Authority's Decision

10.42. The responsible authority should notify the complainant, the child (if he is of sufficient understanding), the independent person and any other person whom the local authority consider has a sufficient interest in the child of the proposed result of their consideration (Regulation 8(1)). The letter should be clear and simple and give reasons, whether or not it changes an earlier decision which gave rise to the complaint, and proposed action. The letter should also remind the complainant of his right to request that the complaint is considered by a panel with an independent person sitting on it. If the complainant does wish to take advantage of this he should be asked in the letter of notification to make a formal written request which should reach the responsible authority no later than 28 days from the date on which the letter of notification was sent (Regulation 8(2)).

Reference to Panel

10.43. If the complainant is dissatisfied with the responsible authority's proposal, whether or not the independent person is in agreement with that decision, he can request that the complaint be considered by a panel. The panel should meet within 28 days of the responsible authority's receipt of the complainant's request for the matter to be referred to a panel and should consist of three persons at least one of whom should be an independent person. Under these Regulations, the responsible authority is required to appoint a panel and arrange for the panel to meet to consider the complaint within 28 days of receipt of the letter from the complainant requesting the complaint to be considered by the panel. If no such letter is received from the complainant then consideration of the complaint is ended.

Notification of Panel Meeting

10.44. It is recommended as part of the arrangements for the meeting, that the complainant and the independent person who considered the complaint at the previous stage (if he is not a member of the panel) are notified in writing of the date, time and venue of the meeting and invited to attend. It would be good practice to inform the complainant of the name and status of the panel members specifying which members are independent persons and which officers of the responsible authority will be present.

Submissions to the Panel

10.45 The complainant may make written submissions to the panel before the meeting and make oral submissions at the meeting. The authority has a corresponding right to make submissions to the panel (Regulation 8(5)). The first stage independent person also has the right to make written and oral submissions to the panel (if he is not a member of the panel). His letter of appointment will have made this clear (see paragraph 10.35). The complainant should also be informed of his entitlement to be accompanied by another person who shall be entitled to be present at the whole meeting and to speak on his behalf if he so wishes (Regulation 8(6)).

Conduct of the Meeting

10.46. It is suggested that the meeting is conducted in as informal an atmosphere as possible. In arranging a meeting, the responsible authority will have to consider whether any special provision needs to be made for complainants from ethnic minorities whose first language may not be English or for complainants with disabilities who may have mobility problems or communication difficulties.

The Panel's Recommendation

10.47. Regulation 9(1) requires that the panel records the reasons for their recommendation in writing. The panel is also required by Regulation 9(1) to decide on its recommendation within twenty four hours of the meeting and to notify in writing the responsible authority, the complainant, the independent person involved in the first stage consideration (if he is not a member of the panel) and any other person who the responsible authority considers has sufficient interest in the case (Regulation 9(2)). The panel may, if they consider it appropriate, make their decision at the meeting. If the panel do not make their decision at the meeting or immediately after the meeting, they must reconvene within the twenty four hour limit to make their decision. The letter of notification should explain simply and clearly the reasons for the decision. The letter should also advise the complainant that the responsible authority are required to consider and have due regard to the panel's recommendation.

Reconsideration of Decision by the Responsible Authority

10.48. The responsible authority are required to consider what action should be taken in the light of the panel's findings, in conjunction with an independent person from the panel (Regulation 9(3)). The Act requires that the responsible authority should "have due regard to the findings of those considering the representations;" (section 26(7)(a)). Authorities will also wish to take account of the effect of the findings and the outcome of their considerations upon the child (and complainant if not the child). There may be aspects of the complaint which require further enquiry under different procedures.

Notification of Responsible Authority's Consideration of Panel's Recommendation

10.49. The responsible authority should notify the complainant, the child (if he is considered to have sufficient understanding) and such other persons as the responsible authority consider appropriate (section 26(7)(b)). This notification should be given within 28 days of the date of the panel's recommendation. The notification should be clear and simple, explaining the responsible authority's reasons for the decision. Those whom the responsible authority should consider notifying may include the panel, the independent person involved in the first stage consideration (if he is not a panel member), relevant members of staff in the responsible authority and other agencies. The responsible authority may also wish to notify a child's independent visitor or someone in another agency working with the child, particularly where the child will need support to come to terms with the decision. The responsible authority should arrange for explanations to be given in advance of formal notifications wherever possible to the child and to parents and to other complainants if appropriate. In particular, the child may need reassurance and should be given opportunities to discuss his feelings about the outcome of the consideration. This will be the case whether or not the outcome is one that the child or complainant welcomes. Where it is appropriate the responsible authority should advise the complainant of other avenues of complaint or appeal that may be open to him. Informative leaflets could be provided with the notice of decision. Equally, members of a responsible authority's staff who were involved in the matter complained of should receive an explanation of the outcome of the considerations.

Subsequent Action

10.50. The responsible authority should take any action decided upon as a result of the findings in an individual case as soon as possible after the decision has been reached. Delay would undermine confidence in the procedure and might well become the subject of another complaint or cause the complainant to seek another remedy.

10.51. The responsible authority will wish to take note of aspects of the case complained about that require action under other procedures or that have general implications for policies or practice. In the first instance the relevant procedure should be identified and other authorities should be informed and appropriate arrangements made. Where issues of policy and practice arise, the authority will need to consider how best to address the issue and the timescale for action. Serious matters will need immediate attention.

MONITORING

10.52. Regulation 10 sets out requirements for responsible authorities to monitor the operation and effectiveness of their representations procedure. A record should be kept of each complaint received which details the nature of the complaint, the action taken, the outcome of each complaint and whether there was compliance with the time limits specified in Regulations 6, 8(4) and 9(1) (Regulation 10(1)). Local authorities should use this information to provide the Social Services Committee with regular and anonymised information about numbers and types of complaint received, the time taken to deal with them and their outcome. All responsible authorities should devise systems locally to provide for:

● the dissemination of this information to line managers;

● its use as a measure of performance and means of quality control;

● information derived from complaints about services subject to statutory regulation (such as residential care homes), or where services purchased under contract are concerned, to the person responsible for monitoring the contract.

Information about complaints that are dealt with and resolved at the first stage may be of equal value to information about the smaller number of complaints referred to the panel. Where such (first stage) complaints raise policy, resource management, staffing or other issues, line managers should be informed.

10.53. Information collected during the monitoring process and during consideration of individual complaints will provide feedback on management and operational matters such as how policies are interpreted by staff and service users, how effective communication is within the responsible authority and to the public, where staff training is required and whether resources are targeted correctly.

10.54. An annual report dealing with the operation of the complaints procedure should be compiled and in the case of local authorities be presented to the Social Services Committee. In the case of a voluntary organisation or registered children's home, the report should be available, with a copy of the procedure, at any inspection authorised by the Secretary of State. The report should include:

● a summary of the statistical and other information which may have been supplied at more frequent intervals to the Committee;

● a review of the effectiveness of the procedure.

In preparation for making the annual report, or separately, responsible authorities should consider inviting comment from those consulted during the setting up of the procedure on the question of its effectiveness and on the scope for possible improvements.

10.55. All or part of the periodic reports made to the Council or Social Services Committee by local authorities should be open to inspection by members of the public under the terms of the Local Government (Access to Information) Act 1985. They should be anonymised where necessary to ensure there is no breach of confidentiality.

10.56. The responsible authority should consider inviting comment from those consulted during the setting up of the procedure (community groups, service users etc – see paragraph 10.4) on the effectiveness of the procedure and ask for suggestions for improvement. Regular consultation with such groups and sharing information on the outcome of the monitoring process will help to build confidence in the operation of the procedure.

STATUTORY INSTRUMENTS

1991 No. 890

CHILDREN AND YOUNG PERSONS

ARRANGEMENTS FOR PLACEMENT OF CHILDREN (GENERAL) REGULATIONS 1991

Made	*2nd April 1991*
Laid before Parliament	*10th April 1991*
Coming into force	*14 October 1991*

ARRANGEMENT OF REGULATIONS

SCHEDULES

The Secretary of State for Health in exercise of the powers conferred by sections 23(2)(a) and (f)(ii) and (5), 59(2) and (3) and 104(4) of, and paragraphs 12, 13 and 14 of Schedule 2, 4(1) and (2)(d) of Schedule 4, 7(1) and (2)(g) of Schedule 5 and paragraph 10(1) and (2)(f) of Schedule 6 to the Children Act 1989(*a*) and of all other powers enabling him in that behalf hereby makes the following Regulations:—

Citation, commencement and interpretation

1.–(1) These Regulations may be cited as the Arrangements for Placement of Children (General) Regulations 1991 and shall come into force on 14 October 1991.

(2) In these Regulations, unless the context otherwise requires–

"the Act" means the Children Act 1989;

(*a*) 1989 c.41. Paragraph 14 of Schedule 2 was amended by paragraph 26 of Schedule 16 to the Courts and Legal Services Act 1990 (c.41).

"area authority" means, in relation to a child who is or is to be placed, the local authority (*b*) in whose area the child is or is to be placed, where the child is looked after by a different authority;

"care case" means a case in which in the child is in the care of a local authority (*c*);

"placement" subject to regulation 13 means

(a) the provision of accommodation and maintenance by a local authority for any child whom they are looking after by any of the means specified in section 23(2)(a), (b), (c), (d) or (f) of the Act (accommodation and maintenance of child looked after by a local authority);

(b) the provision of accommodation for a child by a voluntary organisation by any of the means specified in section 59(1)(a), (b), (c), (d) or (f) of the Act (provision of accommodation by voluntary organisations), and

(c) the provision of accommodation for a child in a registered children's home,

and the expressions "place" and "placed" shall be construed accordingly;

"responsible authority" means–

(a) in relation to a placement by a local authority (including one in which the child is accommodated and maintained in a voluntary home or a registered children's home), the local authority which place the child,

(b) in relation to a placement by a voluntary organisation of a child who is not looked after by a local authority, the voluntary organisation which place the child, and

(c) in relation to a placement in a registered children's home of a child who is neither looked after by a local authority nor accommodated in such a home by a voluntary organisation, the person carrying on the home.

(3) Any notice required under these Regulations is to be given in writing and may be sent by post.

(4) In these Regulations, unless the context otherwise requires–

(a) any reference to a numbered regulation is to the regulation in these Regulations bearing that number and any reference in a regulation to a numbered paragraph is to the paragraph of that regulation bearing that number;

(b) any reference to a numbered Schedule is to the Schedule to these Regulations bearing that number.

Application of Regulations

2. These Regulations apply to placements–

(a) by a local authority of any child;

(b) by a voluntary organisation of a child who is not looked after by a local authority;

(c) in a registered children's home of a child who is neither looked after by a local authority nor accommodated in such a home by a voluntary organisation, by a person carrying on the home.

Making of arrangements

3.–(1) Before they place a child the responsible authority shall, so far as is reasonably practicable, make immediate and long-term arrangements for that placement, and for promoting the welfare of the child who is to be placed.

(*b*) "local authority" is defined in section 105(1) of the Act as the council of a county, a metropolitan district, a London Borough or the Common Council of the City of London. Pursuant to section 2 of the Local Authority Social Services Act 1970 (c.42) local authority functions under the Children Act 1989 stand referred to the social services committee of a local authority.

(*c*) *See* the definition of "care order" in section 105(1) of the Children Act 1989 and paragraphs 15 and 16 of Schedule 14 to that Act.

(2) Where it is not practicable to make those arrangements before the placement, the responsible authority shall make them as soon as reasonably practicable thereafter.

(3) In the case of a child to whom section 20(11) of the Act applies (child aged 16 or over agreeing to be provided with accommodation) the arrangements shall so far as reasonably practicable be agreed by the responsible authority with the child before a placement is made and if that is not practicable as soon as reasonably practicable thereafter.

(4) In any other case in which a child is looked after or accommodated but is not in care the arrangements shall so far as reasonably practicable be agreed by the responsible authority with—

(a) a person with parental responsibility for the child, or

(b) if there is no such person the person who is caring for the child

before a placement is made and if that is not practicable as soon as reasonably practicable thereafter.

(5) Any arrangements made by the responsible authority under this regulation shall be recorded in writing.

Considerations on making and contents of arrangements

4.–(1) The considerations to which the responsible authority are to have regard so far as reasonably practicable in making the arrangements referred to in regulation 3 in each case are the general considerations specified in Schedule 1, the considerations concerning the health of a child are specified in Schedule 2 and the considerations concerning the education of a child specified in Schedule 3.

(2) Except in a care case, the arrangements referred to in regulation 3 shall include, where practicable, arrangements concerning the matters specified in Schedule 4.

Notification of arrangements

5.–(1) The responsible authority shall, so far as is reasonably practicable, notify the following persons in writing of the arrangements to place a child, before the placement is made–

(a) any person an indication of whose wishes and feelings have been sought under section 22(4), section 61(2) or section 64(2) of the Act (consultation prior to decision making in respect of children looked after by a local authority, provided with accommodation by a voluntary organisation or in a registered children's home);

(b) the district health authority for the district in which the child is living;

(c) the local education authority for the area in which the child is living;

(d) the child's registered medical practitioner;

(e) the local authority for the area in which the child is living where the child is not placed by such an authority;

(f) the area authority;

(g) any person, not being an officer of a local authority, who is caring for a child immediately before the arrangements are made;

(h) except in a care case, any person in whose favour a contact order is in force with respect to the child, and

(i) in a care case, any person who has contact with the child pursuant to section 34 of the Act (contact with a child in care by parents etc) or to an order under that section.

(2) Where it is not practicable to give the notification before the placement, it shall be given as soon as reasonably practicable thereafter.

(3) The responsible authority shall send a copy of the arrangements referred to in regulation 3 or such part of the arrangements as they consider will not

prejudice the welfare of the child with the notification referred to in paragraph (1) but in the case of notification to those specified in paragraph (1)(b) − (i) applies they shall send details of only such part of the arrangements as they consider those persons need to know.

Arrangements for contact

6. In operating the arrangements referred to in paragraph 6 of Schedule 4, a voluntary organisation or a person carrying on a registered children's home shall, unless it is not reasonably practicable or consistent with the child's welfare, endeavour to promote contact between the child and the persons mentioned in that paragraph.

Health requirements

7. A responsible authority shall, so far as reasonably practicable before a placement is made and if that is not reasonably practicable as soon as practicable after the placement is made−

   (a) ensure that arrangements are made for the child to be examined by a registered medical practitioner and

   (b) require the practitioner who has carried out the examination to make a written assessment of the state of health of the child and his need for health care

unless the child has been so examined and such assessment has been made within a period of three months immediately preceding the placement or the child is of sufficient understanding and he refuses to submit to the examination.

(2) During the placement of the child the responsible authority shall ensure that arrangements are made for a child to be provided with health care services, including medical and dental care and treatment.

Establishment of records

8.−(1) A responsible authority shall establish, if one is not already in existence, a written case record in respect of each child whom it places.

(2) The record shall include−

   (a) a copy of the arrangements referred to in regulation 3;

   (b) a copy of any written report in its possession concerning the welfare of the child;

   (c) a copy of any document considered or record established in the course of or as a result of a review of the child's case;

   (d) details of arrangements for contact, of contact orders and of other court orders relating to the child; and

   (e) details of any arrangements whereby another person acts on behalf of the local authority or organisation which placed the child.

Retention and confidentiality of records

9.−(1) A case record relating to a child who is placed shall be retained by the responsible authority until the seventy-fifth anniversary of the date of birth of the child to whom it relates or, if the child dies before attaining the age of 18, for a period of 15 years beginning with the date of his death.

(2) The requirements of paragraph (1) may be complied with either by retaining the original written record, or a copy of it, or by keeping all of the information from such record in some other accessible form (such as by means of a computer).

(3) A responsible authority shall secure the safe keeping of case records and shall take all necessary steps to ensure that information contained in them is treated as confidential, subject only to−

(a) any provision of or made under or by virtue of, a statute under which access to such records or information may be obtained or given;

(b) any court order under which access to such records or information may be obtained or given.

Register

10.–(1) A local authority, shall, in respect of every child placed in their area (by them and any other responsible authority) and every child placed by them outside their area enter into a register to be kept for the purpose–

(a) the particulars specified in paragraph (3), and

(b) such of the particulars specified in paragraph (4) as may be appropriate.

(2) A voluntary organisation and a person carrying on a registered children's home shall, in respect of every child placed by them, enter into a register to be kept for the purpose–

(a) the particulars specified in paragraph (3), and

(b) such of the particulars specified in paragraph (4) as may be appropriate.

(3) The particulars to be entered into the register in accordance with paragraphs (1) or (2) are–

(a) the name, sex and date of birth of the child;

(b) the name and address of the person with whom the child is placed and, if different, of those of the child's parent or other person not being a parent of his who has parental responsibility for him;

(c) in the case of a child placed on behalf of a local authority by a voluntary organisation or in a registered children's home, the name of the authority;

(d) whether the child's name is entered on any local authority register indicating that the child is at risk of being abused;

(e) whether the child's name is entered on the register maintained under paragraph 2 of Schedule 2 to the Act (register of disabled children);

(f) the date on which each placement of the child began and terminated and the reason for each termination;

(g) in a care case of a child the name of the local authority in whose care the child is;

(h) the legal provisions under which the child is being looked after or cared for.

(4) The additional particulars to be entered in the register, where appropriate in accordance with paragraphs (1) or (2) are–

(a) in the case of a child placed by a local authority in respect of whom arrangements have been made for the area authority to carry out functions pursuant to regulation 12 a note that the arrangements were made and the name of the other local authority with whom they were made; and

(b) in the case of a child who has been placed, in respect of whom arrangements have been made for supervision of the placement to be carried out on behalf of a responsible authority (otherwise than pursuant to Regulation 12), a note that the arrangements were made and the name of person with whom the arrangements were made.

(5) Entries in registers kept in accordance with this regulation shall be retained until the child to whom the entry relates attains the age of 23 or, if the child has died before attaining 23, the period of 5 years beginning with the date of his death.

(6) The requirements of paragraph (1) may be complied with either by retaining the original register, or a copy of it, or by keeping all of the

information from such a register in some other accessible form (such as by means of a computer).

(7) A responsible authority shall secure the safe keeping of registers kept in accordance with this regulation and shall take all necessary steps to ensure that information contained in them is treated as confidential, subject only to–

(a) any provision of or made under or by virtue of a statute under which access to such registers or information may be obtained or given;

(b) any court order under which access to such registers or information may be obtained or given.

Access by guardians ad litem to records and register

11. Each voluntary organisation, where they are not acting as an authorised person (a), and every person carrying on a registered children's home shall provide a guardian ad litem of a child–

(a) such access as may be required to–

(i) case records and registers maintained in accordance with these Regulations; and

(ii) information from such records or registers held in whatever form (such as by means of computer)

(b) such copies of the records or entries in the registers as he may require.

Arrangements between local authorities and area authorities

12. Where arrangements are made by a local authority which is looking after a child with an area authority for the area authority to carry out functions in relation to a placement on behalf of the local authority–

(a) the local authority shall supply the area authority with all such information as is necessary to enable the area authority to carry out those functions on behalf of the local authority;

(b) the area authority shall keep the local authority informed of the progress of the child and, in particular, shall furnish reports to the local authority following each visit to the home in which the child is placed and following each review of the case of the child carried out by the area authority on behalf of the local authority;

(c) the local authority and the area authority shall consult each other from time to time as necessary, and as soon as reasonably practicable after each such review of the case of the child, with regard to what action is required in relation to him.

Application of Regulations to short-term placements

13.–(1) This regulation applies to a series of short-term placements at the same place where the following conditions are satisfied–

(a) all the placements occur within a period which does not exceed one year;

(b) no single placement is for a duration of more than four weeks; and

(c) the total duration of the placements does not exceed 90 days.

(2) Any series of short-term placements to which this regulation applies may be treated as a single placement for the purposes of these Regulations.

Signed by authority of
the Secretary of State for Health   Minister of State for Health

---

(a) For access by guardians ad litem to local authority and authorised person's records *see* section 42 of the 1989 Act as amended by paragraph 18 of Schedule 16 to the Courts and Legal Services Act 1990 (c.41). "Authorised person" is defined in section 31 of the 1989 Act.

SCHEDULE 1   Regulation 4(1)

CONSIDERATIONS TO WHICH RESPONSIBLE AUTHORITIES TO HAVE REGARD

1. In the case of a child who is in care, whether an application should be made to discharge the care order.

2. Where the responsible authority is a local authority whether the authority should seek a change in the child's legal status.

3. Arrangements for contact, and whether there is any need for changes in the arrangements in order to promote contact with the child's family and others so far as is consistent with his welfare.

4. The responsible authority's immediate and long term arrangements for the child, previous arrangements in respect of the child and whether a change in those arrangements is needed and consideration of alternative courses of action.

5. Where the responsible authority is a local authority, whether an independent visitor should be appointed if one has not already been appointed.

6. Whether arrangements need to be made for the time when the child will no longer be looked after by the responsible authority.

7. Whether plans need to be made to find a permanent substitute family for the child.

SCHEDULE 2   Regulation 4(1)

HEALTH CONSIDERATIONS TO WHICH RESPONSIBLE AUTHORITIES ARE TO HAVE REGARD

1. The child's state of health.

2. The child's health history.

3. The effect of the child's health and health history on his development.

4. Existing arrangements for the child's medical and dental care and treatment and health and dental surveillance.

5. The possible need for an appropriate course of action which should be identified to assist necessary change of such care, treatment or surveillance.

6. The possible need for preventive measures, such as vaccination and immunisation, and screening for vision and hearing.

SCHEDULE 3   Regulation 4(1)

EDUCATIONAL CONSIDERATIONS

1. The child's educational history.

2. The need to achieve continuity in the child's education.

3. The need to identify any educational need which the child may have and to take action to meet that need.

4. The need to carry out any assessment in respect of any special educational need under the Education Act 1981 (a) and meet any such needs identified in a statement of special educational needs made under section 7 of that Act.

(a) 1981 c.60

MATTERS TO BE INCLUDED IN ARRANGEMENTS TO ACCOMMODATE CHILDREN WHO ARE NOT IN CARE

1. The type of accommodation to be provided and its address together with the name of any person who will be responsible for the child at that accommodation on behalf of the responsible authority.

2. The details of any services to be provided for the child.

3. The respective responsibilities of the responsible authority and–

    (a) the child;

    (b) any parent of his; and

    (c) any person who is not a parent of his but who has parental responsibility for him.

4. What delegation there has been by the persons referred to in paragraph 3(b) and (c) of this Schedule to the responsible authority of parental responsibility for the child's day to day care.

5. The arrangements for involving those persons and the child in decision making having regard–

    (a) to the local authority's duty under sections 20(6) (involvement of children before provision of accommodation) and 22(3) to (5) of the Act (general duties of the local authority in relation to children looked after by them);

    (b) the duty of the voluntary organisation under section 61(1) and (2) of the Act (duties of voluntary organisations); and

    (c) the duty of the person carrying on a registered children's home under section 64(1) and (2) of the Act (welfare of children in registered children's homes).

6. The arrangements for contact between the child and–

    (a) his parents;

    (b) any person who is not a parent of his but who has parental responsibility for him; and

    (c) any relative, friend or other person connected with him,

and if appropriate the reasons why contact with any such person would not be reasonably practicable or would be inconsistent with the child's welfare.

7. The arrangements for notifying changes in arrangements to any of the persons referred to in paragraph 6.

8. In the case of a child aged 16 or over whether section 20(11) (accommodation of a child of 16 or over despite parental opposition) applies.

9. The expected duration of arrangements and the steps which should apply to bring the arrangements to an end, including arrangements for rehabilitation of the child with the person with whom he was living before the voluntary arrangements were made or some other suitable person, having regard in particular, in the case of a local authority looking after a child, to section 23(6) of the Act (duty to place children where practicable with parents etc.) and paragraph 15 of Schedule 2 to the Act (maintenance of contact between child and family).

EXPLANATORY NOTE

(This note does not form part of the Regulations)

These Regulations make provision for the arrangements for placement of children by local authorities, voluntary organisations and persons carrying on registered children's homes. These placements are with foster parents, in community homes, voluntary children's homes or registered children's homes and under other arrangements (but not in a home provided in accordance with arrangements made by the Secretary of State under section 82(5) of the Children Act 1989). The Regulations make provision for the application of the regulations (regulation 2); the making of arrangements for accommodation and maintenance of and promotion of the welfare of children (regulation 3); the considerations to be given on making the arrangements and except in a care case the contents of those arrangements (regulation 4); notification of the arrangements (regulation 5); the arrangements for contact in respect of children placed by voluntary organisations or in a registered children's home (regulation 6); the health requirements (regulation 7); establishment of records (regulation 8); the retention and confidentiality of records (regulation 9); registers of relevant information (regulation 10); the access by guardians ad litem to records and registers (regulation 11); arrangements made between local authorities and other authorities for carrying out responsibilities in respect of those arrangements on their behalf (regulation 12) and short-term placements (regulation 13).

STATUTORY INSTRUMENTS

1991 No. 910

CHILDREN AND YOUNG PERSONS

THE FOSTER PLACEMENT (CHILDREN) REGULATIONS 1991

Made	*3rd April 1991*
Laid before Parliament	*10th April 1991*
Coming into Force	*14th October 1991*

ARRANGEMENT OF REGULATIONS

PART I   GENERAL

PART II   APPROVALS AND PLACEMENTS

PART III   RECORDS OF FOSTER PARENTS

PART IV   LOCAL AUTHORITY VISITS

PART V   REVOCATION

SCHEDULES

The Secretary of State for Health, in exercise of the powers conferred by sections 23(2)(a) and (9), 59(2) and 62(3) of, and paragraph 12(a), (b), (c), (d), (e), (f), and (g) of Schedule 2 to, the Children Act 1989 (*a*) and of all other powers enabling him in that behalf, hereby makes the following Regulations: –

PART I   GENERAL

Citation, commencement and interpretation

1.–(1) These Regulations may be cited as the Foster Placement (Children) Regulations 1991 and shall come into force on 14th October 1991.

(2) In these Regulations, unless the context otherwise requires –

"the Act" means the Children Act 1989;

"approving authority", in relation to a foster parent, means the local authority (*b*) or voluntary organisation responsible under regulation 3 for approving (or not approving) the foster parent;

"area authority", in relation to a child (and foster parent), means the local authority in whose area the child is placed where that authority is not also the responsible authority;

"foster parent" means the person with whom a child is or is proposed to be placed under these Regulations;

"foster placement agreement" means an agreement referred to in regulation 5(6);

"responsible authority", in relation to a child, means the local authority or voluntary organisation responsible for the placement of the child under (as the case may be) section 23(2)(a) or 59(1)(a) of the Act.

(3) Any notice or consent required under these Regulations is to be given in writing and may be sent by post.

(4) In these Regulations –

(a) any reference to a numbered regulation is to the regulation in these Regulations bearing that number and any reference in a regulation to a numbered paragraph is to the paragraph of that regulation bearing that number;

(b) any reference to a numbered Schedule is to the Schedule to these Regulations bearing that number.

Scope of the Regulations

2.–(1) These Regulations apply (subject to paragraph (2)) to any placement of a child –

(a) by a local authority under section 23(2)(a) of the Act;

(b) by a voluntary organisation under section 59(1)(a) of the Act (unless they are acting on behalf of a local authority).

(2) These Regulations do not apply to any placement of a child –

(a) to which the Placement of Children with Parents etc. Regulations 1991 (*c*) apply;

(b) if the child is not in the care of a local authority, with a parent of his or other person having parental responsibility for him;

(c) for adoption pursuant to the Adoption Act 1976 (*d*).

(*a*) 1989 c.41.
(*b*) "local authority" is defined in section 105(1) of the Act as the council of a county, a metropolitan district, a London Borough or the Common Council of the City of London. Pursuant to section 2 of the Local Authority Social Services Act 1970 (c.42) local authority functions under the Children Act 1989 stand referred to the social services committee of a local authority.
(*c*) SI 1991/893.
(*d*) 1976 c.36.

(3) Where a care order is in force the application of these Regulations is subject to any directions given by a court (whether before or after the Regulations come into force).

(4) Nothing in these Regulations requires the temporary removal of a child from a person with whom he is already living before placement under these Regulations.

PART II   APPROVALS AND PLACEMENTS

Approval of foster parents

3.–(1) Except in the case of an immediate placement under regulation 11, a child is not to be placed unless the foster parent is approved under this regulation.

(2) Subject to paragraph (3), any local authority and any voluntary organisation which is also a responsible authority may approve a foster parent.

(3) A local authority or voluntary organisation –

(a) are not to approve a foster parent who is already approved by another local authority or voluntary organisation;

(b) are not to approve a foster parent in the area of an area authority unless they first consult with, and take into account the views of, that authority whom they are also to notify of their decision.

(4) A local authority or voluntary organisation are not to give any approval under this regulation unless they have first –

(a) required the prospective foster parent to supply the names and addresses of two persons to provide personal references for him and have arranged for them to be interviewed;

(b) obtained so far as practicable, the information specified in Schedule 1 relating to him and other members of his household and family,

and (having had regard to these matters) are satisfied that the person is suitable to act as a foster parent and that his household is suitable for any child in respect of whom approval is given

(5) An approval given under this regulation may be in respect of a particular named child or children, or number and age range of children, or of placements of any particular kind or in any particular circumstances.

(6) Where an approving authority approve a person as a foster parent they –
(a) shall give him notice which specifies whether the approval is in respect of a particular named child or children or number and age range of children or of placements of any particular kind or in any particular circumstances;

(b) shall nevertheless place no child with him unless he enters into a written agreement with them covering the matters specified in Schedule 2.

(7) Where an approving authority decide not to approve a person as a foster parent they shall give him notice of the decision.

Reviews and terminations of approvals

4.–(1) Where a foster parent has been approved under regulation 3 the approving authority are to review, at intervals of not more than a year, whether the foster parent and his household continue to be suitable (as mentioned in regulation 3(4)).

(2) When undertaking a review under this regulation the approving authority are to seek, and take into account, the views of the foster parent and of any responsible authority who have placed a child with the foster parent within the

preceding year or who have an earlier placement with the foster parent which has not been terminated.

(3) At the conclusion of the review the approving authority are to prepare a report and give notice to the foster parent of their decision (including any revision of the terms of the approval under regulation 3(6)(a)).

(4) Where on a review the approving authority are no longer satisfied –

(a) that the terms of the approval under regulation 3(6)(a) are appropriate they shall revise the terms;

(b) that the foster parent and his household are suitable they shall terminate the approval from a date to be specified in the notice under paragraph (3).

(5) Where a foster parent notifies the approving authority that he no longer wishes to act as a foster parent, or where the authority are otherwise satisfied that this is the case, the authority are to terminate the approval from a date to be specified by notice to the foster parent.

(6) A copy of any notice given under paragraph (3) or (5) is to be sent to any other local authority or voluntary organisation who have a child placed with the foster parent.

Placements

5.–(1) A responsible authority are not to place a child with a foster parent unless they are satisfied that –

(a) that is the most suitable way of performing their duty under (as the case may be) section 22(3) or 61(1) (a) and (b) of the Act; and

(b) placement with the particular foster parent is the most suitable placement having regard to all the circumstances.

(2) In making arrangements for a placement a responsible authority are to secure that where possible the foster parent is –

(a) of the same religious persuasion as the child, or

(b) gives an undertaking that the child will be brought up in that religious persuasion.

(3) Consistent with the terms of any approval given under regulation 3, a responsible authority may place a child with a foster parent whom they have themselves approved or, provided the conditions specified in paragraph (4) are satisfied, with a foster parent approved by another local authority or voluntary organisation.

(4) The conditions referred to in paragraph (3) are that –

(a) the approving authority consent to the placement;

(b) any other local authority or voluntary organisation who already have a child placed with the foster parent also consent to the placement; and

(c) the area authority (if they are not also the approving authority) are consulted, and their views taken into account, and are given notice of the placement.

(5) A responsible authority which places a child after consulting an area authority under paragraph (4)(c) shall give notice of the placement to the area authority.

(6) Except in the case of an emergency or immediate placement under regulation 11, a responsible authority are not to place a child unless the authority and the foster parent have entered into a written agreement relating to that child covering the matters specified in Schedule 3.

Supervision of placements

6.–(1) A responsible authority are to satisfy themselves that the welfare of each child placed by them continues to be suitably provided for by the placement and for this purpose the authority are to –

(a) make arrangements for a person authorised by the authority to visit the child, in the home in which he is placed, from time to time as circumstances may require and when reasonably requested by the child or the foster parent and in particular (but subject to regulation 9(2)) –

(i) in the first year of the placement, within one week from its beginning and then at intervals of not more than six weeks,

(ii) subsequently, at intervals of not more than 3 months;

(b) give such advice to the foster parent as appears to the authority to be needed.

(2) In the case of an emergency or immediate placement under regulation 11 the responsible authority are to arrange for the child to be visited at least once in each week during the placement.

(3) On each occasion on which the child is visited under this regulation the responsible authority shall cause the authorised person, if they consider it appropriate, to arrange to see the child alone.

(4) On each occasion on which a child is visited under this regulation the responsible authority are to cause a written report to be prepared by the person who made the visit.

Termination of placements

7.–(1) A responsible authority are not to allow the placement of a child with a particular foster parent to continue if it appears to them that the placement is no longer the most suitable way of performing their duty under (as the case may be) section 22(3) or 61(1) (a) and (b) of the Act.

(2) Where a child has been placed by some other local authority, or by a voluntary organisation, in the area of the area authority and it appears to the authority that continuation of the placement would be detrimental to the welfare of the child, the area authority are to remove the child forthwith.

(3) An area authority who remove a child under paragraph (2) are forthwith to notify the responsible authority.

Arrangements between local authorities and voluntary organisations as to placements

8.–(1) Where a local authority looking after a child are satisfied that the child should be placed with a foster parent, they may make arrangements under this regulation for the other duties imposed on them under this Part of these Regulations to be discharged on their behalf by a voluntary organisation.

(2) A local authority are not to make arrangements under this regulation unless –

(a) they are satisfied –

(i) as to the capacity of the voluntary organisation to discharge duties on their behalf, and

(ii) that those arrangements are the most suitable way for those duties to be discharged; and

(b) they enter into a written agreement with the voluntary organisation about the arrangements, providing for consultation and for exchange of information and reports between the authority and the organisation.

Short-term placements

9.–(1) This regulation applies to a series of short-term placements of a child with the same foster parent where the following conditions are satisfied –

(a) all the placements occur within a period which does not exceed one year;

(b) no single placement is for a duration of more than four weeks; and

(c) the total duration of the placements does not exceed 90 days.

(2) Any series of short-term placements to which the regulation applies may be treated as a single placement for the purposes of this Part of these Regulations but with the modification that a visit under regulation 6(1)(a)(i) and (ii) and regulation 16 (a) to (c) is to be made –

(a) during the first in the series of placements; and

(b) again, if more than six months pass from the beginning of that first placement when the child is in fact placed.

Placements outside England and Wales

10.–(1) A voluntary organisation are not to place a child outside the British Islands (*a*).

(2) Where a responsible authority make arrangements to place a child outside England or Wales they are to ensure that, so far as reasonably practicable, requirements are complied with in relation to the child which would have applied under these Regulations if the child had been placed in England or Wales.

(3) In the case of a local authority, paragraph (2) is subject to the provisions of paragraph 19 of Schedule 2 to the Act (arrangements by local authorities to assist children to live outside England and Wales).

Emergency and immediate placements by local authorities

11.–(1) Subject to paragraph (2) where arrangements have been made for the placement of a child in an emergency, a local authority may for a period not exceeding 24 hours place them with any person approved under regulation 3.

(2) Before an emergency placement is made pursuant to paragraph (1) the authority shall –

(a) satisfy the provisions of regulation 5(1)(a), and

(b) obtain a written agreement from the person with whom the child is to be placed that that person will carry out the duties specified in paragraph (4) of this regulation.

(3) Where a local authority are satisfied that the immediate placement of a child is necessary they may for a period not exceeding six weeks place the child with a person who has not been approved under regulation 3 provided, after interviewing the person, inspecting the accommodation and obtaining information about other persons living in his household, the authority are also satisfied that –

(a) the person is a relative or friend of the child;

(b) the person has made a written agreement with the local authority to carry out the duties specified in paragraph (4); and

(c) the provisions of regulation 5(1)(a) are satisfied.

(4) The duties referred to in paragraph (2)(b) and (3)(b) are –

(a) to care for the child as if he were a member of that person's family;

(b) to permit any person authorised by the local authority of (if different) the area authority, to visit the child at any time;

(c) where regulation 7(1) or (2) applies, to allow the child to be removed at any time by the local authority or (as the case may be) the area authority;

(d) to ensure that any information which the foster parent may acquire relating to the child, or to his family or any other person, which has been given to him in confidence in connection with the placement is kept confidential and is not disclosed except to, or with the agreement of, the local authority; and

---

(*a*) "British Islands" are defined in the Interpretation Act 1978 (c.30) as meaning the United Kingdom, the Channel Islands and the Isle of Man.

(e) to allow contact with the child in accordance with section 34 of the Act (parental contact etc in relation to a child in care), with any contact order (as defined in section 8(1) of the Act) and with any arrangements made or agreed by the local authority.

PART III   RECORDS

Register of foster parents and others with whom a child is placed

12.–(1) A local authority are to enter, in a register kept for the purpose, the particulars specified in paragraph (2) for each foster parent in their area who is approved under regulation 3 and each person not being an approved foster parent with whom a child is placed pursuant to regulation 11 in their area.

(2) The particulars mentioned in paragraph (1) are –

(a) the name and address of the foster parent (or, where foster parents are approved jointly, of both foster parents or other person with whom the child is placed pursuant to regulation 11);

(b) the date of the approval under regulation 3 or agreement specified in regulation 11(3)(b);

(c) the terms of the notice of approval under regulation 3(6)(a) or of the agreement specified in regulation 11(3)(b) as for the time being in force.

Case records for foster parents and others with whom a child is placed

13.–(1) An approving authority are to compile (if one is not already established) and maintain a record for each foster parent whom they have approved under regulation 3 and for each person, not being an approved foster parent, with whom a child is placed by them pursuant to regulation 11.

(2) Each record compiled under paragraph (1) is to include copies of each of the documents specified in paragraph (3) and the information specified in paragraph (4).

(3) The documents referred to in paragraph (2) are as the case may be a copy of each –

(a) the notice of approval under regulation 3(6)(a);

(b) the agreement under regulation 3(6)(b) and Schedule 2;

(c) any report of review of approval under regulation 4(3);

(d) any notice of termination of approval under regulation 4(3) or (5);

(e) any agreement specified in regulation 11(3)(b).

(4) The information referred to in paragraph (2) is as the case may be –

(a) a record of each placement with the foster parent or person, not being an approved foster parent, with whom a child is placed pursuant to regulation 11, including the name, age and sex of each child placed, the dates on which each placement began and terminated and the circumstances of the termination;

(b) the information obtained by the approving authority in relation to the approval of the foster parent and in relation to any review of termination of the approval;

(c) the information obtained under regulation 11(3).

(5) An approving authority are to compile a record for each prospective foster parent to whom notice is given under regulation 3(7) that he is not approved as a foster parent, the record to include a copy of the notice and the information, as to the foster parent and his household and family, obtained by the authority in connection with the question of approval.

Retention and confidentiality of records

14.–(1) The record for a foster parent or other person compiled under regulation 13, and any entry relating to him in the register maintained under regulation 12, is to be retained for at least 10 years from the date on which his approval is terminated, or until his death if earlier.

(2) The requirements of paragraph (1) may be complied with either by retaining the original written record (or a copy of it) or by keeping all the information from the record in some other accessible form (such as by means of a computer).

(3) The authority or organisation responsible for the maintenance of any register or record under regulation 12 or 13 are to secure its safe keeping and to take all necessary steps to ensure that the information which it contains is treated as confidential subject only to –

    (a) any provision in under or by virtue of a statute under which access to such register, record or information may be obtained or should be granted;

    (b) any court order under which access to such register, record or information may be obtained or given.

(4) Each voluntary organisation, where they are not acting as an authorised person (a), shall provide a guardian ad litem of a child –

    (a) such access as may be required to –

        (i) case records and registers maintained in accordance with these Regulations,

        (ii) the information from such records or registers held in whatever form (such as by means of computer);

    (b) such copies of the records or entries in the registers as he may require.

PART IV   LOCAL AUTHORITY VISITS TO CHILDREN PLACED BY VOLUNTARY ORGANISATIONS

Circumstances necessitating visits by local authorities

15.–(1) Subject to paragraph (2) every local authority shall arrange for one of their officers to visit every child who is accommodated with a foster parent within their area by or on behalf of a voluntary organisation in any of the following circumstances and within the periods specified –

    (a) within 28 days of the placement with the foster parent;

    (b) where the voluntary organisation which made the placement with the foster parent make representations to the local authority that there are circumstances relating to the child which require a visit, within 14 days of the receipt of the representations;

    (c) where the local authority are informed that the welfare of the child may not be being safeguarded or promoted, as soon as reasonably practicable but in any event within 7 days of being informed;

    (d) where the local authority are satisfied, following a visit to a child under this regulation in respect of a placement with the foster parent, that the child's welfare is being safeguarded and promoted, at intervals of not more than six months.

(2) This regulation shall not apply to children in respect of whom the local authority have made arrangements under regulation 8.

Requirements in respect of visits

16. Every local authority shall make arrangements to ensure that in respect of any visit made pursuant to regulation 15 an officer of theirs (but subject to regulation 9(2)) –

(a) For access by guardian ad litem to local authority and authorised person's records *see* section 42 of the 1989 Act as amended by paragraph 18 of Schedule 16 to the Courts and Legal Services Act 1990 (c.41). "Authorised person" is defined in section 31 of the 1989 Act.

(a) sees the child during the course of the visit, unless he considers it unnecessary to do so or the child is not in fact with the foster parents at the time of the visit;

(b) if the child is not there, makes arrangements to see the child as soon as reasonably practicable;

(c) takes steps to discover whether the voluntary organisation which placed the child have made suitable arrangements to perform their duties under these Regulations and there under section 61 of the Act.

PART V   REVOCATION

Revocation

17. Subject to the operation of the transitional provisions of paragaph 21 of Schedule 14 to the Act, the Boarding-out of Children (Foster Placement) Regulations 1988 (a) are hereby revoked.

Signed by authority of the   Minister of State for Health
Secretary of State for Health

SCHEDULE 1   Regulation 3(4)(b)

INFORMATION AS TO PROSPECTIVE FOSTER PARENT AND OTHER MEMBERS OF HIS HOUSEHOLD AND FAMILY

1. His age, health (supported by a medical report), personality and marital status (including any previous marriage).

2. Particulars of the other adult members of his household.

3. Particulars of the children in his family, whether or not members of his household, and any other children in his household.

4. Particulars of his accommodation.

5. His religious persuasion, the degree of his religious observance and his capacity to care for a child from any particular religious persuasion.

6. His racial origin, cultural and linguistic background and his capacity to care for a child from any particular origin or cultural or linguistic background.

7. His past and present employment or occupation, his standard of living and leisure activities and interests.

8. His previous experience of caring for his own and other children and his ability in this respect.

9. (If any, and subject to the Rehabilitation of Offenders Act 1974(b)) his previous criminal convictions and those of other adult members of his household.

10. The outcome of any request or application made by him or any other member of his household to foster or adopt children or for registration under section 71 of the Act or any previous enactment of that section.

11. Particulars of any previous approval under regulation 3, or refusal of approval or termination of approval under regulation 4, relating to him or any other member of his household.

MATTERS AND OBLIGATIONS IN FOSTER CARE AGREEMENTS

1. The support and training to be given to the foster parent.

2. The procedure for the review of approval of a foster parent.

3. The procedure in connection with the placement of foster children, and in particular –

   (a) the matters to be covered in foster placement agreements and the respective obligations, under any such agreements, of the responsible authority and the foster parent;

   (b) the authority's arrangements for meeting any legal liabilities of the foster parent arising by reason of a placement; and

   (c) the procedure available to foster parents for making representations to the local authority in whose area that child is placed.

4. To give written notice to the authority forthwith, with full particulars, of –

   (a) any intended change of his address;

   (b) any change in the composition of his household;

   (c) any other change in his personal circumstances and any other event affecting either his capacity to care for any child placed or the suitability of his household; and

   (d) any further request or application of a kind mentioned in paragraph 10 of Schedule 1.

5. Not to administer corporal punishment to any child placed with him.

6. To ensure that any information relating to a child placed with him, to the child's family or to any other person, which has been given to him in confidence in connection with a placement is kept confidential and is not disclosed to any person without the consent of the responsible authority.

7. To comply with the terms of any foster placement agreement, to care for the child placed with the foster parent as if he were a member of the foster parent's family and to promote his welfare having regard to the responsible authority's long and short-term arrangements for the child.

8. To notify the responsible authority immediately of any serious illness of the child or of any other serious occurrence affecting the child.

9. Where regulation 7(1) or (2) applies, to allow the child to be removed from the foster parent's home by the responsible authority or (as the case may be) the area authority.

MATTERS AND OBLIGATIONS TO BE COVERED IN FOSTER PLACEMENT AGREEMENTS

1. The provision by the responsible authority of a statement containing all the information which the authority considers necessary to enable the foster parents to care for the child and, in particular, information as to –

   (a) the authority's arrangements for the child and the objectives of the placement;

   (b) the child's personal history, religious persuasion and cultural and linguistic background and racial origin;

   (c) the child's state of health and need for health care and surveillance; and

   (d) the child's education needs

including a requirement for the statement to be provided either at the time of the signing of the agreement or, where this is not practicable, within the following 14 days.

2. The responsible authority's arrangements for the financial support of the child during the placement.

3. Any arrangements for delegation of responsibility for consent to the medical or dental examination or treatment of the child.

4. The circumstances in which it is necessary to obtain in advance the approval of the responsible authority for the child to live, even temporarily, away from the foster parent's home.

5. The arrangements for visits to the child, in connection with the supervision of the placement, by the person authorised by or on behalf of the responsible authority or area authority and the frequency of visits and reviews under the Review of Children's Cases Regulations 1991 (a).

6. The arrangements for the child to have contact with his parents and other persons, including any arrangements in pursuance of section 34 of the Act (parental contact etc for children in the care of local authority in relation to a child in care, or any contact under (as defined in section 8(1) of the Act)).

7. Compliance by the foster parent with the terms of the agreement set out in Schedule 2.

8. Cooperation by the foster parent with any arrangements made by the responsible authority for the child.

EXPLANATORY NOTE

(This note is not part of the Regulations)

These Regulations replace with modifications the Boarding-out of Children (Foster Placement) Regulations 1988 ("the 1988 Regulations").

The main changes are that under these Regulations:

(a) there is approval of foster parents and not households in which a child is to live and foster parents may now be approved only by one local authority or voluntary organisation at any one time;

(b) an emergency placement may be made with any approved foster parent for not more than 24 hours while an immediate placement may be made with a relative or friend for not more than six weeks. Previously emergency placements only were permitted with a person in a household which was approved outside the normal approval procedure;

(c) local authority responsibilities in respect of children placed by voluntary organisations are enhanced.

They apply to placements of children by local authorities and voluntary organisations, other than placements to which the Placement of Children with Parents etc Regulations 1991 apply and placements for adoption or with a person having parental responsibility for the child (regulation 2).

Part II of the Regulations relates to approvals and placements and requires the foster parent with whom a child is placed to be approved by a local authority or voluntary organisation (regulation 3); makes provision for reviews and terminations of approval (regulation 4); for the placement of a child with a foster parent (regulation 5) and for the supervision and termination of placements (regulations 6 and 7); allows a local authority to make arrangements with a voluntary organisation to be responsible for the placement of the child (regulation 8); the application of the Regulations to short-term placements (regulation 9) and placements outside England and Wales (regulation 10); and, by local authorities only, emergency and immediate placements (regulation 11).

(a) SI 1991/895.

Part III of the Regulations provides for local authorities to maintain a register of foster parents approved in their area (regulation 12), for local authorities and voluntary organisations to maintain a record for each foster parent they approve (regulation 13) and for the retention and confidentiality of the registers and records (regulation 14).

Part IV of the Regulations makes provision for visits to children placed with foster parents by voluntary organisations (regulations 15 and 16).

Part V of the Regulations revokes the 1988 Regulations (regulation 17).

STATUTORY INSTRUMENTS

1991 No. 893

CHILDREN AND YOUNG PERSONS

THE PLACEMENT OF CHILDREN WITH PARENTS ETC REGULATIONS 1991

Made	*2nd April 1991*
Laid before Parliament	*10th April 1991*
Coming into force	*14th October 1991*

ARRANGEMENT OF REGULATIONS

SCHEDULES

The Secretary of State for Health, in exercise of the powers conferred by sections 23(5), and (9) and 104(4) of, and paragraph 14 of Schedule 2 to, the Children Act 1989(*a*) and of all other powers enabling him in that behalf hereby makes the following Regulations:—

Citation, commencement and interpretation

1.–(1) These Regulations may be cited as the Placement of Children with Parents etc Regulations 1991 and shall come into force on 14th October 1991.

(*a*) 1989 c.41. Section 23 was amended by the insertion of new subsection (5A) by paragraph 12(2) of Schedule 16 to the Court and Legal Services Act 1990 (c.41). Paragraph 14(d) of Schedule 2 to the 1989 Act was inserted by paragraph 26 of Schedule 16 to the 1990 Act.

(2) In these Regulations, unless the context otherwise requires –

"the Act" means the Children Act 1989;

"area authority" means, in relation to a child who is or is to be placed, the local authority (a) in whose area the child is or is to be placed where the child is in the care of a different authority;

"guardian and litem" means a guardian ad litem appointed pursuant to section 41 of the Act (representation of child and his interests in certain proceedings) or under rules made under section 65 of the Adoption Act 1976(b) (panels for selection of guardians ad litem and reporting officers);

"placement" means the act of allowing a child who is in the care of a local authority to live pursuant to section 23(5) of the Act (placement of a child in care with parents etc.) with

(a) a parent of the child,

(b) a person who is not a parent of the child but who has parental responsiblity for him, or

(c) where there was a residence order in force with respect to him immediately before the care order was made a person in whose favour the residence order was made,

and the expressions "place" and "placed" shall be construed accordingly and "placed with" a person means being allowed to live with that person pursuant to that section;

"placement decision" means a decision to place a child which is made in accordance with regulation 5(2) (placement decisions by director of social services or nominated person);

"supervisory duties" means the duties imposed by regulation 9 (support and supervision of placements).

(3) Any notice required under these Regulations is to be in writing and any such notice may be sent by post.

(4) In these Regulations, unless the context otherwise requires –

(a) any reference to a numbered regulation is to the regulation in these Regulations bearing that number and any reference in a regulation to a numbered paragraph is to the paragraph of that regulation bearing that number;

(b) any reference to a numbered Schedule is to the Schedule to these Regulations bearing that number.

Scope of Regulations

2.–(1) These Regulations shall apply to every child who is in the care of a local authority (c) and who is or is proposed to be placed.

(2) Where a child who is to be placed is aged 16 or over regulations 3, 6, 7, 8, 9 and 12 shall not apply.

(3) These Regulations shall not apply to the placement of a child for adoption pursuant to the Adoption Act 1976.

(4) Nothing in these Regulations shall require the temporary removal of a child from the person with whom he is already living and with whom he may be placed, before a placement decision is made concerning him.

(5) These Regulations shall not apply in a case to the extent that they are incompatible with any order made by a court under section 34 of the Act (parental contact with children in care etc), or any direction of a court which

---

(a) "local authority" is defined in section 105(1) of the Act as the council of a county, a metropolitan district, a London Borough or the Common Council of the City of London. Pursuant to section 2 of the Local Authority Social Services Act 1970 (c.42) local authority functions under the Children Act 1989 stand referred to the social services committee of a local authority.
(b) 1976 c.36.
(c) See the definition of "care order" in section 105(1) of the Children Act 1989 and paragraphs 15 and 16 of Schedule 14 to that Act.

has effect under paragraph 16(5) of Schedule 14 to the Act (transitional provision as to directions) in that case.

Enquiries and assessment

3.–(1) Before a placement is made, a local authority shall make all necessary enquiries in respect of –

    (a) the health of the child;

    (b) the suitability of the person with whom it is proposed the child should be placed;

    (c) the suitability of the proposed accommodation, including the proposed sleeping arrangements;

    (d) the educational and social needs of the child; and

    (e) the suitability of all other members of the household, aged 16 and over, in which it is proposed a child will live.

(2) In considering the suitability of a person as required in paragraph (1)(b) or (e), the local authority shall, so far as practicable, take into account the particulars specified in paragraphs 1 and 2 respectively of Schedule 1.

Duties of local authorities in relation to placements

4. A local authority shall satisfy themselves that the placement of a child is the most suitable way of performing their general duty under section 22(3) of the Act (general duty of local authority in respect of children looked after by them) and that the placement is the most suitable having regard to all the circumstances.

Placement decisions by director of social services or nominated person

5.–(1) A placement shall be made only after a placement decision has been made.

(2) The decision to place a child shall be made on behalf of the local authority by the director of social services appointed by the authority under section 6 of the Local Authority Social Services Act 1970(a) (director of social services) or by an officer of the local authority nominated in writing for that purpose by the director.

Immediate Placements

6.–(1) Subject to paragraph (2), nothing in Regulation 3 shall prevent the immediate placement of a child pursuant to a placement decision in circumstances in which the local authority consider that to be necessary and in accordance with their duty under section 22(3) of the Act and in such a case the authority shall take steps to ensure that the provisions of these Regulations that would otherwise have to be complied with before the placement decision is made are complied with as soon as practicable thereafter.

(2) Before an immediate placement is made pursuant to this regulation a local authority shall –

    (a) arrange for the person with whom the child is to be placed to be interviewed in order to obtain as much of the information specified in paragraph 1 of Schedule 1 as can be readily ascertained at the interview, and

    (b) arrange to obtain as much of the information specified in paragraph 2 of Schedule 1 in relation to other members of the household aged 16 and over, in which it is proposed the child will live, as can be readily ascertained at the time of that interview.

(a) 1970 c.42.

Provisions of agreements

7. Following a placement decision the local authority shall seek to reach agreement with the person with whom the child is to be placed on all the particulars, so far as is practicable, specified in Schedule 2 and the placement shall not be put into effect unless and until such an agreement on all such particulars has been reached and recorded in writing and a copy of it has been given or sent to that person.

Notification of placements

8.–(1) Subject to paragraph (3) the local authority shall, so far as practicable, give notice to all the persons whose wishes and feelings have been sought in relation to the decision to place the child pursuant to section 22(4) of the Act (persons to be consulted concerning local authority decisions) and those persons specified in paragraph (4) of –

    (a) the placement decision, and

    (b) details of where the child is to be placed.

(2) Where the child is placed with a person other than a parent the local authority's notice under paragraph (1) to the persons referred to in that paragraph shall contain –

    (a) the name and address of the person with whom the child is placed;

    (b) particulars of arrangements for contact with the child;

    (c) any other particulars relating to the care and welfare of the child which it appears to the local authority ought to be supplied.

(3) A local authority shall not be required to give notice under paragraph (1) in the case of a person whose whereabouts are unknown to the authority, or cannot be readily ascertained, or in any case where the authority determine that to give such notice would not be in accordance with their duty under section 22(3) of the Act.

(4) For the purposes of paragraph (1) the persons specified are –

    (a) the district health authority for the district in which the child is living;

    (b) the local education authority for the area in which the child is living;

    (c) the child's registered medical practitioner;

    (d) the area authority;

    (e) any person, not being an officer of a local authority, who has been caring for the child immediately before the placement, and

    (f) where there was a residence order in force with respect to the child immediately before the care order was made, the person in whose favour the residence order was made.

Support and supervision of placements

9.–(1) A local authority shall satisfy themselves that the welfare of each child who has been placed by them continues to be appropriately provided for by his placement and for that purpose the authority shall –

    (a) give such advice and assistance to the person with whom the child is placed as appears to the local authority to be necessary;

    (b) make arrangements for a person authorised by the local authority to visit the child from time to time as necessary but in any event –

        (i) within one week of the beginning of the placement,

        (ii) at intervals of not more than 6 weeks during the first year of the placement,

        (iii) thereafter at intervals of not more than three months and also whenever reasonably requested by the child or the person with whom the child is placed

and for the person so authorised to make arrangements, so far as practicable, on each visit to see the child alone.

(2) On each occasion on which a child is visited in pursuance of this regulation by any person authorised by the local authority which placed the child the local authority shall cause a written report on the child to be prepared by that person.

Placements outside England and Wales

10. A local authority which makes arrangements to place a child outside England and Wales in accordance with the provisions of paragraph 19 of Schedule 2 to the Act (placement of child in care outside England and Wales) shall take steps to ensure that, so far as is reasonably practicable, requirements corresponding with the requirements of these Regulations are complied with in relation to that child as would be required to be complied with under these Regulations if the child were placed in England and Wales.

Termination of placements

11.–(1) If it appears to a local authority that the placement is no longer in accordance with the duty of the authority in respect of the child under section 22(3) of the Act or would prejudice the safety of the child, they shall terminate the placement and shall remove the child forthwith from the person with whom he is placed

(2) Where, in the case of a child who has been placed in the area of an area authority by another local authority, it appears to the area authority that it would be detrimental to the welfare of the child if he continued to be so placed, the area authority may remove the child forthwith from the person with whom he is placed.

(3) Where a child is removed under paragraph (2) the area authority shall forthwith notify the other authority of that fact and that authority shall make other arrangements for the care of the child as soon as is practicable.

Notification of termination of placements

12. In relation to termination of a placement a local authority shall, so far as is reasonably practicable –

(a) give notice in writing of any decision to terminate the placement before it is terminated to –

(i) the child, having regard to his age and understanding,

(ii) the other persons whose wishes and feelings have been sought in relation to the decision to terminate the placement pursuant to section 22(4) of the Act,

(iii) to the person with whom the child is placed,

(iv) to the other pesons to whom regulation 8(1) refers; and

(b) give notice in writing of the termination of the placement to all those persons, other than the child, and the person with whom the child was placed.

Application of Regulations to short-term placements

13.–(1) This regulation applies to a series of short-term placements with the same person where the following conditions are satisfied –

(a) all the placements occur within a period which does not exceed one year;

(b) no single placement is for a duration of more than four weeks; and

(c) the total duration of the placements does not exceed 90 days.

(2) Any series of short-term placements to which this regulation applies may be treated as a single placement for the purpose of these Regulations.

(3) Regulation 9(1)(b) shall apply in relation to short-term placements to which this regulation applies as if for paragraphs (1)(b)(i) to (iii) of that regulation there were substituted –

"(i) during the first of the series of short term placements to which this regulation applies, and

(ii) on one other occasion while the child is in fact placed during the series of short-term placements."

Signed by authority of the
Secretary of State for Health

Minister of State for Health

SCHEDULE 1   Regulation 3(2)

PARTICULARS TO BE TAKEN INTO ACCOUNT IN CONSIDERING SUITABILITY OF PERSONS AND HOUSEHOLDS

1. In respect of a person with whom it is proposed the child should be placed –

 (a) age;

 (b) health;

 (c) personality;

 (d) marital status and particulars of any previous marriage;

 (e) previous experience of looking after and capacity to look after children and capacity to care for the child;

 (f) the result of any application to have a child placed with him or to adopt a child or of any application for registration under section 71 (registration as child-minder) of the Act and details of any prohibition on his acting as a child-minder, providing day care, or caring for foster children privately or children in a voluntary or registered children's home;

 (g) details of children in his household, whether living there or not;

 (h) religious persuasion and degree of observance, racial origin and cultural and linguistic background;

 (i) past and present employment and leisure activities and interests;

 (j) details of the living standards and particulars of accommodation of his household;

 (k) subject to the provisions of the Rehabilitation of Offenders Act 1974, any criminal conviction.

2. In respect of members of the household aged 16 and over of a person with whom a child is to be placed, so far as is practicable, all the particulars specified in paragraph 1(a), (b), (c), (d), (f), (i), and (k) of this Schedule.

SCHEDULE 2   Regulation 7

PARTICULARS ON WHICH THERE SHOULD BE AGREEMENT WITH THE PERSON WITH WHOM A CHILD IS TO BE PLACED

1. The authority's plans for the child and the objectives of the placement.

2. The arrangements for support of the placement.

3. Arrangements for visiting the child in connection with the supervision of the placement by the person authorised by or on behalf of the local authority or area authority, and frequency of visits and reviews of the child's case under regulations made under section 26 of the Act (*a*) (review of cases).

4. Arrangements for contact, if any, (including prohibition of contact) in pursuance of section 34 of the Act (parental contact etc for children in care).

(*a*) SI 1991/895.

5. Removal of the child from the placement in the circumstances specified in regulation 11.

6. The need to notify the local authority of relevant changes in circumstances of the person with whom the child is placed, including any intention to change his address, changes in the household in which the child will live and any serious occurrence involving the child such as injury or death.

7. The provision of a statement concerning the health of the child, the child's need for health care and surveillance, and the child's educational needs and the local authority's arrangements to provide for all such needs.

8. Any arrangements for any delegation and exercise of responsiblity for consent to medical examination or treatment.

9. The need to ensure that any information relating to any child or his family or any other person given in confidence to the person with whom the child is placed in connection with the placement is kept confidential and that such information is not disclosed to any person without the consent of the local authority.

10. The circumstances in which it is necessary to obtain in advance the approval of the local authority for the child living, even temporarily, in a household other than the household of the person with whom the child has been placed.

11. The arrangements for requesting a change in the agreement.

EXPLANATORY NOTE

(This Note is not part of the Regulations)

These Regulations provide for the accommodation of children in the care of a local authority with a parent, person who is not a parent but has parental responsibility and a person in whose favour there was a residence order immediately before the care order was made.

They make provision for the children to whom the regulations apply (regulation 2); the enquiries and assessment to be made by local authorities before making decisions to place children in such accommodation (regulation 3); the duties of local authorities in relation to placements in those circumstances (regulation 4); the taking of such decisions by the director of social services or a person nominated by him (regulation 5); immediate placements (regulation 6): the provision of and particulars to be included in agreements between local authorities and those who are to accommodate the children (regulation 7); notification of placements (regulation 8); support and supervision of placements by local authorities (regulation 9); the application of the regulations to placements which may be made outside England and Wales (regulation 10); the circumstances in which there may be termination of placements (regulation 11); notification of termination of placements (regulation 12); and the application of these Regulations to short-term placements (regulation 13).

STATUTORY INSTRUMENTS

1991 No. 891

CHILDREN AND YOUNG PERSONS

CONTACT WITH CHILDREN REGULATIONS 1991

Made	*2nd April 1991*
Laid before Parliament	*10th April 1991*
Coming into force	*14th October 1991*

The Secretary of State for Health, in exercise of the powers conferred by section 34(8) of the Children Act 1989(*a*), and all other powers enabling him in that behalf, hereby makes the following Regulations:

Citation, commencement and interpretation

1.–(1) These Regulations may be cited as the Contact with Children Regulations 1991, and shall come into force on 14th October 1991.

(2) Any notice required under these Regulations is to be given in writing and may be sent by post.

(3) In these Regulations unless the context requires otherwise –

    (a) any reference to a numbered section is to the section in the Children Act 1989 bearing that number;

    (b) any reference to a numbered regulation is to the regulation in these Regulations bearing that number; and

    (c) any reference to a Schedule is to the Schedule to these Regulations.

(3) Any notice required under these Regulations is to be given in writing and may be sent by post.

Local authority refusal of contact with child

2. Where a local authority has decided under section 34(6) to refuse contact with a child that would otherwise be required by virtue of section 34(1) or a court order, the authority shall, as soon as the decision has been made, notify the following persons in writing of those parts of the information specified in the Schedule as the authority considers those persons need to know –

    (a) the child, if he is of sufficient understanding;

    (b) the child's parents;

    (c) any guardian of his;

    (d) where there was a residence order in force with respect to the child immediately before the care order was made, the person in whose favour the order was made;

    (e) where immediately before the care order was made, a person had care of the child by virtue of an order made in the exercise of the High Court's inherent jurisdiction with respect to children, that person; and

    (f) any other person whose wishes and feelings the authority consider to be relevant.

(*a*) 1989 c.41.

Departure from terms of court order on contact under section 34

3. The local authority may depart from the terms of any order under section 34 (parental contact etc with children in care) by agreement between the local authority and the person in relation to whom the order is made and in the following circumstance and subject to the following condition –

(a) where the child is of sufficient understanding, subject to agreement also with him; and

(b) a written notification shall be sent to the persons specified in regulation 2 containing those parts of the information specified in the Schedule as the authority considers those persons need to know, within seven days of the agreement to depart from the terms of the order.

Notification of variation or suspension of contact arrangements

4. Where a local authority varies or suspends any arrangements made (otherwise than under an order made under section 34) with a view to affording any person contact with a child in the care of that local authority, written notification shall be sent to those persons specified in regulation 2 containing those parts of the information specified in the Schedule as the authority considers those persons need to know, as soon as the decision is made to vary or suspend the arrangements.

Signed by authority of the Secretary of State for Health.

Minister of State for Health.

SCHEDULE Regulations 2, 3, and 4

Information to be contained in written notification

1. Local authority's decision.
2. Date of the decision.
3. Reasons for the decision.
4. Duration (if applicable).
5. Remedies available in case of dissatisfaction.

EXPLANATORY NOTE

(This note is not part of the Regulations)

These Regulations provide for the steps to be taken by a local authority who have refused to allow contact between a child in care and parents and others specified in section 34(1), which include notifying those persons and anyone else whose wishes and feelings they consider to be relevant (regulation 2).

They provide for the authority to depart from the terms of any order as to contact, by agreement between the authority and the person about whom the order was made, where the child agrees, if he is of sufficient understanding, and where a written notification of details of the decision is sent to the person specified in regulation 2 (regulation 3). They provide for the authority to notify those persons of details of any decision to vary or suspend any arrangements made, other than under an order under section 34, so as to allow any person contact with a child in care (regulation 4).

The Schedule provides for the details of the information which may be given in each case.

STATUTORY INSTRUMENTS

1991 No. 892

CHILDREN AND YOUNG PERSONS

DEFINITION OF INDEPENDENT VISITORS
(CHILDREN) REGULATIONS 1991

Made	*2nd April 1991*
Laid before Parliament	*10th April 1991*
Coming into Force	*14th October 1991*

The Secretary of State for Health, in exercise of the powers conferred by paragraph 17(7) of Schedule 2 to the Children Act 1989(*a*) and of all other powers enabling him in that behalf hereby makes the following Regulations:

Citation and commencement

1. These Regulations may be cited as the Definition of Independent Visitors (Children) Regulations 1991 and shall come into force on 14th October 1991.

Independent visitors

2. A person appointed by a local authority as an independent visitor under paragraph 17(1) of Schedule 2 to the Children Act 1989 shall be regarded as independent of the local authority appointing him in the following circumstances:

(a) where the person appointed is not connected with the local authority by virtue of being –

(i) a member of the local authority or any of their committees or sub-committees, whether elected or co-opted; or

(ii) an officer of the local authority employed in the Social Services Department of that authority; or

(iii) a spouse of any such person;

(b) where the child who is to receive visits from the person appointed is accommodated by an organisation other than the local authority, and the person appointed is not –

(i) a member of that organisation; or

(ii) a patron or trustee of that organisation; or

(iii) an employee of that organisation, whether paid or not; or

(iv) a spouse of any such person.

Signed by authority of the
Secretary of State for Health

Minister of State for Health

(*a*) 1989 c.41.

These Regulations prescribe the circumstances in which a person appointed as an independent visitor is to be regarded as independent of the local authority appointing him.

Regulation 2(a) provides that certain local authority members, employees and their spouses, are not to be regarded as independent. Regulation 2(b) provides that where the child is accommodated by some organisation other than a local authority, certain persons connected with that organisation shall not be regarded as independent.

STATUTORY INSTRUMENTS

1991 No. 895

CHILDREN AND YOUNG PERSONS

REVIEW OF CHILDREN'S CASES REGULATIONS 1991

Made	*2nd April 1991*
Laid before Parliament	*10th April 1991*
Coming into force	*14th October 1991*

ARRANGEMENT OF REGULATIONS

SCHEDULES

The Secretary of State for Health in exercise of the powers conferred by sections 26(1) and (2), 59(4)(a) and (5) and 104(4) of and paragraph 10(1) and (2)(l) of Schedule 6 to the Children Act 1989 (*a*) and of all other powers enabling him in that behalf hereby makes the following Regulations:

Citation, commencement and interpretation

1.–(1) These Regulations may be cited as the Review of Children's Cases Regulations 1991 and shall come into force on 14th October 1991.

(2) In these Regulations, unless the context otherwise requires –

"the Act" means the Children Act 1989;

"guardian ad litem" means a guardian ad litem appointed pursuant to section 41 of the Act or rules made under section 65 of the Adoption Act 1976 (*b*);

"independent visitor" means an independent visitor appointed under paragraph 17 of Schedule 2 to the Act;

(a) 1989 c.41.   (b) 1976 c.36.

"responsible authority" means in relation to –

(a) a child who is being looked after by a local authority (a), that authority,

(b) a child who is being provided with accommodation by a voluntary organisation otherwise than on behalf of a local authority, that voluntary organisation,

(c) a child who is being provided with accommodation in a registered children's home otherwise than on behalf of a local authority or voluntary organisation, the person carrying on that home;

(3) Any notice required under these Regulations is to be given in writing and may be sent by post.

(4) In these Regulations, unless the context otherwise requires –

(a) any reference to a numbered regulation is to the regulation in these Regulations bearing that number and any reference in any regulation to a numbered paragraph is to the paragraph of that regulation bearing that number;

(b) any reference to a numbered Schedule is to the Schedule to these Regulations bearing that number.

Review of children's cases

2. Each responsible authority shall review in accordance with these Regulations the case of each child while he is being looked after or provided with accommodation by them.

Time when case is to be reviewed

3.–(1) Each case is first to be reviewed within four weeks of the date upon which the child begins to be looked after or provided with accommodation by a responsible authority.

(2) The second review shall be carried out not more than three months after the first and thereafter subsequent reviews shall be carried out not more than six months after the date of the previous review.

Manner in which cases are to be reviewed

4.–(1) Each responsible authority shall set out in writing their arrangements governing the manner in which the case of each child shall be reviewed and shall draw the written arrangements to the attention of those specified in regulation 7(1).

(2) The responsible authority which are looking after or providing accommodation for a child shall make arrangements to coordinate the carrying out of all aspects of the review of that child's case.

(3) The responsible authority shall appoint one of their officers to assist the authority in the coordination of all the aspects of the review.

(4) The manner in which each case is reviewed shall, so far as practicable, include the elements specified in Schedule 1.

(5) Nothing in these Regulations shall prevent the carrying out of any review under these Regulations and any other review, assessment or consideration under any other provision at the same time.

Considerations to which responsible authorities are to have regard

5. The considerations to which the responsible authority are to have regard so far as is reasonably practicable in reviewing each case are the general

---

(a) "local authority" is defined in section 105(1) of the Act as the council of a county, a metropolitan district, a London Borough or Common Council of the City of London. Pursuant to section 2 of the Local Authority Social Services Act 1970 (c.42) local authority functions under the Children Act 1989 stand referred to the social services committee of a local authority.

considerations specified in Schedule 2 and the considerations concerning the health of the child specified in Schedule 3.

Health reviews

6. The responsible authority shall make arrangements for a child who continues to be looked after or provided with accommodation by them to be examined by a registered medical practitioner and for a written assessment on the state of health of the child and his need for health care to be made –

> (a) at least once in every period of six months before the child's second birthday, and

> (b) at least once in every period of twelve months after the child's second birthday,

unless the child is of sufficient understanding and he refuses to submit to the examination.

Consultation, participation and notification

7.–(1) Before conducting any review the responsible authority shall, unless it is not reasonably practicable to do so, seek and take into account the views of –

> (a) the child;

> (b) his parents;

> (c) any person who is not a parent of his but who has parental responsibility for him; and

> (d) any other person whose views the authority consider to be relevant;

including, in particular, the views of those persons in relation to any particular matter which is to be considered in the course of the review.

(2) The responsible authority shall so far as is reasonably practicable involve the persons whose views are sought under paragraph (1) in the review including, where the authority consider appropriate, the attendance of those persons at part or all of any meeting which is to consider the child's case in connection with any aspect of the review of that case.

(3) The responsible authority shall, so far as is reasonably practicable, notify details of the result of the review and of any decision taken by them in consequence of the review to –

> (a) the child;

> (b) his parents;

> (c) any person who is not a parent of his but who has parental responsibility for him; and

> (d) any other person whom they consider ought to be notified.

Arrangements for implementation of decisions arising out of reviews

8. The responsible authority shall make arrangements themselves or with other persons to implement any decision which the authority propose to make in the course, or as a result, of the review of a child's case.

Monitoring arrangments for reviews

9. Each responsible authority shall monitor the arrangements which they have made with a view to ensuring that they comply with these Regulations.

Recording review information

10. Each responsible authority shall ensure that –

> (a) information obtained in respect of the review of a child's case,

> (b) details of the proceedings at any meeting arranged by the authority at which the child's case is considered in connection with any aspect of the review of that case, and

(c) details of any decisions made in the course of or as a result of the review

are recorded in writing.

Application of Regulations to short periods of care

11.—(1) This regulation applies to cases in which a child is looked after or provided with accommodation by a responsible authority for a series of short periods at the same place where the following conditions are satisfied –

(a) all the periods are included within a period which does not exceed one year;

(b) no single period is for a duration of more than four weeks; and

(c) the total duration of the period does not exceed 90 days.

(2) Cases to which this regulation applies may be treated as a single case of a child being looked after or provided with accommodation by a responsible authority for the purpose of these Regulations.

Signed by authority of the
Secretary of State for Health   Minister of State for Health

SCHEDULE 1   Regulation 4(4)

ELEMENTS TO BE INCLUDED IN REVIEW

1. Keeping informed of the arrangements for looking after the child and of any relevant change in the child's circumstances.

2. Keeping informed of the name and address of any person whose views should be taken into account in the course of the review.

3. Making necessary preparations and providing any relevant information to the participants in any meeting of the responsible authority which considers the child's case in connection with any aspect of the review.

4. Initiating meetings of relevant personnel of the responsible authority and other relevant persons to consider the review of the child's case.

5. Explaining to the child any steps which he may take under the Act including, where appropriate—

(a) his right to apply, with leave, for a section 8 order (residence, contact and other orders with respect to children),

(b) where he is in care, his right to apply for the discharge of the care order, and

(c) the availability of the procedure established under the Act for considering representations.

6. Making decisions or taking steps following review decisions arising out of or resulting from the review.

SCHEDULE 2   Regulation 5

CONSIDERATIONS TO WHICH RESPONSIBLE AUTHORITIES ARE TO HAVE REGARD

1. In the case of a child who is in care, whether an application should be made to discharge the care order.

2. Where the responsible authority are a local authority whether they should seek a change in the child's legal status.

3. Arrangements for contact, and whether there is any need for changes in the arrangements in order to promote contact with the child's family and others so far as is consistent with his welfare.

4. Any special arrangements that have been made or need to be made for the child, including the carrying out of assessments either by a local authority or other persons, such as those in respect of special educational need under the Education Act 1981(*a*).

5. The responsible authority's immediate and long term arrangements for looking after the child or providing the child with accommodation (made pursuant to the provisions of the Arrangements for Placement of Children (General) Regulations 1991 (*b*)), whether a change in those arrangements is needed and consideration of alternative courses of action.

6. Where the responsible authority are a local authority, whether an independent visitor should be appointed if one has not already been appointed.

7. The child's educational needs, progress and development.

8. Whether arrangements need to be made for the time when the child will no longer be looked after or provided with accommodation by the responsible authority.

9. Whether plans need to be made to find a permanent substitute family for the child.

SCHEDULE 3   Regulation 5

HEALTH CONSIDERATIONS TO WHICH RESPONSIBLE AUTHORITIES
ARE TO HAVE REGARD

1. The child's state of health.

2. The child's health history.

3. The effect of the child's health and health history on his development.

4. Existing arrangements for the child's medical and dental care and treatment and health and dental surveillance.

5. The possible need for an appropriate course of action which should be identified to assist necessary change of such care, treatment or surveillance.

6. The possible need for preventive measures, such as vaccination and immunisation, and screening for vision and hearing.

EXPLANATORY NOTE

(*This Note is not part of the Regulations*)

These Regulations provide for the review of the cases of children who are looked after by a local authority or provided with accommodation by a voluntary organisation or in a registered children's home.

They make provision for the review of such cases (regulation 2); the time when cases are to be reviewed (regulation 3); the manner in which cases are to be reviewed (regulation 4); the considerations to which there should be regard (regulation 5); health reviews (regulation 6); consultation, participation and notification (regulation 7); the arrangements for implementation of decisions arising out of reviews (regulation 8); monitoring the arrangements for reviews (regulation 9); recording review information (regulation 10); and application of the Regulations to short periods (regulation 11).

(*a*) 1981 c.60.
(*b*) SI 1991/890

STATUTORY INSTRUMENTS

1991 No. 894

CHILDREN AND YOUNG PERSONS

REPRESENTATIONS PROCEDURE (CHILDREN) REGULATIONS 1991

Made	*2nd April 1991*
Laid before Parliament	*10th April 1991*
Coming into force	*14th October 1991*

ARRANGEMENT OF REGULATIONS

The Secretary of State for Health, in exercise of the powers conferred by sections 24(15) and 26(5) and (6), 59(4) and (5) and 104(4) of, and paragraph 10(2)(l) of Schedule 6 and paragraph 6 of Schedule 7 to, the Children Act 1989 (*a*), and all other powers enabling him in that behalf, hereby makes the following Regulations:

PART I INTRODUCTORY

Citation and Commencement

1. These Regulations may be cited as the Representations Procedure (Children) Regulations 1991, and shall come into force on 14th October 1991.

(*a*) 1989 c.41. section 24(14) and (15) were inserted by paragraph 9 of Schedule 16 to the Courts and Legal Services Act 1991 c.41.

Interpretation

2.–(1) In these Regulations, unless the context otherwise requires –

"the Act" means the Children Act 1989;

"complainant" means a person qualifying for advice and assistance about the discharge of their functions by a local authority under Part III of the Act in relation to him, or a person specified in section 26(3)(a) to (e) of the Act making any representations;

"independent person" means in relation to representations made to, or treated as being made to, a local authority, a person who is neither a member nor an officer of that authority;

"panel" means a panel of 3 persons;

"representations" means representations referred to in sections 24(14) or 26(3) of the Act.

(2) Any notice required under these Regulations is to be given in writing and may be sent by post.

(3) In these Regulations unless the context requires otherwise –

(a) any reference to a numbered section is to the section in the Act bearing that number;

(b) any reference to a numbered regulation is to the regulation in these Regulations bearing that number, and any reference in a regulation to a numbered paragraph is to the paragraph of that regulation bearing that number.

PART II   REPRESENTATIONS AND THEIR CONSIDERATION

Local authority action

3.–(1) The local authority shall appoint one of their officers to assist the authority in the coordination of all aspects of their consideration of the representations.

(2) The local authority shall take all reasonable steps to ensure that everyone involved in the handling of the representations, including independent persons, is familiar with the procedure set out in these Regulations.

Preliminaries

4.–(1) Where a local authority receive representations from any complainant, except from a person to whom section 26(3)(e) may apply, they shall send to the complainant an explanation of the procedure set out in these Regulations, and offer assistance and guidance on the use of the procedure, or give advice on where he may obtain it.

(2) Where oral representations are made, the authority shall forthwith cause them to be recorded in writing, and sent to the complainant, who shall be given the opportunity to agree that they are accurately recorded in writing.

(3) For all other purposes of these Regulations the written record to which paragraph (2) refers shall be deemed to be the representations.

(4) Where a local authority receive representations from a person to whom they consider section 26(3)(e) may apply they shall –

(a) forthwith consider whether the person has a sufficient interest in the child's welfare to warrant his representations being considered by them;

(b) if they consider that he has a sufficient interest, cause the representations to be dealt with in accordance with the provisions of these Regulations, and send to the complainant an explanation of the procedure set out in the Regulations, and offer assistance and guidance on the use of the procedure, or give advice on where he may obtain it;

(c) if they consider that he has not got a sufficient interest they shall notify him accordingly in writing, and inform him that no further action will be taken;

(d) if they consider it appropriate to do so having regard to his understanding, they shall notify the child of the result of their consideration.

(5) Where paragraph (4)(b) applies, the date at which the authority conclude that the person has a sufficient interest shall be treated for the purpose of these Regulations as the date of receipt of the representations.

Appointment of independent person

5. Where the local authority receive representations under regulation 4 they shall appoint an independent person to take part in the consideration of them, unless regulation 4(4)(c) applies.

Consideration by local authority with independent person

6.–(1) The local authority shall consider the representations with the independent person and formulate a response within 28 days of their receipt.

(2) The independent person shall take part in any discussions which are held by the local authority about the action (if any) to be taken in relation to the child in the light of the consideration of the representations.

Withdrawal of representations

7. The representations may be withdrawn at any stage by the person making them.

Notification to complainant and reference to panel

8.–(1) The local authority shall give notice within the period specified in regulation 6 to –

(a) the complainant;

(b) if different, the person on whose behalf the representations were made, unless the local authority consider that he is not of sufficient understanding or it would be likely to cause serious harm to his health or emotional condition;

(c) the independent person;

(d) any other person whom the local authority consider has sufficient interest in the case

of the proposed result of their consideration of the representations and the complainant's right to have the matter referred to a panel under paragraph (2).

(2) If the complainant informs the authority in writing within 28 days of the date on which notice is given under paragraph (1) that he is dissatisfied with the proposed result and wishes the matter to be referred to a panel for consideration of the representations, a panel shall be appointed by the local authority for that purpose.

(3) The panel shall include at least one independent person.

(4) The panel shall meet within 28 days of the receipt by the local authority of the complainant's request that the matter be referred to a panel.

(5) At that meeting the panel shall consider –

(a) any oral or written submissions that the complainant or the local authority wish to make; and

(b) if the independent person appointed under regulation 5 is different from the independent person on the panel, any oral or written submissions which the independent person appointed under regulation 5 wishes to make.

(6) If the complainant wishes to attend the meeting of the panel he may be accompanied throughout the meeting by another person of his choice, and may nominate that other person to speak on his behalf.

Recommendations

9.–(1) When a panel meets under regulation 8, they shall decide on their recommendations and record them with their reasons in writing within 24 hours of the end of the meeting referred to in regulation 8.

(2) The panel shall give notice of their recommendations to –

    (a) the local authority;

    (b) the complainant;

    (c) the independent person appointed under regulation 5 if different from the independent person on the panel;

    (d) any other person whom the local authority considers has sufficient interest in the case.

(3) The local authority shall, together with the independent person appointed to the panel under regulation 8(3) consider what action if any should be taken in relation to the child in the light of the representation, and that independent person shall take part in any decisions about any such action.

PART III   REVIEW

Monitoring of operation of procedure

10.–(1) Each local authority shall monitor the arrangements that they have made with a view to ensuring that they comply with the Regulations by keeping a record of each representation received, the outcome of each representation, and whether there was compliance with the time limits specified in regulations 6(1), 8(4) and 9(1).

(2) For the purposes of such monitoring, each local authority shall, at least once in every period of twelve months, compile a report on the operation in that period of the procedures set out in these Regulations.

(3) The first report referred to in paragraph (2) shall be compiled within twelve months of the date of coming into force of these Regulations.

PART IV   APPLICATION OF REGULATIONS TO VOLUNTARY ORGANISATIONS AND REGISTERED CHILDREN'S HOMES AND IN SPECIAL CASES

Application to voluntary organisations and registered children's homes

11.–(1) The provisions of Parts I to III of these Regulations shall apply where accommodation is provided for a child by a voluntary organisation, and he is not looked after by a local authority, as if –

    (a) for references to "local authority" there were substituted references to "voluntary organisation";

    (b) for the definition in regulation 2(1) of "complainant" there were substituted –

" "complainant" means

        (a) any child who is being provided with accommodation by a voluntary organisation;

        (b) any parent of his;

        (c) any person who is not a parent of his but who has parental responsibility for him;

(d) such other person as the voluntary organisation consider has a sufficient interest in the child's welfare to warrant his representations being considered by them.";

(c) for the definition in regulation 2(1) of "independent person" there were substituted—

" "independent" person means in relation to representations made to, or treated as being made to a voluntary organisation, a person who is not an officer of that voluntary organisation nor a person engaged in any way in furthering its objects, nor the spouse of any such person;" and

(d) for the definition in regulation 2(1) of "representations" there were substituted –

" "representations" means representations referred to in section 59(4) about the discharge by the voluntary organisation of any of their functions relating to section 61 and any regulations made under it in relation to the child.";

(e) for the reference in regulation 4(1) and (4) to a person to whom section 26(3)(e) may apply or to whom the local authority consider section 26(3)(e) may apply there was substituted a reference to a person who may fall within sub-paragraph (d) in the definition of "complainant" in these Regulations.

(2) The provisions of Parts I to III of these Regulations shall apply where accommodation is provided for a child in a registered children's home, but where a child is neither looked after by a local authority nor accommodated on behalf of a voluntary organisation, as if –

(a) for references to "local authority" there were substituted references to "the person carrying on the home;"

(b) for the definition in regulation 2(1) of "complainant" there were substituted –

" "complainant" means

(i) any child who is being provided with accommodation in a registered children's home;

(ii) a parent of his;

(iii) any person who is not a parent of his but who has parental responsibility for him;

(iv) such other person as the person carrying on the home considers has a sufficient interest in the child's welfare to warrant his representations being considered by them;"

(c) for the definition in regulation 2(1) of "independent person" there were substituted –

" "independent person" means in relation to representations made to a person carrying on a registered children's home, a person who is neither involved in the management or operation of that home nor financially interested in its operation, nor the spouse of any such person;

(d) for the definition in regulation 2(1) of "representations" there were substituted –

" "representations" means any representations (including any complaint) made in relation to the person carrying on the registered children's home by a complainant about the discharge of his functions relating to section 64.";

(e) for the reference in regulation 4(1) and (4) to a person to whom section 26(3)(e) may apply or to whom the local authority consider section 26(3)(e) may apply there was substituted a reference to a person who may fall within sub-paragraph (d) in the definition of "complainant" in these Regulations.

12.–(1) Where representations would fall to be considered by more than one local authority, they shall be considered by the authority which is looking after the child or by the authority within whose area the child is ordinarily resident where no authority has that responsibility.

(2) The provisions of Parts I and III of, and of regulation 12(1) of, these Regulations, shall apply to the consideration by a local authority of any representations (including any complaint) made to them by any person exempted or seeking to be exempted under paragraph 4 of Schedule 7 to the Act (foster parents: limits on numbers of foster children) about the discharge of their functions under that paragraph as if –

    (a) for the definition in regulation 2(1) of "complainant" there were substituted: "a person exempted or seeking to be exempted under paragraph 4 of Schedule 7 to the Act making any representations;"

    (b) for the definition in regulation 2(1) of "representations" there were substituted: "representations referred to in paragraph 6 of Schedule 7 to the Act.";

    (c) in regulation 4(1) the words "except from a person to whom section 26(3)(e) may apply" were omitted;

    (d) regulation 4(4) and (5) were omitted.

Signed by authority of the Secretary of State for Health.

Minister of State for Health

EXPLANATORY NOTE

(this note is not part of the Regulations)

These Regulations establish a procedure for considering representations (including complaints) made to local authorities about the discharge by the authority of any of their functions –

    (a) under Part III of the Act in relation to a child looked after by them or in need;

    (b) where section 24(14) of the Act applies (representations concerning advice and assistance for certain children aged 18 to 21);

    (c) under paragraph 4 of Schedule 7 to the Act (foster parents: limits on number of foster children) in relation to exemption from the usual fostering limit.

The Regulations make provision to include consideration of representations by an independent person and for reference of representations to a panel which is to make recommendations to the authority, organisation or person carrying on the home.

The Regulations also make provision for a record to be kept of all representations received and their outcome to monitor the operation of the procedure and for a report on the operation of the procedure to be prepared every twelve months.

The Regulations apply the procedure for considering representations (including complaints) made to voluntary organisations and persons carrying on registered children's homes with modifications.

Printed in the United Kingdom for HMSO
Dd293813 4/91 C280 G3392 10170